Taylor & Beyond...

Taylor & Beyond...

Malcolm Knox

Published by ABC Books for the
AUSTRALIAN BROADCASTING CORPORATION
GPO Box 9994 Sydney NSW 2001

Copyright © Malcolm Knox 2000

First published August 2000

All rights reserved. No part of this publication
may be reproduced, stored in a retrieval system
or transmitted in any form or by any means,
electronic, mechanical, photocopying, recording
or otherwise, without the prior written permission
of the Australian Broadcasting Corporation.

National Library of Australia
Cataloguing-in-Publication entry
Knox, Malcolm. 1966- .
  Taylor and beyond.

  Includes index.

  ISBN 0 7333 0775 2

  1. Cricket – Australia – History – 20th century.
  2. Cricket players – Australia. 3. Cricket – History –
  20th century. 4. Cricket-Psychological aspects.
  I. Australian Broadcasting Corporation. II. Title.

  796.358

Designed by Jim Shepherd
Set in 10.5/15.5pt Rotis by
Midland Typesetters, Maryborough, Victoria
Text colour separations by Finsbury, Adelaide
Cover film by Pageset, Victoria
Printed and bound in Australia by
Australian Print Group, Maryborough, Victoria

5 4 3 2 1

Contents

Introduction: The Hidden Histories	vii
Pakistan: The Grudge Match	1
The West Indies: The Crown in Dispute	39
South Africa: The Throat Ball	81
England: The Ashes of the Ashes	131
Sri Lanka: Under the Skin	169
New Zealand: A Minor Theme	202
India: The Last Frontier	229
Two Teams or One?	257
The Captains	266
Further Reading	282
Index	283

Introduction: The Hidden Histories

THE WORLD LEARNED a lot about how the Australian cricket team operates when their game plan was slipped under a New Zealand businessman's hotel door in February 2000. Attention was paid to the thoroughness of the Australians' approach. Their dossiers on each New Zealand player covered every technical strength and mental flaw, advising on how specifically to nullify the former and exploit the latter. Much had been said, over the years, on how Australia modified their tactics for individual opponents: never sledge Brian Lara; test Sachin Tendulkar early with rising balls outside off stump; leave Daryll Cullinan to Shane Warne. But never before had the champion team's game plans been made public, and nor was it known that the ruthless dissection of opponents reached down to the most modest of rivals, from the Laras and Tendulkars down to the likes of Roger Twose and Simon Doull. Perhaps Chris Harris might have been flattered to know that the World Cup holders believed the New Zealand team's spirit hung on the language expressed by his slim shoulders.

The scouting report relied heavily on Australia's previous series against New Zealand, in Australia in 1997–98. For instance, Stephen Fleming was characterised as 'lazy early' in his innings. This shortcoming had been evident in 1997–98, when Fleming had been caught several times wafting outside the off stump to balls sliding across him early in his innings. But since that time, Fleming had matured as a batsman, tightening his early technique and playing some tough, long innings on the subcontinent. Similarly, the notes praised Craig McMillan's timing and aggression. This again was based on the excellent start to his Test career he had made, as a 21-year-old, in Australia in 1997-98. But McMillan had since fallen on harder times, his looseness against the moving ball exposed in a disappointing World Cup and Test series in England in 1999.

Sure enough, however, Fleming and McMillan returned to their entrenched patterns against the Australians. Fleming again struggled to fulfill his potential, while McMillan counterpunched with a near-match-winning innings in Auckland. It was as if the intervening years had not happened, and the players were reverting to a continuation of their previous encounters with this opponent.

An international bush telegraph does exist in cricket, but the Australians still relied mostly on their own experience, more than two years old, against New Zealand. The attention on Harris reached back even further, to his marvellous 130 off 124 balls against Australia in the 1996 World Cup.

What the world learned from this is a self-evident truth in cricket: that there is a second continuity, running parallel with the chronological passage, that underpins the psychology of the game. This second continuity runs between each pair of rival nations. Ongoing battles are resumed whenever the two teams meet. On their 2000 tour of New Zealand, the Australians picked up narrative threads that had been set on their previous encounter; to ready themselves to take on New Zealand once more, they forced themselves, to a certain extent, to clear the intervening two years from their mind in order to resume an interrupted contest.

Cricket is full of these interrupted contests. Notoriously, Lara ended his 1996-97 tour of Australia with the words: 'When they come to the West Indies, we won't be losers.' Defying all the evidence provided by his mediocre batting in the interim, Lara settled his personal score with Australia in 1999 by enjoying a stunning series, ensuring that his team would not, indeed, be losers. Conversely, the Australians might have been expected to sail into their home series against India in 1999-2000 in a supremely confident, almost complacent, frame of mind after defeating Pakistan at home 3-0. But no, they were not thinking necessarily of their winning home run, but rather switched into revenge mode, recalling all the pain of their humbling loss in India in 1998.

From the other side, a series against Australia became, during the period of Mark Taylor's captaincy, from 1994 to 1999, the supreme contest in cricket. Just as the West Indies had been in the 1980s and early 1990s, Australia became the yardstick for other teams. All the best players – Lara, Tendulkar, Saeed Anwar – might have suffered indifferent form against other opponents, but they lifted themselves to play at their very best against Australia. South Africa's Allan Donald said, before coming to Australia in 1997–98, that defeating Taylor's team in a Test series was the dearest wish in his career – above World Cups, above beating England, above beating the West Indies. Early in 2000, Donald decided to retire from international one-day cricket so as to reserve his energies and concentrate his mind upon one last effort to knock off the Australians in 2001–02. Like golfers arranging their calendars around the four 'major' tournaments, the best cricketers from other nations set themselves for the ongoing, interrupted contest against Australia. Every player has his favourite opponents and venues – the records show extreme variation between players' performances against certain teams – and it is fair to say that the narrative of the Australia–South Africa cricket contest, for instance, has been a radically different story from that of Australia–India, Australia–England and Australia–Pakistan rivalries. The one common element is that each of these contests became, during the late 1990s, the marquee event of the cricketing year.

For that reason, I have chosen to 'cut up' the past six years of the Australian team's performances by opponent, rather than by chronology. For one, this affords a more interesting and meaningful analysis than simply following the team on its random travels through the world. In addition, it affords an insight into motivations which may not be apparent in the contemporaneous flux, a good example of this being the extreme antagonism between the Australian team and certain Pakistani players dating back to the 1994 series when Salim Malik offered Warne, Tim May and Mark Waugh money to play poorly. It has been often overlooked that this enmity permeated not only the subsequent clash in 1995–96, but also the 1998 tour and, to a waning extent, the confrontations in the 1999 World Cup final and the 1999–2000 Australian series, when ill feeling broke out again over the issues of sledging and the questioning of Shoaib Akhtar's action. This book opens its story by examining that ongoing rivalry between Australia and Pakistan – the most pungent, in terms of world cricket's wider context of racial and cultural complications, of all rivalries.

Each of the contests we shall follow has a particular flavour. Australia and the West Indies continued to fight for what was unofficially the world crown; while the West Indians faded badly in most of their away series, they remained undefeated at home against all teams except Taylor's in 1995, and they still won a higher proportion of Tests against Australia in this period than did any other nation. The Ashes series has a narrative of its own, given England's decline as a cricketing power and the questions hanging over that trophy's pre-eminence. For the last few years of the 20th century, the split widened between the importance of the Ashes in the spirituality of cricket and its importance as an on-field contest.

India and Australia had the most bizarre rivalry, torn by political antagonism after the Indians' 1991–92 tour to Australia and repaired, tenuously, by the inauguration of the Border–Gavaskar Trophy in 1996. The strangeness of this contest is that India were able to inflict Australia's worst loss in 60 years, in Calcutta in 1998, but were barely able to provide a spectacle when they returned to Australia, after an eight-year hiatus, in 1999–2000. Geography and off-field touring conditions play their own part in what we see in the arena; Australia and India are the most different of all cricketing nations, and this difference helps to explain the wild divergence between the outcomes of the series.

Other rivalries were shaped by deeper movements in the game. Australia's clashes with Sri Lanka in 1995 and 1996 are placed in the context of the revolution in one-day cricket inspired by Sri Lanka's slash-and-burn batting strategy. Aside from winning the World Cup in 1996, Sri Lanka's tactic prompted Australia to imitate it and thus set in train the 'two-teams policy' that caused such upheaval in Taylor's last years as captain. Australia's loss in Lahore in 1996 was the first step towards their win at Lord's in 1999.

In a similar mode, the Australian players' dispute with their employer over payments and working conditions overshadowed New Zealand's tour in 1997–98 to such a degree that the cricket that summer became a minor theme to the more important business of industrial reform.

Taylor And Beyond . . . The captain and author.   Mark Ray

Richie Benaud has said that cricket is the most controversial game. Active players would wish it were otherwise. As Steve Waugh has lamented, Australia's pre-eminence as a cricket-playing team is often overlooked by a public obsessed with the troubles courted by, or forced upon, players off the field. Warne likened his life to a soap opera, but the same could be said of the team as a whole. At various times Taylor, the Waughs, Glenn McGrath, Stuart MacGill, Michael Slater and Ricky Ponting – the cream of the cream – found themselves at the centre of stories which had ramifications far beyond the boundaries of the games they played. The Australian Cricket Board became more than a governing body or a custodian of the game; it became an active player in these controversies.

This book is an attempt to look a wonderful era of Australian cricket squarely in the eye. Without any self-interest at stake, it is timely to assess the period without fear or favour. On the field and off, life with the Australian cricket team in the Taylor-Waugh era was anything but dull.

At the time this book is going to press, the news has just broken that Hansie Cronje has been allegedly taped by Indian police in early 1999 discussing ways of cheating on one-day matches with an illegal bookmaker. The tapes, if authentic, show that Cronje was involved deeply in fixing scores, telegraphing tactics to gamblers, and possibly taking measures to rig the results of matches. In April 2000, days after the Indian police released transcripts of these conversations, Cronje made a partial admission – that he had received money in South Africa earlier in the year for providing a bookmaker with pitch and weather forecasts – and was suspended from the South African captaincy. He continued to deny the substantial accusations.

The story is unfolding rapidly. Indian police are comparing their tapes with other recordings of Cronje's voice, and have issued warrants for his arrest, along with three other South African players he named in the tapes as complicit in the fraud – Herschelle Gibbs, Peter Strydom and Nicky Boje.

Within a week, the conflagration spread throughout world cricket. Mohammed Azharuddin, Nayan Mongia and Ajay Jadeja were named in the Indian press as having bet against their own team. A former Indian cricket board chief, Inderjit Singh Bindra, accused ICC president Jagmohan Dalmiyah of being in the grip of mafia elements. England's Chris Lewis revealed that a bookmaker had told him three English players had taken money to fix scores. The three names were believed to be Alec Stewart, Michael Atherton and Darren Gough. Perhaps they were mentioned because they were the only regular English players! The English Cricket Board had dismissed Lewis's claim as hearsay, but Scotland Yard mounted an investigation in early 2000. Malik Mohammed Qayyum, the Pakistani judge whose report into match-fixing there had disappeared into the national President's office, threatened to take his document to the ICC in London. In it, he recommended severe punishments for a number of Pakistani players, including Salim Malik, Wasim Akram, Ijax Ahmed and Mushtaq Ahmed. The cancer continued to grow when South African cricket boss Ali Bacher said he had been told by players that two 1999 World Cup matches, between Pakistan and Bangladesh and Pakistan and India, were intentionally lost by Pakistan. Doubt was cast over the Australia/South Africa Super Six game in which Gibbs famously dropped a catch off Steve Waugh, and over the rain-shortened Test match between South Africa and England at Pretoria when England won on a one-innings-a-side final day. And a former South African player told newspapers he believed Cronje had rigged the recent Sharjah Cup final. This highlighted what a scourge match-fixing is: doubt metastasises quickly, tainting a great number of probably genuine matches. Against this backdrop, Australian cricket claimed a high ground, having conducted its inquiry into betting after the Mark Waugh/Shane Warne scandal broke in 1998. Aside from Mark Waugh's extended and ill-advised dalliance with the bookmaker in 1994 and 1995, no Australian had been accused of treading so close to the line of cheating. Yet the Australian Cricket Board had been no more proactive than anyone else, except Pakistan's. The ACB only reacted to the story when they were exposed by a journalist, the *Australian*'s Malcolm Conn. South Africa and India only reacted when caught by the police. No cricket authority, least of all the toothless ICC, has appeared to want to take any proactive measure, with the exception of the Qayyum initiative in Pakistan in 1998–99.

More will be heard of the story, probably much more, by the time this book is released. Cronje, at the very least, is facing the prospect of criminal charges in South Africa for foreign currency violations. By late 2000, we may be witnessing a concerted effort by cricket's administrators to cut match-fixing out of the game. Or we may be witnessing yet more official inaction and prevarication, with administrators unable or unwilling to put aside their national interest for the good of the game as a whole. They could show no greater contempt for the paying public. But, as this book shows, self-interest and inaction have been characteristic of all cricket administrations, not least Australia's, since the match-fixing scandal first broke in Mark Taylor's first series as captain. Recent history gives more reason for pessimism than hope. We shall see.

Pakistan: The Grudge Match

IT CAN BE said that the key moments of the Taylor years occurred in Pakistani hotels. It was in the Karachi Pearl Continental on the night of 1 October 1994 that Shane Warne received a telephone call from the Pakistan captain, Salim Malik, from his room on another floor. Malik invited Warne to his room and made him an offer that was to create more than mere scandal; it was to undermine the very basis of international cricket, the notion that both teams always try their hardest in every competitive match.

It was also in Pakistani hotel rooms that Warne and Mark Waugh, on the same tour, received a number of telephone calls from an Indian bookmaker named 'John' or 'Pinky', seeking pre-match information to help him frame markets and place bets in the illegal – but lucrative – cricket gambling scene in the subcontinent. It was in Pakistani hotel rooms, on that tour, that new captain Mark Taylor faced his first off-field crisis, addressing the team passionately on the bribery issue even while he was ignorant of the money Warne and Mark Waugh had been receiving from the illegal punter.

Four years later, on the night of 16 October 1998, it was in another Pakistani hotel, Room 428 of the Pearl Continental in Peshawar, that Taylor lay awake in bed and made a decision which did not so much shape his future as confirm his standing as a leader of attacking instinct and a man with a deep sense of obligation. By declaring Australia's first innings of the second 1998 Test at 4/599, denying himself the chance to progress from his overnight 334 past the Australian record of Sir Donald Bradman (and possibly Brian Lara's world record of 375), Taylor restated to the cricket world what he had stated continuously since 1994: that he placed winning Test matches and Test series above all individual aspirations. At the same time, he was continuing to repay, to his teammates, a debt he had incurred during his horrendous loss of form in 1997. At that time, they had made sacrifices for him, and allowed him to act at times selfishly. This time, he was going to commit a conspicuously unselfish act, even though many of them were urging him to bat on.

It was also in Pakistani hotel rooms, in Rawalpindi and Peshawar in 1998, that the circle of illegal betting closed in on Taylor himself, as he became the target of gamblers wishing to influence his on-field decisions. Rumours swirled around him in Pakistan, alleging that he had declared his innings for a bribe. It was not until the hearings before a Pakistani judge in Melbourne in 1999, coinciding almost to the day with the end of Taylor's Test career, that the odour of betting on cricket which had spread to his team was finally addressed.

The Pearl Continental is Pakistan's only five-star hotel chain, providing oases of comfort and modern convenience in a poor country. Hotels of such grandeur signify different things to different cricket teams. To the touring Australians, luxury hotels are quickly taken for granted; they assume a generic air and tend to be noticed more for their occasional shortcomings than for their opulence. For Pakistani cricketers, on the other hand, staying in five-star hotels served to underline both the privileges and the transience of their position. Hotel luxury, to the Australians, was a compensation for gruelling tour schedules. To the Pakistanis, who would invite their friends and families to visit and marvel at the hotel's interior, this lifestyle was a rare and precious prize. It could be easily lost, and one could be cast out, like an angel from heaven, into a more difficult life outside. The difference between being inside and outside the gilded fortress bred an insecurity and a money hunger which governed many of their otherwise less explicable actions.

It was in the Pearl Continental in Peshawar, two nights before Taylor's agonising decision to declare, standing over the barbecue, that Malcolm

Conn, chief cricket writer from *The Australian* newspaper, asked Mark Waugh about a letter the Pakistan Cricket Board had received alleging that Waugh had been involved with Indian bookmakers. Conn had been spending too much time, in his own opinion, in Pakistani hotels. While Taylor was smashing the bowlers for two days in Peshawar, Conn had been able only to catch up with highlights on television in his hotel in Lahore, where he had been seconded by News Limited to cover the High Court hearings into match-fixing instead of watching the cricket. Conn was annoyed that he had missed the Taylor innings, but the letter he had been shown in Lahore and the conversation with Mark Waugh over the Peshawar barbecue were to set in train a cataclysmic series of events which caused irrevocable damage to the reputations of Waugh, Warne and Australian cricket. It was to end, indirectly, in Taylor's resignation. Among other reasons for his retirement, he had lost the appetite for dealing with four-year cycles of controversy which were no fault of his own. A year after breaking the story, Conn was to become the first cricket writer to win a Walkley Award, the most prestigious award in Australian journalism.

The Judge ... Justice Malik Mohammed Qayyum of the Lahore High Court. The man charged with cleaning up Pakistani cricket – and his own desk. Mark Ray

The accolade could have easily gone to the *Sydney Morning Herald*'s Phil Wilkins, who wrote in February 1995 that a Pakistani player – later identified as Salim Malik – had tried unsuccessfully to bribe May, Warne and Mark Waugh in October 1994. The identity of Wilkins's source has been one of the lasting mysteries of Australian cricket in the Taylor years. One theory points to Australian coach Bob Simpson, who was believed by some to have leaked the story as a 'retirement present' to Wilkins after the journalist's three decades as an international cricket correspondent. Simpson had been a key source for some members of the Australian press during his time as coach and selector, and it was theorised that he may have given the veteran writer the scoop of the century as a parting gesture to make up for missed opportunities in the past.

Another theory had it that Wilkins's source was umpire Steve Randell. The pair dined together at the end of the 1994–95 Ashes series in Australia, after which Randell was to be sent to Zimbabwe to officiate on Pakistan's tour there. It was possible that Randell, having been briefed by the International Cricket Council on the rumours of match-fixing in the Pakistan team, mentioned this to Wilkins.

There are other theories, none conclusive. Simpson denies being Wilkins's 'Deep Throat', Randell went to jail in Hobart in 1999 for sexually molesting minors, and Wilkins, being a responsible and ethical journalist, kept his source to himself.

The news took a tortuous route from the Pakistani hotel rooms to the public eye. It was not revealed to cricket authorities in a direct manner either. At around 10.30 on the night of 1 October 1994, Warne and May were sharing a room when the call came from Malik. May was dozing. Warne collected the phone, and Malik said: 'We'd like to meet you and your good friend Tim May and have an interesting chat.' May was too tired, and sent Warne 'to represent me'. Warne went to Malik's room, where the Pakistani captain offered Warne and May $US200,000 to bowl outside off stump, ensuring a draw. At that juncture of the Test match, which venerable English umpire Dickie Bird called the greatest he had seen, and which was the first of Taylor's captaincy, Pakistan were 3/155 chasing 314 to win. Malik insisted to Warne three times that 'We can't lose.' When Warne failed to take the hint, Malik said baldly that the money would be in Warne's room before midnight if he and May agreed.

Warne told Malik to 'get stuffed'. When he returned to the room, May showed joking interest, saying, 'I bowl outside off stump anyway. I'd be getting $200,000 for nothing.' Warne phoned Malik back and told him to 'get fucked'.

Pakistan won the match, aided by the fact that May had ricked his neck overnight and Australia's strike bowler, Craig McDermott, was not playing due to an ingrown toenail. It required a record last-wicket partnership of 57 between Inzamam-ul-Haq and Mushtaq Ahmed, and a missed stumping by Ian Healy on what proved to be the last ball, bowled by Warne, for Pakistan to achieve a remarkable win.

After the match Malik told Warne, 'You should have taken the money.' Malik was certainly in a playful mood. At the presentation ceremony, David Boon says Malik invited him to come to a party and – it seemed – smoke hashish.

'I remember vividly,' Boon wrote later, 'at the presentation ceremony, the Pakistani captain approached me and asked me what I was doing that night. "What is there to do in Pakistan – nothing," I replied. "We've got a bit of a party going on. Do you smoke?" was his rejoinder. I told him that I enjoyed the occasional Benson & Hedges, but I think I was being offered something else. I thanked him for the invitation to the party, but declined. "You can still come. We can talk about all sorts of things," the Pakistan skipper said.'

Boon declined again, and what might have been the third bribery offer to an Australian player failed to eventuate.

What happened then is subject to dispute. Taylor went to a disciplinary hearing with fast bowler Jo Angel, who was to face a charge of dissent from ICC referee John Reid. Taylor contended that Warne and May informed their captain of the bribery offer after the match. May's version differed slightly. In an unpublished interview with *Inside Sport* magazine's Graem Sims in 1998, May said he 'didn't say anything more about the whole issue' until some weeks later. May said the details of the offer did not come out until 22 October, in Rawalpindi. At a ministerial function before that game, Malik had approached Mark Waugh and through him offered Warne, May and the Waugh twins $US50,000 each to play poorly. Waugh brushed Malik away, and an hour and a half later repeated his refusal.

Australia scored 250 the next day, Mark Waugh making 121 not out off 132 balls. Pakistan replied with what May called 'the most extraordinary batting display I've ever seen in my life', losing one wicket and passing Australia on the last ball of the 39th over.

It was only as the Australians returned to their rooms, according to May, that the information came out. 'Junior walked in the rooms – we hadn't told anybody about these bribes and that sort of stuff, we thought it was just ... hush. Like, "Christ, did this really happen?" And Mark Waugh said (jokingly), "Ah, would've been better off taking the bribes, guys." And the manager and the coach were there – "What? What are you talking about?" And so that's where it all sort of came from.'

It was only then that Simpson and the manager, Australian Cricket Board member Col Egar, heard of the bribery offers. If Taylor's recollection is correct, and he was told of Malik's 1 October offer on 2 October; that left three full weeks during which the captain kept the matter to himself. The only cogent reason for this is that Taylor, in his first tour as captain, did not appreciate the ramifications of Malik's offer. In his 1999 memoir, *Time To Declare*, Taylor writes: 'Some people have asked me: "Why was such a big fuss made? Why didn't you just forget about it?"'

The evidence suggests that, at first, Taylor did try to 'just forget about it'. It was only when Mark Waugh let the news slip in Rawalpindi on 22 October that it leaked to Simpson, Egar and, presumably, Australian-born ICC chief executive David Richards, who was in Pakistan at the time.

Taylor wrote in 1999: 'Increasingly in those difficult days, I knew that there was no other way. What had happened was deeply alarming just in itself – and especially so in the climate existing in cricket at that time. But there was the additional fact that we had lost both of the games in question – the Test and the one-dayer ... We had to go public and let cricket officialdom know what had gone on. Not to have done that would have left us wide open to all sorts of suspicions and insinuations.'

Unfortunately, the captain was writing with four years' hindsight. The Australian leadership's attitude at the time was to go anything but 'public'. Taylor made a rousing speech at a team meeting before the third Test in Lahore, starting on 1 November, along the lines of 'let's stuff these cheats'. They could not – Malik stood in their way and ensured a second draw, as he had done in the previous Test. Pakistan now had a 1–0 home victory. But the bribery issue went no further. The Australian players, led by Taylor, wanted simply to forget the murkiness of Pakistan and concentrate on their cricket. If Egar and Simpson told Richards, the ICC chief did nothing about it. Somewhere in the link between May and Warne, Taylor, Egar and Simpson, and Richards, was a total breakdown in the process of addressing the most serious imaginable contravention of the game.

The issue would bubble along for another few months, boiling over in Zimbabwe when wicketkeeper Rashid Latif and batsman Basit Ali quit the Pakistan team, alleging match-fixing against senior players, principally Malik. Pakistan lost the first Test there, in Harare, by an innings and 64 runs. It was the most suspicious of Test match results, especially given Pakistan's status as favourite and the fact that they won the second and third Tests convincingly. After the Harare loss, Rashid approached a South African journalist and offered to sell his story. The journalist asked Rashid who had been arranging the match-fixing. Rashid pointed at Malik.

Warne, May and Mark Waugh did not volunteer any information when Wilkins broke the Malik bribe story in February 1995. They were subsequently praised for their courage in speaking against match-fixing, but they only did so under the greatest duress. May was fairly candid when pushed, Waugh and Warne less so. Only Waugh and Warne knew, at that stage, that they had other reasons for holding their tongues.

That other matter – the secondary compromise of Waugh and Warne – was also covered up until the fateful night over the Peshawar barbecue in 1998. By this time, the corrupt Bhutto government in Pakistan had been displaced and a concerted move was under way to root out any match-fixing. Malik, Wasim Akram and Malik's brother-in-law Ijaz Ahmed were named as conspirators, while the heart of the team – Inzamam-ul-Haq, Waqar Younis, Mushtaq Ahmed, Moin Khan and Saqlain Mushtaq – was named in a judicial report as participants in match-fixing.

Malcolm Conn was shown the anonymous letter alleging Mark Waugh's involvement with illegal bookmakers on the subcontinent, but that was not enough in itself to raise suspicions. Dean Jones had been similarly named – even though it was well known that Jones had rejected an approach from bookmakers in 1992 – and the ludicrous statement was made that Dennis Lillee and Rod Marsh had been suspended from the Australian team after their infamous wager on the English at Headingley in 1981. Waugh and Taylor had the previous week given evidence to the inquiry in Lahore, and nothing new had emerged about Waugh's past. Conn put the matter to Waugh over the barbecue, and the batsman said he had never bet on a cricket match.

Conn wrote in the *Australian* that the allegations against Waugh were far-fetched. Two nights later – after Taylor's incredible 334 – Waugh asked Conn what he had written. When Conn told him, Waugh mumbled 'That's all right, then', and walked away.

This reaction was what first aroused Conn's suspicions. It contrasted so markedly with that of Jones, who had been accused in the inquiry of selling information to bookmakers, and who responded by angrily threatening to sue his accuser, former Pakistan medium-fast bowler Sarfraz Nawaz, that Conn felt uneasy. Was there something in the allegation? Conn began asking questions in the Australian cricket fraternity. After the team returned to Australia, the ACB held a function to launch the 1998–99 Ashes series at Brisbane's City Hall. Afterwards, at Ian Healy's nightclub Adrenalin, Conn was told that Mark Waugh had been fined secretly by the board, on 28 February 1995, for accepting money to supply information to an illegal Indian bookmaker.

In the next four weeks, Conn gathered enough hard information to write the story. He did not know that Shane Warne had been fined at the same time for the same misdemeanour. When Conn told the ACB's chief executive, Malcolm Speed, that he was going to 'out' Mark Waugh for the four-year-old fine, the ACB could not then protect Warne. On the night of 8 December 1998, the ACB released the information that both Warne and Waugh had been disciplined in February 1995.

Even then, the board could not grasp the importance of the story. Speed told the ACB media liaison officer, former AAP cricket journalist Patrick Keane, that he thought the issue would blow over quickly. Shocked, Keane told his boss that this would be a major scandal. Keane's instincts were right. Waugh and Warne – the latter at the time out of the Australian team, nursing his right shoulder after an operation – were pilloried. The ACB's chairman, Denis Rogers, tried to evade responsibility by saying that a different administration had decided to keep the fine secret: the 1995 chairman Alan Crompton and the then chief executive Graham Halbish. When it was pointed out that Rogers had been on the board in 1995, he replied that times had changed and he would henceforth conduct board business with the transparency demanded in 1998. Under intense pressure during a media conference in Adelaide in December 1998, Rogers announced an inquiry into the affair, to be headed by a Brisbane barrister, Rob O'Regan QC.

Naive And Stupid . . . Shane Warne and Mark Waugh tried to think up some words their lawyers hadn't written, match-fixing enquiry, 1999.   Wayne Taylor/Fairfax

O'Regan questioned about 60 current and former players and administrators, but uncovered no new information apart from Taylor's revelation that he had rebuffed an unknown caller in Pakistan in 1998.

'In Rawalpindi a couple of nights before the first Test,' Taylor said, 'I took a call from a friendly fellow who chatted to me about Pakistan cricket, and told me he didn't like the Pakistanis much. They were all bigheads, he said. The Australians were his favourite team. "How are you fellows going?" he asked. "We're going all right ... yeah, we're in good shape," I said. "What do you think is going to happen in this Test?" he inquired. "Well, mate, I hope we score more runs than they do," I replied, keeping it polite and light. He pressed on. "How's the ground ... how's the wicket looking?" The warning lights flickered just a little, and I cut short the conversation. "Mate, I'm busy ... I'm going to have to go."

'He rang me again before the last Test. I don't recall his name, but he was on the line bright and chirpy. "It's me again," he said. He chatted on: "You did well in the first Test ... and that was a wonderful innings in Peshawar." On he went. And then: "What about this Test? How is the wicket looking?" I thought to myself: I'm definitely not going down that track again. I thanked him for the call, excused myself, and hung up.'

O'Regan's criticisms of the board and of Warne and Mark Waugh were strong. He said they should have received 'substantial suspensions' rather than the secret fines. Yet, his condemnation did not damage their standing in the board's eyes. Shortly after they were exposed for the secret fines, Warne and Waugh were appointed captain and vice-captain of Australia's one-day team in the absence of Steve Waugh, whose reputation was infinitely sounder than his hamstrings. The board was in an impossible position. It had effectively condoned Warne's and Mark Waugh's indiscretion for four years. It could not suddenly punish them again on the basis that that indiscretion was now a public matter. If it had denied Warne and Waugh the one-day leadership, the ACB would be admitting its own complicity.

Even after the scandal, which played its part in influencing Taylor's thoughts as he considered retirement, the dominant view among Australian players and administrators was that Warne and Mark Waugh had been unfairly punished by being exposed. After all, none of the alleged match fixers from the subcontinent had received any punishment. Many Australian cricketers, past and present, could not understand the commotion, holding the view that as the key issue was match-fixing rather than providing information to bookmakers, then those involved in match-fixing, foremost among them Malik, should be brought to account. They believed it unjust that Warne and Waugh, who had merely been paid for providing bland information about pitch conditions and weather, should be linked to the darker matter.

Boon typified this view when he wrote, 'It created huge pressure on all three players in the summer of '95–96, when the matter became public property. Warney was tremendously upset, Maysie similarly, and while Mark (Waugh) didn't appear so on the surface, that's his character. In the end, the ACB backed their players to the hilt, which was tremendous.'

This attitude had governed Australian cricket since 1994. When Warne and May received the original offer from Malik, they preferred to concentrate on their cricket. When they told Taylor – assuming, as he says, that this happened on 2 October 1994 – he also preferred to keep it to himself and concentrate on his first series as captain. When Simpson and Egar heard of the bribe offer, on 22 October 1994, they did little to investigate it or root out the cancer. Indeed, a Pakistani official told the judicial inquiry that Egar had played down the issue deliberately, saying there was 'nothing in' the accusations against Malik. When the ICC's Richards heard about it, he took no official action. For the next three months, Warne and particularly Mark Waugh had continued to talk to 'John', the illegal bookmaker they had met in Sri Lanka in 1994. Even though 'John's' original approach had been made in a casino, and even though the Australians suspected their match against Pakistan in Colombo at the time was rigged – this was the Singer World Series game which a bookmaker, Salim Pervez, claimed to have bribed Pakistani players to lose – the Australians continued to treat the matter lightly. Warne gave 'John' information about pitch conditions and team composition three times until he was caught and fined in February 1995. Mark Waugh spoke to the illegal bookmaker on approximately ten occasions during the Pakistan series, the home Ashes series, the short tour to New Zealand in February 1995, and – astonishingly, after he had been fined – even during the 1995 tour to the West Indies.

Even when the relationship between Warne and Waugh and 'John' came to the ACB's attention, during the short tour to New Zealand, cricket was put above propriety. Australia was about to tour the West Indies, after all, and the ACB did not want to jeopardise its team's chances by publicising the misbehaviour of two star players. This was why Crompton and Halbish kept the fines small (the players paid back approximately the amounts the bookmaker had paid them) and secret. The ACB was to argue that player discipline was routinely dealt with 'in-house'. As Mark Ray wrote in *Wisden Australia*, 'To the Board, there was apparently little difference between breaking a team curfew, for instance, and becoming involved with illegal bookmakers.'

Taylor held ambivalent views. On the one hand, he was content to pass the buck for action to the board. 'I doubt I could have done more than I did ... Once they were disclosed, both matters rightly became the matter of official policy and action. That was not my territory.'

On the other hand, he still wanted to be kept inside the policy circle, and was aggrieved when the fact that Warne and Waugh had been fined was withheld from him at first.

'As captain, I was disappointed that I hadn't been told. I was the one who carried the responsibility of fronting the media and letting people know what was going on, and where we stood on various issues. To be left in the dark on something so serious, with the potential of exploding into a huge headache for the game, was not pleasing. That's the way I felt then, and feel now.'

And yet, 'To be totally honest, I also hoped for the sake of Mark and Shane that the bookmaker story would never become public.'

As O'Regan was to find, nobody in the inner circle of Australian cricket judged these matters sufficiently important to help the Pakistani reformers eradicate match-fixing. Even in October 1998, when everyone concerned had had ample time to reflect on the seriousness of the matter, and by which time the rumours of match-fixing were so strong as to undermine the validity of many of Pakistan's international matches between around 1992 and 1996, even then, Taylor and Waugh did not volunteer all the information they held to the Pakistani inquiry. Australian cricket's view was that it had nothing to do with them, and Taylor and Waugh excused themselves on the basis that Judge Malik Mohammed Qayyum had not asked them the question. At ICC meetings and in public pronouncements, Australia was presumptuous enough to take the high moral ground on match-fixing, illegal bowling and other contentious issues, yet it did not help cut out the most serious violation of the game. If match-fixing was not a serious enough issue to unite international cricket, then nothing was. No Australian player has been connected with match-fixing, yet the greed of Warne and Mark Waugh established them in the eyes of the fixers as characters whose morality was for sale. This was almost certainly why they were offered money in Pakistan: because they were known to accept money from illegal sources.

As O'Regan reported, 'I do not see how the ACB, when it later came to deal with the matter, would confidently conclude that there was no connection between 'John's' payments and the alleged attempted bribes. Both the chronology of events and the symmetry of the contacts, the two players being both the recipients of the bookmaker payments and the targets of the alleged attempted bribes, suggest that there may well have been such a connection.'

Warne and Waugh kept their silence to save their own skins. Little more could be expected of them, though O'Regan condemned the pair for having 'failed lamentably to set the sort of example one might expect from senior players and role models for many young cricketers'. Taylor kept his silence because he wanted to concentrate his energies on winning cricket matches, and because he had passed the responsibility for action to his employers. The ACB and the ICC kept their silence because they did not trust the Pakistani inquiry and because they wanted to protect their own players. As a consequence, by the end of 1999 no action had been taken against any player for match-fixing or bribery. Salim Malik had reached the end of his natural cricketing life after the 1999 World Cup, and Wasim Akram and Ijaz Ahmed defied rumours of impending retirement to continue their weighty contributions to Pakistani cricket, Akram, intermittently as captain. The vagaries of Pakistani politics no doubt had much to do with this, but so did Australia's official inaction. And so, one of the true golden ages of Australian cricket will forever carry a blemish. Some of their wins may have been in matches where the opposition was not trying. Some matches around the world at the time may have been won by payment in cash, not runs and wickets. Even Australia's World Cup win over Pakistan in 1999 was tainted by rumours that some of the Pakistani players, who had been tailed by their own country's secret service through nightclubs and casinos during the World Cup, had taken bribes to lose the final. There was no evidence, on or off the field, that Pakistan had thrown the World Cup final. But that is why match-rigging is such a cancer: it affects even the healthy cells around it. The very basis of the game during the Taylor years, and beyond, was eroded. Cheating happened. Australia, through self-interest and sheer ignorance, was an accomplice to the fraud.

In varying degrees, members of the ACB and the Australian team neglected their duty to a covenant, coined by Bradman, to which they often paid lip service: that they are mere custodians of the game for a short time before passing its guardianship on to a new generation. Were they true custodians, the Australians would have acted in the game's interest and helped eradicate match-fixing. Instead, they put their cricketing self-interest first, and acted in a parochial manner, as if these issues were just another contest between themselves and Pakistan.

Only in retrospect, it seems, did Taylor realise fully the magnitude of what was happening. In *Time To Declare*, Taylor recalls 'daily talk of bribery and the throwing of matches – with the Pakistan team at the heart of the rumours' in 1994. Australia played Pakistan at the Sinhalese Sports Ground in Colombo on 7 September 1994 in the game most heavily compromised by the bribery allegations.

Afterwards, Taylor wrote, 'We came off feeling very pleased with ourselves; we'd played very good cricket with the ball and we had brought off what seemed to be a quality victory. It was not until later that the thought started to take shape: did we really play well enough to win the game ... or did they throw it? That day in Colombo we probably won fair and square, and they probably lost fair and square. But I don't really know ... and I guess I never will.'

There can be no deeper scar on a team's otherwise peerless record.

Much as Taylor and his teammates liked to draw a firm line between on-field and off-field conflicts, the implications of the Malik bribery affair were to flow onto the field for the next four years.

Taylor writes: 'Salim Malik's place at the centre of the rumour allegations added to the general unease. He was the opposing captain, after all. The Australian players were upset about what they knew, heard and read, and there was some sledging of Malik, though nothing too dramatic. My own relationship with him, captain to captain, was uneasy. He was a bloke I didn't know too well, and frankly, I didn't spend much time talking to him after the things I was told following the First Test (in 1994). I'll just say this: whatever else he may or may not be, he proved himself a great batsman in that series.'

Salim Malik's career is the barometer of how the bribery offers affected the chemistry of encounters between the two nations. In 1994, he scored 557 runs at 92.83 in the Tests. His scores were 26, 43, 33, 237, 75 and 143. Those latter four scores were made with the sound of Australian voices saying 'Cheat! Cheat!' in his ears. He was the difference between the sides in the only series Australia was to lose between 1992-93 and 1998. His limited-overs scores that season were 32, 62 not out, 56, 7 and 35. That season, his 13th in Test cricket, his batting average hit a career high of 47.43. Thereafter, it was all downhill. Facing the constant stream of rumour and allegation, he only scored two more Test centuries, against the second-rank nations England and Sri Lanka. When he came to Australia in 1995-96, his scores were 0, 36 and 45. He was in and out of the Pakistan team for the next few years, but played Australia in 1998 at home. His scores were 10, 52 not out, 49, and a pair of ducks in his last match against them in Karachi.

The Pakistanis were Australia's most talented opponent during the Taylor years. The West Indies were fading and the South Africans yet to fully emerge; Pakistan, meanwhile, ripened a crop of gifted players, headed by Wasim Akram at times, and a string of other captains at other times. Yet, after the 1994 series, Australia reserved their very best for Pakistan. In 1995-96, Australia reached a high-water mark to beat Pakistan 2-1. At that time, Taylor had Glenn McGrath, Craig McDermott and Warne at their peaks, and he was combining with Boon and Michael Slater at the top of a rock-solid batting order. It was the best team Taylor had during his five years. In 1998, the Australians avenged their 1994 loss with a 1-0 series win, without Warne, but propelled by Taylor's monumental 334 not out in Peshawar. The trend was to continue after Taylor's retirement. In the 1999 World Cup final, Steve Waugh's team put together their own version of a 334 - a performance the new captain ranked as the best in his 18 months since taking the one-day reins from Taylor. In the 1999-2000 home series, which Waugh entered under some personal pressure, having drawn a series in the Caribbean and lost in Sri Lanka, Pakistan played with brilliance but Australia countered with an aura of invincibility. Australia had to play some near-perfect cricket to beat Pakistan 3-0 - its seventh whitewash in 123 years and its first since Taylor's team defeated Sri Lanka 3-0 in 1995-96. After 1994, whatever Pakistan could do, Australia could do better. A special motivation existed, born in those faraway hotel rooms.

Australia in Pakistan, 1994
What amazed the Australian players, once the series was underway, was Malik's ability to shut from his mind the distractions he had brought on himself and still dominate the series. The Pakistani captain, shunned by his opponents and undergoing questionable relations with some of his own men, had the best series of his long career. Australia played well enough to win in Pakistan for the first time since 1959, and after their nerve-tingling loss in Karachi held reasonable hopes of doing so. But

Malik was an insurmountable obstacle, blunting Australia's first-innings leads in Rawalpindi and Lahore to ensure draws there and a 1–0 Pakistan win.

Without Allan Border for the first time since 1978, Australia's team and management set out on a fresh course. Anxious to avoid repeating the mistakes of the 1988 tour, when unhappiness with umpiring and other tour conditions had led the Australians to the brink of abandoning the enterprise, the ACB tutored its players on how to take the best attitude into Pakistan and, of equal importance, how to say the right things to the media.

Patrick Keane of AAP obtained a copy of the comical 'media tips' supplied at a pre-tour camp in Adelaide by Sydney public relations firm Rogen Communications. The tips included giving pat answers such as 'Harsh conditions are part of international cricket', 'Weather conditions during a hot Australian summer are just as challenging for touring teams', and 'Conditions in Pakistan are very comfortable: five-star accommodation, hotel-prepared food at the grounds and bottled water'. Even before leaving Australia, the team was putting on its happy face.

Taylor's appointment also breathed fresh life into the team, though not at first into his batting. His scores in the drawn lead-up match in Rawalpindi were 4 and 1, and then he notched a pair in his first Test as captain. Pakistan might have been a premonition of his career's great crisis two years later – the impact of captaincy on batting – but Taylor did recover in the second and third Tests to score 111 runs for the series.

Karachi was the best Test English umpire 'Dickie' Bird had seen. Pakistan's three great bowlers, Wasim Akram, Waqar Younis and Mushtaq Ahmed, were at their peak on the first day, but Australia batted with confident counter-aggression to make 7/325 in the three sessions. Left-handed debutant Michael Bevan handled the pacemen immaculately to score 82, Steve Waugh hit the ball as well as he ever had with 73 from 85 balls, and Ian Healy scored 57 to shepherd the tail to a final score of 337.

Craig McDermott had withdrawn on match morning with an ingrown toenail, leaving Australia to open with a novice pace attack of Glenn

McGrath and Jo Angel. Saeed Anwar (85) launched Pakistan to a typically fluent start, but Australia's spinners, May and Warne, bowled beautifully to claw the hosts back. The spinners dismissed most of the top order, after which Angel and McGrath came back to clean up the tail. Leading by 81, Australia were in the driver's seat, and seemed set for an easy victory when David Boon and Mark Waugh had them at 2/171, effectively 2/252, just before stumps on the third day. This was not allowing for the great Wasim and Waqar, however. Boon and Waugh had hit the ball around just enough to rough it up by the 60th over, enabling Waqar and Wasim to exploit their reverse swing talents. Reverse swing is so called because the ball will swing towards, not away from, the shiny side, as it does with a new ball. Conventional swing operates on the principle that the shiny half will slide quicker through the air than the rough half, causing the ball's path to bend towards the rough. With reverse swing, the rough side of an old ball reaches a threshold where it becomes so rough that a film of air bubbles forms around the roughness. This film acts as a kind of slipstream on the rough side, so suddenly the shinier side – also laden down with moisture from the bowler's sweat – moves more slowly, and the ball swings 'reverse', or away from the rougher side.

Waqar bowled the match-turning ball when he swung one through Mark Waugh (61). That was the end of the over, and Boon hit three off Wasim's next ball, putting the new man, Bevan, on strike. Wasim bowled him first ball, and trapped Steve Waugh leg-before with the next. Impregnable at 2/171, Australia were wobbling overnight at 5/181. They still had Boon there next morning, but he could do little except farm the strike to protect the tail from the Wasim–Waqar blitz. He added 29, taking his score past his 19th Test century, but watched helplessly as the tail folded. Australia made just 232, Wasim and Waqar cleaning up eight wickets between them with the old ball. Instead of the expected 400-odd, Pakistan needed 314 in five sessions to win.

At stumps they were 3/155, having just lost Malik for 43, caught by Taylor at slip off the tireless Angel. This was the infamous fourth night, when Malik made his call to Warne. Next day, McGrath was troubled with a strained hamstring and May with a ricked neck, but Warne and

Angel were able to steadily pick off Pakistani wickets. Nightwatchman Akram Raza fell at 157, top-scorer Saeed Anwar at 174, Wasim at 179, Basit Ali at 184. Rashid Latif put on 52 with an ill Inzamam-ul-Haq to take them to 7/236, but Steve Waugh trapped Latif and Warne got Waqar at 258. Mushtaq, not a complete bunny but not far off, joined Inzamam with 56 needed. The Australians celebrated when Angel thundered through Inzamam and hit him apparently plumb in front. Pakistani umpire Khizar Hayat rejected the appeal, triggering an angry reaction from Angel which later earned him the meeting with referee John Reid.

Inzamam monopolised the strike and pushed Warne and Angel away. It soon became desperate for the Australians, as Mushtaq connected with some big swipes and the score kept rattling along. In 40 minutes the pair had taken Pakistan to one shot from victory. Warne lobbed one up to Inzamam, the batsman charged – and missed – but the ball kept low and spun past Healy too, for four byes. Bird signalled them legbyes, but television replays cast doubt on whether the ball had hit the pad. Healy said it hadn't. And that was that. Pakistan had seized victory from a match the Australians had dominated at every turn except for the vital ones, when Wasim and Waqar wrecked the second innings and when Inzamam and Mushtaq refused to die. It was a lesson Taylor and his team had to learn if they were not to repeat the agonising losses of the Border years: winning teams win the big points.

Australia travelled to Islamabad optimistic and determined. Taylor won the toss and added 176 with Slater, who went on to a prized century. Mark Waugh (68), Bevan (70) and Healy (58) were again in fine touch, and Steve Waugh made 98 before Waqar hit him with a sharp bouncer. Waugh fended it off his throat, and it travelled via bicep and heel to dribble onto the leg stump. Australia's 521 looked matchwinning when Pakistan could muster only 260 in reply, the rejuvenated McDermott and debutant Damien Fleming taking four wickets apiece. Australia's first-Test attack was feeling the toll: McGrath and May had been omitted, and the exhausted Angel and Warne could take only one wicket between them.

Then Taylor made another of the decisions that turned this into such an important formative tour. Having taken 76 overs to dismiss Pakistan first time around, he sent them in again. Aamir Sohail and Saeed Anwar opened comfortably before Sohail retired hurt on 30. No 3 Zahid Fazal went cheaply, and Malik entered at 1/79. Pakistan did not lose another wicket until Anwar edged Mark Waugh at 227, but Sohail returned to add another 109 with Malik. Every time a wicket fell, the Australians summoned up a bigger effort, Taylor calling his bowlers together for an on-field conference. It was a new departure for a captain who had felt nervous about talking to any of his men, who had known no Test captain other than Border. But the fielders offered poor support, Taylor dropping Malik and Warne putting down Sohail at deep fine leg. Australia could not get going until 469, when Aamir Malik's fall for 65, caught by Bevan off Fleming, precipitated a first-ball dismissal for Inzamam. By then, though, it was too late. Pakistan were 200 ahead with three hours remaining.

Salim's double century was one of the great Test innings. He started in a blaze, hitting his first century off 139 balls with 19 fours – perhaps he was unsettled by the things the Australians were saying to him! He hit his second hundred off the same number of balls, but settled into a pattern of gliding the fast bowlers and pushing Warne onto the off side. He eschewed hitting against the leg-spin, waiting for Warne to bowl at the stumps and letting his soft wrists turn the ball through the off. It was a lesson in batting against Warne, and gave Malik such confidence that he later claimed that Warne only raised the bribery allegations because he was bitter at his inability to get Malik out.

Fleming did, eventually, with an unusual hat-trick. After taking Aamir Malik and Inzamam, Fleming watched as Salim and Wasim Akram took nine runs off the next over. Fleming's next ball was to Malik, then on 237. Famously, the bowler said at the top of his mark: 'Salim Malik, you're about to become part of history.' In Fleming's account, he closed his eyes in delivery and hoped to bowl his stock outswinger. Malik edged to Healy, and Fleming became the first Australian to take a hat-trick on debut. It was all academic by that stage, however: Pakistan had drawn the match.

As tended increasingly to occur, there was then a one-day series, before the third Test. Australia continued their good form by beating South Africa in Lahore and Pakistan in Multan, then South Africa again in Faisalabad. Pakistan hit back in Rawalpindi, the match where Mark Waugh turned down Malik's money and made a century – but unwittingly revealed the offer after Pakistan had chased 251 runs in 39 overs. Healy broke his thumb during the chase, and NSW veteran Phil Emery flew over – but not in time for the next match, in Peshawar, where Australia beat South Africa with the aid of wicketkeeper Justin Langer. Australia's last preliminary game, against Pakistan in Gujranwala, was cancelled due to overnight rain. A crowd of 20,000 became so restless that the local deputy police commissioner begged the Australian management: 'Please, you must play ... or they will kill us!' A 15-over hit-out was arranged, with bowlers coming in only from the dry end, and Pakistan won – using 12 bowlers.

South Africa lost their sixth match in six attempts, to Pakistan in Faisalabad, setting up a high-quality final in Lahore. Australia won by 65, thanks to a flying start from Taylor and Slater and a five-wicket spree from McGrath, but lost Steve Waugh to a dislocated shoulder suffered while throwing from the deep field.

Wasim and Waqar fed the fuel of suspicion when both withdrew from Pakistan's team on the morning of the third Test in Lahore. Rashid Latif also pulled out, but his replacement, Moin Khan, scored 115 not out to shore up a first innings of 373. Australia replied with 455, led by Bevan's 91, but Malik and Sohail, whose lives were to follow such divergent paths in the next few years, both scored second-innings hundreds to seal the draw and a series win. Australia had been unable to break the hoodoo in Pakistan, but on this tour they learned the lessons which they were to put to effective use in the next four years.

Pakistan in Australia, 1995–96
As had happened so often in the past, the Pakistanis arrived woefully underprepared for a three-Test series and did not find their form until the dead rubber. They found it so resoundingly, however, that they had some claims – which they did not, of course, leave unspoken – to be a better

team than Australia, and left the country muttering that a five-Test series would have ended in their favour.

Between 1994 and this series, Pakistan had fallen into disarray, losing a home series to Sri Lanka and an away Test to South Africa. The team became a revolving door as the political winds shifted to and fro. Malik was now in, now out. Rashid Latif and Basit Ali were alternately punished and rewarded for their whistleblowing. Waqar Younis, whose early career was the most prodigious in modern cricket – he had taken a wicket every 35 balls – was restricted by back and groin injuries.

When they came to Australia, the Pakistanis' priority was to prepare for their World Cup defence on home soil at the end of the southern summer.

Salim Malik was omitted from the original Pakistan touring squad on grounds of 'poor discipline'. In fact, the ever-shifting factionalism of Pakistani cricket had moved against Malik for a few months, the Pakistan Cricket Board launching an inquiry into the match-fixing allegations against him. He had been left out of the Pakistan team for the home series against Sri Lanka in September, which Pakistan lost humiliatingly. Malik was subsequently cleared of wrongdoing – after such a bad home loss, the winds shifted back in the leading batsman's favour – and added to the squad for the Australian tour on a supplementary basis. The Pakistan inquiry, headed by supreme court judge Fakhruddin G. Ibrahim, said the allegations against Malik were 'concocted'. The accusers, Mark Waugh, Shane Warne and Tim May, did not travel to Pakistan, fearing for their safety, though May was to release a statement on 31 October saying: 'I am ready, willing and able to attend any independent hearing convened by the ICC and give sworn evidence as to what transpired in Pakistan.' The ICC's impotence was again exposed, however, the international body having to admit that it had no jurisdiction to override the wishes of the PCB.

As the Pakistanis meandered through their early matches, in Perth and Adelaide, a constant watch was kept for Malik's late arrival. Several unfortunate Pakistani and Indian gentlemen were beset by television news cameras in Perth as Malik-spotting built to a frenzy. Finally he arrived for the second lead-up match, in Adelaide, and scored seven and 16. In the second innings he was stumped off May.

The Pakistanis' indifferent form was a concern for the ACB leading into a season in which they were the top attraction. They had the worse of their drawn matches in Perth and Adelaide, only Basit Ali of the batsmen showing any consistency. Waqar bowled just five overs before the first Test in Brisbane. They folded meekly there. Australia's team, which had beaten England and, triumphantly, recaptured the Frank Worrell Trophy in the Caribbean, was bolstered by Craig McDermott's return, and was probably the strongest team to play during Taylor's years. They were aided by eight dropped catches in their first innings in Brisbane as they piled up 463 runs, Steve Waugh top-scoring with an unbeaten 112. Malik's contribution was an excellent diving catch at mid-wicket to remove Taylor for 69, but in doing so he split the base of his thumb and required six stitches. He absented himself from Pakistan's innings of 97. A rampant Warne took 7/23 as the Pakistanis capitulated in 41 overs. Malik was scorned most of all for a perceived lack of courage. Ian Chappell, in the television commentary box, noted that absent injured counts as an innings, so Malik would have had nothing to lose by at least trying to bat, and Warne said that if it had been an Australian, nothing short of a broken leg would have stopped him batting. The events of 1994 were at the top of the Australians' minds. Taylor had learned, at Rawalpindi in 1994, that it was best to bat again and let the opposition face Warne in a fourth innings; but this time, the deficit was so immense that he enforced the follow-on. Apart from Aamir Sohail's 99 and Inzamam's 62, there was little improvement on the first time around – Pakistan made 240 and lost by an innings and 126. Malik batted at No 8 and faced four balls, the last of which he scooped to mid-off. The jubilant bowler was Warne.

Pakistan's bowling improved in the second Test, in Hobart, an affair drained of much of its drama because Malik did not play and Warne did not bowl after Waqar broke his toe during Australia's first innings. Pakistan recalled Mushtaq Ahmed, and the effervescent leg-spinner's nine wickets were to trigger an incredible two-year period in which he bamboozled batsmen around the world and laid fair claim to being the most destructive spinner in the game, Warne included. Mushtaq could not stop the Australians sealing the series, however. A run-a-minute 120 partnership from Taylor (123) and Slater (73) in Australia's second innings broke the visitors' spirit, as did some poor umpiring decisions against Ramiz Raja and Ijaz Ahmed. McGrath confirmed his rise as Australia's No 1 strike bowler when he took his two-Test tally to 13 wickets, as opposed to McDermott's three.

Another bad loss – inside three days to Victoria – spread the belief that the Pakistanis were counting the days before they could get home and commence the final stage of their World Cup preparation. Their team was divided into factions, too. On one side were those who were to make the key allegations of match-fixing two years later: Aamir Sohail, Rashid Latif, Basit Ali, Ata-ur-Rehman, and Aaqib Javed. On the other were the accused: Malik, Wasim Akram, Ijaz, Moin Khan, Mushtaq Ahmed, and Waqar. If ever a team was ripe for disaster, it was this one. Almost inevitably, then, Pakistan defeated Australia soundly in the third Test.

Malik's brother-in-law, Ijaz, had always been a thorn in Australia's side, and top-scored for the match with a first-innings 137. 'The Axeman', so known because of his awkward-looking, chopping-bottom-hand batting style, was one of the main accused in the match-fixing saga, and like several of his teammates, he batted as if for his very life over the next four years.

Instability was building in the Australian batting order, with the form of Slater, Boon and Greg Blewett tailing off. Slater was, in fact, four Tests away from omission, Boon three away from a semi-enforced retirement, and Blewett ran out of chances altogether when, after an unhappy time against Mushtaq's looping wrong'uns, he was bowled on the last day by a searing, inswinging Waqar full toss. McDermott had kept Australia in the match with five second-innings wickets, but chasing 247 in the fourth innings, Australia never looked likely, losing 7/51 on the last morning. Pakistan's first win in Australia since 1981–82 was enough to give them the belief, made public by captain Akram, that in a five-Test series they would have come home over the top of the waning Australians.

Australia in Pakistan, 1998

The psychological landscape between the two teams had changed irrevocably by the time of their next meeting. Key players in the bribery scandal were either retired (Tim May), absent injured (Warne, recovering from shoulder surgery in May 1998), or marginalised (Malik was a ghostly presence in the Pakistan team, kept on in the hope that this would deter him from carrying out threats to sue the PCB).

Yet this was also the series, four years after the fact, that was most directly affected by the controversy. The fall of the Bhutto government had led to an authentic Pakistani judicial inquiry into match-fixing, the interim report of which had been leaked during the Commonwealth Games in Kuala Lumpur, where Australia's cricket team took silver behind South Africa's gold. By the time the Australians arrived in Pakistan, the inquiry, under Justice Malik Mohammed Qayyum, was in full swing, questioning Pakistan players, bookmakers, administrators and former players.

The political breeze was blowing hard against the suspected match-fixers. Pakistan's 'Mr Clean', opening batsman Aamir Sohail, had been appointed national captain. For the time being, Pakistan seemed to be trying to achieve a steady transition from the murky Malik–Akram days into a new era, where young players could join the team and not be immediately taken under the wing of corrupting influences.

Alas for Sohail, Australia again thwarted the progress of ethical cleansing, this time by the fair and honest means of playing excellent cricket. By winning the series, the Australians set back the progress of corruption-fighting in Pakistan.

Having learnt, from their unsuccessful 1998 tour of India, that they had to arrive in the subcontinent ready to play and win every single game, the Australians crushed a Karachi selection by 333 runs in their first encounter and never looked back. They did not lose a game of any kind on this tour. Their only loss before returning home was in an ill-planned sortie to Bangladesh for an ICC-sponsored one-day tournament.

NSW leg-spinner Stuart MacGill, selected in place of the injured Warne, took nine wickets in the momentum-establishing game in Karachi. MacGill, originally from Perth, was a different kind of bowler from Warne. He flung the ball with a flatter action and aimed at middle and off stumps rather than Warne's leg-stump line. MacGill relied less on loop and drift, and more on the savage side-spin he imparted on the ball. He also had a well-disguised wrong'un.

A Couple Of Rogues ... Salim Malik tries to sweet-talk Inzamam, Pakistan, 1998. Salim's brother-in-law Ijaz Ahmed listens in for a tip. Mark Ray

In the first and, ultimately, decisive Test match in Rawalpindi, played on just that one game's preparation, MacGill took another nine wickets. Sensing the potential for disunity in a Pakistan team led by Sohail but containing a surly Akram and Malik, the Australian bowlers launched themselves ferociously into their work on the first morning. McGrath and Fleming punched holes in the top order, and while the left-handed strokeplayer Saeed Anwar was blazing a fine 145 at one end, MacGill made timely incursions at the other. Australia had surprised by picking 34-year-old journeyman Colin Miller for his first Test, fresh out of semi-professional league cricket in Holland. Miller had taken 67 Sheffield Shield wickets in 1997–98, giving the lie to his age and passing Chuck Fleetwood-Smith's 63-year-old domestic record, bowling outswingers and off-spinners. It was with the former variety that Miller captured his first wicket, the batsman edging a cover drive for Taylor to take an excellent catch at first slip. The unlucky batsman, out for 10, was Salim Malik.

Chasing 269, Australia's moment of truth came when they had lost Taylor, new No 3 Justin Langer, and Mark Waugh for a combined three runs. Steve Waugh joined Slater and together, Waugh wrote, they batted 'as well as we've ever done' to add 198 for the fourth wicket. Slater made 108, Waugh 157, and Darren Lehmann flooded through to stroke a masterly 98 before misjudging a sweep and being bowled. Sohail's timid captaincy was easily spooked, falling back on deep field placings and over-bowling his own left-arm tweakers for 23 overs, and Australia's 513 put them in total command. The seam of McGrath, Fleming and Miller knocked out the Pakistani top four for 32 runs on the fourth day, leaving the tail for MacGill, whose match analysis of 9/113 laid to rest any feelings that Warne's absence would be pivotal.

Australia's first Test win in Pakistan since 1959–60 was achieved through a two-pronged process of mental preparation. On the field, the team had often struggled to find the key to unlocking what they saw as an impenetrable Indo-Pakistani cast of mind. Against South Africa and England there was no language barrier, and the Australians could probe the evident weaknesses of players they could almost consider cricketing cousins. Also, the South Africans and English regarded the Australians with obvious respect. The South Africans even referred to Steve Waugh as 'The Man', and when Australia faced these sides they took the field with the arrogance they had copied from the great West Indian teams of the 1980s.

Pakistan, Sri Lanka and India, on the other hand, held them in no awe. On their own turf and in front of their own people, these teams had a cocky spirit which flummoxed the Australians. Ian Healy said the Indians in 1998 were the most confident opponents he had faced since the West Indies in the 1980s. Sri Lanka had crushed Australia in the 1996 World Cup, transforming themselves on home and neighbouring soil, and had overrun Australia again later in 1996.

How could the Australians counter this? First of all, they prepared themselves for an attacking, aggressive outlook on their cricket and their life in Pakistan in 1998. On the field, the Australian fielders and bowlers revived the old tactic of 'sending off' Pakistani batsmen, not in the ugly and fine-attracting manner with which Warne had 'sent off' South Africa's Andrew Hudson in 1994, but using the more subtle strategy of celebrating wildly in the batsman's face as he departed the centre. When they dismissed Pakistan's free-hitting opener, Shahid Afridi, for example, they celebrated with cries of 'Take that, Mister Big Shot!' The Australians felt they had been too timid in India in 1998, and wanted to tread Pakistani soil as if it were their own.

In order to kid themselves into this kind of confidence, the Australians had tried to adopt a new attitude to off-field life. As Steve Waugh wrote, 'In my early touring days to India and Pakistan we used to count down the days left on tour, starting from our second day; nowadays on these tours we look forward to our next challenge.'

This was easier for some than for others. Waugh himself had overcome homesickness and an unworldly fear of food, people and culture in Pakistan and India earlier in his career, by throwing himself into his diary-writing and photo-snapping activities on the streets of the sub-continental cities. With increased maturity, he was able to enjoy himself taking excursions such as that to the Khyber Pass and to Murree, in the mountains near Rawalpindi, on this tour. He took with him a small group of acolytes, including Justin Langer, Gavin Robertson and Glenn McGrath, who adopted the Steve Waugh way of opening oneself to new experiences. Indeed, Waugh and Robertson had put together a team newsletter, called 'The No Whinge, No Wine Tour', in 1994. Not all Australian players could quite stretch their imaginations so far, and several chose to remain in their comfortable hotels keeping in constant touch with home. But rather than factionalise the team, the outward-looking approach of this tour seemed to unite the players in a general optimism.

It had become harder for Taylor and Healy to take a leadership role in this process, since they had been omitted from the one-day team in 1997. For instance, they were unable to share the one-day team's excitement in being part of the Commonwealth Games atmosphere prior to the Pakistan tour. They had to join up with a team which was becoming used to seeking leadership from Steve Waugh. And then they had to depart again as the one-day team flew to Bangladesh. But those two senior players made their own contributions in returning to the fold.

Healy, first of all, broke Rod Marsh's Australian and world record for Test dismissals in the first Test. On the fourth day, Miller's off-break got Wasim Akram's edge, and Healy leapt forward for dismissal number 356. Healy admitted to having struggled with his concentration once he equalled Marsh's 355 with a catch off Fleming during the first innings. 'I was ready for nothing the whole day and then the dream half-hour start got me into expectation mode. I was a bit anxious and battled with my footwork all day after that,' he said. When he caught Akram three days later, he said it had been 'like being on 99 for 150 overs'. Between times, he had cracked a vital 82 in Australia's first innings. When he left the field on day four, a bottle of champagne was waiting, attached to it a note from Rod Marsh saying: 'Congratulations, Heals. Well deserved. PS Don't drop this one.' Alan Knott had made the same gesture to Marsh when the Australian passed his world record at Headingley in 1981, and no doubt Healy will do the same for his successor. (At time of writing, South Africa's Mark Boucher had just effected his 100th Test dismissal, a week after his 23rd birthday, in his 23rd Test. Given another 10 years in the game, Boucher could expect to pass Healy's record around 2005 and end up with as many as 600 dismissals.)

Taylor, meanwhile, had a lot on his mind in Pakistan. For one, his unhappiness at not being able to lead the one-day team was still evident, only partially eased by a crisis meeting with the ACB before the Pakistan tour. After the first Test he and Mark Waugh were joined by the ACB chief executive, Malcolm Speed, and the trio flew from Rawalpindi to Lahore to face the High Court inquiry. Annoying them profoundly was the presence of Pakistani media and even Salim Malik, who was able to instruct his lawyer's cross-examination in the judge's chambers. Little came from the hearing, with Waugh repeating his four-year-old allegations and Taylor passing on what he had heard second-hand. Taylor recalled it as 'a bloody awful day' – he was 'never happier to be back in the heart of my team than ... that night'. Taylor said he was 'filthy' about the

We'll Carve You Guys Up . . . Pakistani butchers and cricket optimists, Peshawar, 1998.
Mark Ray

presence of Pakistani media, which was 'a violation of a firm agreement', on safety grounds, to keep the Lahore visit secret. Unfortunately, this breach was later raised by ACB chairman Denis Rogers when the Mark Waugh–Shane Warne bookmaker affair came into the open as a reason why Taylor and Waugh had not disclosed their full knowledge to the inquiry. In fact, the reason they did not come forward was that they were not asked, and it is to their discredit, particularly Waugh's, that they did not. This was Australia's golden opportunity to provide new information to help the inquiry, but, partly due to self-interest and partly due to the antagonistic atmosphere caused by Salim Malik's presence, they decided not to help.

The Australian media on tour, including Ray and Conn, were also incensed, but because they had not been told about the hearing and thus had not been there. Conn's masters at *The Australian* were so aggrieved, in fact, that they directed him to cover the inquiry instead of the cricket a week later. Ray had taken the same decision earlier. That line of investigation was to culminate, two months later, in the Waugh–Warne exposé.

Taylor was also concerned about his batting form. His tour innings had been 1, 19 and 3, and he scored 13 in the first innings of the next tour match after his appearance at the inquiry, against the Rawalpindi Cricket Association. Already there were stirrings about a new 'slump', with Taylor's near-fatal lapse in 1997 still fresh in many minds. As a consequence, he decided to bat on in the second innings of the Rawalpindi tour match, making 63 not out, batting at No 5, as the game petered out.

'For the first time in my life,' he told the media after the day's play, 'I made a selfish decision. I felt I needed a hit.' Four days later, he stepped out into the hazy morning light at the Arbab Niaz Stadium in the frontier city of Peshawar, and showed how much good the hit had done him.

Spot The Ball #547 ... Devotees find time to turn to Mecca during practice before the third Test, Australia v Pakistan, Karachi, 1998. Mark Ray

History records Taylor's 334 alongside Sir Donald Bradman's identical score at Leeds in 1930. Taylor took almost twice as long to do it, and admitted modestly that this would be the only time his batting would be compared with Bradman's. The finer details are also revealing. Wasim Akram withdrew from the Pakistan team on the morning of the match, apparently with influenza but according to rumour because he found it intolerable to play under Sohail, who had fingered him as a match-fixer before Judge Qayyum. On a flat, hard pitch, the Pakistan attack consisted of two speedy tyros, Shoaib Akhtar and Mohammed Zahid, the latter of whom was carrying an injury. An injured and out-of-form Mushtaq Ahmed bowled 46 fruitless overs of leg-spin, while part-timers Sohail and Salim Malik bowled 58 overs between them. Taylor was dropped twice, on 18 and 27, both times by Saeed Anwar. Peter Roebuck wrote in *Wisden Australia* that 'in some respects it was neither an exciting nor an exceptional innings. Resourcefulness was not needed because the bowling was threadbare and the pitch gentle.'

That being said, many Test matches are played on easy pitches against teams with weakened bowling, and still only four batsmen had scored more runs than Taylor. The threadbare attack removed Slater and the Waughs cheaply, and Langer for 116. Twelve-hour innings do not just happen. Taylor's 334 was a supreme combination of mental effort, physical fitness and pure, enjoyable ball-striking.

His first runs came off an inside edge which just missed the off stump. Akhtar and Zahid bowled with extreme pace, and Slater was caught for two. Langer could well have been judged lbw first ball. Taylor struggled into the forties, giving Anwar chances at cover and bat-pad. But suddenly, for no clear reason, he found himself in the 'zone'. He later told *Sports Illustrated* that he felt he had almost a supernatural prescience about the position of the ball – both where the bowler would bowl it and where he would place his shot. Whatever clicked in his mind is of course a mystery. Batsmen do enter that 'zone' from time to time, but most do not make triple centuries. It took something extra for Taylor to keep his concentration for six sessions. He compiled 112 by an early, dark stumps on the first day, and added another 100 by lunch on the second – a century in a session, albeit a three-hour one. By the middle of day two, the placement of his strokes was coming so easily that he was able to save some mental energy for reminding himself, simply, not to play a tired stroke. He was aided, in his own belief, by the strenuous physical training he had done with Sydney trainer Kevin Chevell in the 1998 off-season. And no doubt there was a sense of making up for lost time. In 1997 Taylor had spent

'A Supernatural Prescience' ... During his 334 at Peshawar, Mark Taylor said he almost felt as if he knew where the ball would be bowled. Ben Radford/Allsport

many days watching his teammates bat from the dressing room; now, he was savouring every moment.

'It was only when I got to the 290s,' he wrote, 'that I started to get a little nervous. All of a sudden I was a bit weary and overwhelmed.' He punched Mushtaq through cover off the back foot and was past 300. The records continued falling: Bradman's 304, Bob Cowper's 307, Bob Simpson's 311. His teammates cheered loudly as he passed the mark set by the former coach. Ricky Ponting, then Taylor's batting partner, asked 'Who's left?' The only Australian Taylor could think of was Bradman.

He was dropped again on 325, a leg-side chance to keeper Moin Khan. With two balls left on the second day, Taylor was on 334 and facing Sohail. He tried to flick both past Ijaz Ahmed, who as a fielder is pretty much what Taylor is as a bowler. Incredibly, Ijaz stopped the shots, and Taylor was left on the Bradman score.

In *Time To Declare*, Taylor dispels the myth that he finished deliberately on 334: 'Of course I am proud of the wonderful historical coincidence of that day, and that score. Yet, you know, all of it was fate. I ended up on the same score by chance, then finally decided to declare – as I'm sure Sir Donald Bradman would have done – for the good of the team.'

While Taylor tossed and turned in bed that night, and his teammates backed any decision he would make, and while Peshawaris and other fans around the world urged him to bat on, most informed viewers on the spot expected Taylor to declare. He could not sacrifice a Test, and possibly a historic win in Pakistan, on the altar of his own glory. Individual world records are fine things, but undoubtedly they are finer in Pakistan, India and the West Indies, Taylor thought, than in Australia, which prizes the team effort over the individual's. Taylor would have faced some justified criticism had he batted into a third day. As it turned out, Pakistan made 580 and the Test was dead; but Taylor could not have known that on the second night. He spoke to his father, Tony, and his wife, Judi. He said it was easier to have to make the decision for himself than if, say, Steve Waugh or Michael Slater had been 334 not out. But batting on for personal

Time To Declare ... Mark Taylor after batting two days straight in Peshawar.
Ben Radford/Allsport

milestones, he said, 'was not how I ever played the game – and it was not the way I wanted the Australian side to play the game either'.

Australia won the series 1–0 with a draw in Karachi. Slater ground out a tough 96 on the first day, before losing his head in sight of a century and being stumped, to set Australia up with a competitive 280. Only Sohail, heroic with 133, batted well in Pakistan's reply. Even though they were demoralised and disunited, the Pakistanis fought back and may have squared the series if not for Mark Waugh's 117 in his last innings of a barren series. Taylor, Langer and Robertson added useful scores to put Australia out of reach on 390, and Ijaz batted out the final day for a safe draw.

As a footnote, Salim Malik made a pair in Karachi. Perhaps he was haunted by the events there four years previously. In the second innings he was trapped lbw by Colin Miller, as honest a player and person as cricket ever knew. 'I had never,' Taylor wrote, 'seen our guys so jubilant.'

Pakistan in Australia, 1999–2000

Beyond Taylor, Australia continued its psychological mastery of its most talented opponent. Steve Waugh entered the first home series after Taylor's retirement under some pressure as a Test captain. He had drawn a series in the West Indies which Australia expected to win; indeed, retaining the Frank Worrell Trophy required a last-ditch comeback in the fourth Test in Antigua. After that, Waugh's one-day team had won the World Cup, giving him a legitimacy Taylor never enjoyed, but their form fluctuated on the springtime tour to Sri Lanka. They lost the first Test badly, Waugh and Jason Gillespie suffering the collision which broke the former's nose and the latter's leg. Rain disrupted the second and third Test matches, and Australia's feeling that their cricket was improving was not put to the full test. They went down 1–0, and deserved to lose the series without any excuses. A short trip to Zimbabwe yielded a convincing Test win, but nobody was under any illusions about the quality of the opposition.

Pakistan arrived under Wasim Akram, who had been officially cleared of match-fixing. So had Ijaz Ahmed and the rest of the team, which included all the usual suspects except Salim Malik. A military coup had unseated the democratic government of Nawaz Sharif, and Pakistani politics – indivisible from its cricket politics – were yet again in flux. At the time of writing, the reports of the various match-fixing inquiries have yet to surface. The last indications were that they had gone to the office of Mohammed Rafiq Tarar, Pakistan's president and sports minister.

Poorly prepared, and not having played a Test match for seven months, the Pakistanis lost both of their lead-up games against State teams. They had their chances in the first two Test matches, but failed to grasp them. In the first match, in Brisbane, they were 3/265 on the first day but collapsed on the second morning. They allowed Slater and Greg Blewett to add 269 for the first wicket in Australia's reply, but fought back to a position where they could achieve first-innings parity. But Test debutant Adam Gilchrist and Shane Warne blasted eighties down the order, and Australia got away again. A Saeed Anwar century eradicated Australia's

Can't Bowl, Can't Throw, Can Catch ... Queenslander Scott Muller was sledged by a Channel Nine cameraman, or a team-mate – but Wasim Akram had nothing to say after gifting this caught and bowled, Gabba, 1999. Craig Golding/Fairfax

big lead and Pakistan were set to breeze ahead with only three wickets down on the fourth afternoon. A thunderstorm, and a collapse on the last morning, put paid to that, though, and Australia won by 10 wickets.

In Hobart, another contest pulsated from first to last. Waugh sent Pakistan in to bat for a second time, and they got themselves out with indiscriminate strokeplay, only Mohammed Wasim's brazen 91 stopping the Australian momentum. When Slater, Blewett and Langer took charge on the second morning, Australia moved to 1/195, fewer than 30 runs from taking a lead. Saqlain Mushtaq's mystery off-spinners tore out six wickets, however, and put Pakistan in surprising command. This was a position they held, through good innings by Inzamam and Ijaz, through to the end of the fourth day. Setting Australia 369 to win, Pakistan carved up the top order to have the home team five wickets down and more than 200 runs short. Only Langer and Gilchrist stood between Pakistan and a squared series; and there they stood until the middle session of the final day, when Australia won a remarkable match by four wickets. Langer survived a confident caught-behind appeal in his sixties – the Pakistan players will always believe the wooden snick they heard was bat hitting ball as he flashed at Shoaib. Gilchrist's unbeaten 149 from 165 balls vindicated the selectors' ruthless decision to urge Healy to retire at the end of the Zimbabwe tour. Many disagreed with the philosophy of showing such a faithful servant the door, but Trevor Hohns was preoccupied with 'staggering' the retirements of the senior players and thus avoiding a repetition of the 1983–84 season, when Dennis Lillee, Rod Marsh and Greg Chappell all retired in the same Test match. Australia took five years to recover from the shock. In 1999, Taylor's and Healy's retirements, nine months apart, allowed Australia to adjust a little bit at a time. Gilchrist adapted smoothly to Test cricket, taking a marvellous leg-side catch in his third Test, in Perth, and doing things with the bat that Healy, for all his doughty virtues, could never have managed.

Australia achieved its 3–0 result easily in Perth, the Pakistani batsmen failing to adjust to the bouncing WACA wicket. As was customary for an Australia–Pakistan series, this one ended with threats and controversy. Shoaib Akhtar had been placed under suspicion for throwing his faster ball and a videotape was sent to the ICC in London. Shoaib had arrived in Australia as the world's fastest bowler, but had become distracted by the expectation that he might equal Jeff Thomson's 100 mph (160 km/h) delivery speed, and took only six expensive wickets in the three-Test series. The illegal-action furore distracted him further, with Pakistani officials upset by the fact that the ICC match referee, John Reid, had not informed them of suspicions against the young speedster. As a counter-allegation, Wasim said the Australians had sledged his players and Reid had failed to take action. Even though Pakistan had lost all three Test matches, the series ended, as usual, with a sense of unfinished business.

The West Indies: The Crown in Dispute

WEST INDIES CRICKET was said to have entered a spiral of destruction when Mark Taylor's team went to the Caribbean and won in 1995. Certainly that win, regaining the Frank Worrell Trophy after two decades, was a symbolic peak of the Taylor years, and the senior players who had felt the brunt of the West Indies at their best – Taylor, Healy, Steve Waugh, David Boon – rate that series as a career highpoint.

The merit of that win was underscored, rather than undermined, by the fact that West Indian cricket was not quite as decrepit as many thought it was. At time of writing, the 1995 Australians are still the only team to win a series in the Caribbean since 1973. And the West Indies are still the only touring team to have won a series in Australia since the mid-1980s. Since Allan Border retired in 1994, the West Indies have the best winning record against Australia, recording five wins in 13 Tests against Australia's seven. The West Indies were supposed to have sent a substandard team to Australia in 1996–97, yet they only lost the series 3–2. They were the only team in this period to win two Tests in a series against Australia twice – and India, in 1998, was the only other team to do it at all. In 1999, West Indian cricket was said to be in utter disarray, yet Australia needed to come from behind to square the four-Test series.

Imitation is the sincerest form of flattery, and the Australians under Taylor and Waugh adopted many of the techniques of the West Indian sides who had so recently ruled world cricket. These techniques included targeting the opposing captain because of the effect that would have on team morale; carrying themselves with an air of arrogance; focusing on the 'big points'; and suddenly lifting the intensity in the field so as to turn one wicket into a collapse. The Australians became the West Indians of the 1990s. And, in a sense, the West Indies became what Australia had been in the 1980s: a team which, while outgunned on paper, still provided the toughest contest around.

Australia in the West Indies, 1995

The most decisive judgment in Australia's reclamation of the Frank Worrell Trophy was not, perhaps, made in Bridgetown or Kingston. It was not Courtney Browne's famous howler, dropping Steve Waugh at Sabina Park when the Australian champion still had 158 runs left in his bat. Nor was it the exquisite execution of Australia's plans to dismiss Brian Lara, Carl Hooper and Richie Richardson through the series.

The decisive judgment was made by the ACB a few days before Taylor's team left for the Caribbean. The ACB chose to play a role as part of the team's support apparatus rather than as custodian of the game's higher principles. In 1998, when that judgment was revealed to the public, the board was criticised widely for 'covering up' the misdeeds of Shane Warne and Mark Waugh. Publicly, the 1998 ACB chairman Denis Rogers expressed contrition for the actions of the 1995 board, of which he was a member. But privately, the inner circle of Australian cricket – from board members to Allan Border, Bob Simpson and Taylor himself – had few regrets. They remembered the circumstances of the decision, circumstances which, in their belief, overrode all the high-minded principles of their 1998 critics. They had felt that something far more important than principle was at stake in 1995.

The match-fixing scandal was a leitmotif of Taylor's captaincy because it played as a four-year 'B' theme to the 'A' theme of his team's success. It was while Taylor was leading the short one-day tour of New Zealand, sandwiched between the Ashes series and the West Indies tour, that the can of worms sprang open. While the Australian team was in New Zealand, manager Ian McDonald carried out, on the board's instruction, an investigation into rumours that Waugh and Warne had an association with an illegal Indian bookmaker. McDonald interviewed Waugh and Warne, who owned up to having received money since late 1994 for providing weather and pitch information to the bookmaker. McDonald relayed this information to the ACB. The team had only two days in Australia between its arrival home from the New Zealand tour and its departure for the West Indies. Chairman Alan Crompton and chief executive Graham Halbish then made the call that was to dog them four years later. They reprimanded and fined Waugh and Warne – roughly recouping the cash the two had been paid by the bookmaker – and decided to keep the matter in-house. Four years later, Halbish and Crompton could offer no explanation for why they covered up the fines, saying, effectively, 'we kept it in-house because we kept those things in-house'. The reason, in fact, was quite clear. They did not want to compromise Australia's chances of winning the Frank Worrell Trophy for the first time since 1975–76.

Whether the ACB was right or wrong in that decision is a vexed question. On the one hand, it can be argued that the board had a responsibility to do everything in its power to ensure the success of Australian cricket. It was in Australian cricket's interest that Waugh and Warne were able to travel to the West Indies without this cloud over them, and that Taylor be able to conduct the tour without having to respond to constant questions about his players' integrity. On the other hand, the captain himself was at first kept in the dark. 'The news,' Taylor wrote, 'came to me like a bolt from the blue from Ian McDonald ... It happened when I got a phone call from Macca as departure day for the West Indies neared. "Mark, what would you think if I told you two of your players have accepted money from a bookie to provide information?" he asked. It stopped me dead. "You're joking," I responded. "No, I'm not," he said. "Shane and Mark have done that."'

In hindsight, then, Australia's wonderful win in the Caribbean is shadowed by a story that remained untold. Freed from that distraction, Taylor's men could concentrate on the toughest challenge in the game.

It is impossible to appreciate how hard it is to win cricket games in the West Indies until you go there. As Paul Reiffel wrote of the 1995 tour, 'The grounds are small and rough, and the crowds are all over you and very parochial. They're not abusive – in fact, they're pretty well mannered – but they're noisy and staunchly pro-West Indian, and they make you feel a little claustrophobic. And of course, the West Indies at that time were still the champions of the world, and not in the mood to give up the title meekly. All in all, the cricket on that tour was the toughest I have ever played.'

The difficulty of winning overseas is axiomatic – yet in Mark Taylor's view, winning in the Caribbean is harder than in Pakistan, India, Sri Lanka or anywhere else.

Playing cricket in the Caribbean can be likened to playing rugby in New Zealand or fighting wars in Russia. There exists in these places such a culture of winning, of expecting to win, and of pride in defending home turf, that otherwise ordinary players can be transformed into supermen. In 1991, a tired, ageing, out-of-form Gordon Greenidge lifted himself for one final series-deciding innings. In 1999, players such as Sherwin Campbell and Jimmy Adams, so diffident away from home, batted as if for their lives, and helped Brian Lara to the brink of recovering the trophy. Even at their lowest, after a belting in South Africa and a crushing loss in the first Test, the 1999 West Indians still believed they could win the series against the world champions – indeed, they did not recognise Australia as world champions. When Lara played his great innings in Jamaica and Barbados, the West Indies did not receive these as surprise gifts, amazing comeback efforts, but rather as a restoration of world cricket's rightful order.

It is these two disappointments – 1991 and 1999 – which cast Australia's 1995 win in its proper light. This series was the high-water mark of Taylor's captaincy, not simply because his players regained the Worrell Trophy, but because they were able to beat the West Indies at all.

In the purely cricketing sense, the series and tour had a little bit of everything. Australia played eight matches before the first Test in Bridgetown, winning two first-class games easily but losing the international one-day series 1–4. Carl Hooper (290 runs at 72.5), Phil Simmons (233 at 46.6) and Lara (256 at 85.3) were in ominous form with the bat, while captain Richie Richardson, recently returned after a year-long fight with chronic fatigue syndrome and now wearing an unfamiliar helmet, sat out all but one match of the series with a shoulder injury. In his absence, Courtney Walsh led the team once again. The West Indian batting had an air of invincibility, enhanced when Damien Fleming wore out his bowling shoulder in Port-of-Spain and Craig McDermott ripped his ankle ligaments in Georgetown during the three-day match – not playing cricket, but jumping to the ground from a one-metre high concrete wall when running along the beach from the Bourda Ground back to the team hotel. Both were sent home, replaced by Brendon Julian and Carl Rackemann. On Test eve, the teams looked so mismatched that Robert Craddock wrote for News Limited that 'even the most ardent Australian fan is now wondering how the tourists' threadbare attack is going to secure enough regular breakthroughs to win a Test match in the Caribbean'.

The Australians had a pivotal meeting in St Lucia, where they addressed their problems honestly. Bob Simpson circulated a questionnaire which illuminated the team's attitude at the time:

Question 1: Why haven't we been playing as well as we can? Answers: Batting – no forward thinking, the cardinal sin of too many wickets being lost together, inconsistency, not being tough enough, not building parnerships, not capitalising on good starts. Bottom line: basics are not being adhered to, and we're not batting as a team. Bowling – not accurate enough, bowling to both sides of the wicket, poor concentration, lack of communication between teammates, lack of aggression, little enjoyment. Fielding – lack of communication, aggression and confidence, not enough enjoyment.

Question 2: What can you do to improve performance? Answers: Pull together, more confidence, train with more focus, communicate more, lift intensity, more pressure at practice. And very important: enjoy the challenge of the series. Assist others, stop the "whinge".

Question 3: What sacrifices are you prepared to make? Answers: Rest more, put cricket first, spend more time with teammates, spend more free time training, assist teammates.

As David Boon reflected:

> This was a big meeting and, to be honest, a few blokes disagreed on some matters – some thought they had been putting in and, simply, that things hadn't been going our way. But while that may or may not have been right, things hadn't been working.

Paul Reiffel had a similar recollection:

> It began to turn around at a team meeting in St Lucia just before we left for Barbados and the First Test. Before the meeting, Bob Simpson asked us all to write down our answers to a few questions about what we were doing wrong and what we might do to put it right. It got us all thinking a bit more deeply, and the meeting itself was pretty frank. The tour had moved to another level.

The team moved on to Barbados where, for the first time in Taylor's captaincy, the Australians refined their ability to switch up a gear when the circumstances demanded it. On Test eve McGrath impressed his captain with his quiet determination. He said he wanted the new ball for Australia; Taylor observed, 'It wasn't really what he said so much as how he said it.' Of a training session in Barbados, Taylor recalls:

> Suddenly everything felt different and better. In the blink of an eye the team's whole attitude had changed. No longer were we just going through the motions at training. I remember watching it happen and thinking, "Something real is taking place here." The switch was back to "on".

The bowlers decided to bowl in the nets as they would in matches – no more no-balls, and as much short-pitched stuff as they wanted. The backs were taken off the nets (which in Bridgetown are in the centre of the field) so as to approximate match conditions. 'We turned training into fun – although fun with a slightly dangerous edge to it,' Taylor said. 'Practice sessions grew closer to real game time. There would be acclaim for a ball "well evaded" as a steepling bumper soared past. We talked about looking ahead, not looking back.'

One significant change was how this team now dealt with the spectre of short-pitched bowling. Simpson's view had always been to avoid the subject, not to dwell on it, reasoning that too much talk would lead to preoccupation and ultimately panic. He believed, as many do, that facing the West Indies bowlers is hardest of all the night before the match. That is, the anticipation is more nerve-racking than the event. Taylor, however, wanted his men to get the bogey out of their systems. He counselled them to talk about their fears and thus put them into a more public perspective; once spoken, fear can lose its edge. In addition, the Australian bowlers decided to 'bounce' their counterparts. In the past, fearing the obvious consequences, Australian fast bowlers had resisted aiming at the heads of the West Indian fast bowlers. This time, McGrath, who did not care if he trod on his own wicket and was out first ball – what was he sacrificing? – put his hand up and promised to return the West Indians' intimidation.

As Reiffel remembers:

The dominant theme in our team meetings was aggression. I hadn't played against the West Indies before, but the senior guys in the squad – Mark Taylor, Steve Waugh, Ian Healy – kept saying that they were sick of copping it from the Windies and that we had to give some back. They kept drumming that into us.

The Australians were ready for the First Test, at the heaving Kensington Oval in Bridgetown, the spiritual home of West Indian cricket, where Australia had not won a Test in five attempts. Despite his willingness, McGrath was not given the new ball. Instead, the more experienced Reiffel and Julian took it, and promptly took the wickets of openers Campbell and Williams, and then Richardson, in the first three overs. Lara and Hooper steadied with 124 counterattacking runs in 116 minutes, but then Hooper, Adams and Lara fell quickly, the last in unhappy circumstances. Lara cut Julian to backward point, where Steve Waugh fumbled the ball against his chest as he fell to ground. He claimed the catch, and umpires Lloyd Barker and Srinivas Venkataraghavan gave Lara out for 65. Television replays showed the ball may have hit the ground. Viv Richards protested in a newspaper article, calling the Australians cheats and saying Lara was 'batting like a dream' and might have made 200. As Taylor observed, Richards's voice probably came from a more confrontational past than the relatively congenial present, but Lara harboured a grudge. The incident added to three other dismissals – a stumping by Healy off Greg Matthews at Brisbane in 1992–93, a catch by Healy at Sydney in 1996–97, and a run-out by Healy at Port-of-Spain in 1999 – which were to convince Lara, over time, that the Australians had dismissed him by dishonest means. There was doubt over all four of the dismissals, but no objective viewer could possibly believe that the Australian players believed Lara was not out. Each was a messy dismissal, the ball and hands jumbled all around. In the passion of the moment, the Australian players – Healy and Waugh – were within their rights to claim the wickets. It was not for them to know the truth beyond reasonable doubt. All they could do was appeal to the umpires. And in each case, the umpires gave Lara out. Even in Trinidad in 1999, when Lara was very likely not out, the decision was made by a third (West Indian) umpire on the basis of a video replay. Nonetheless, Lara nursed a complex about the Australians' honesty which poisoned his relations with them for an entire decade.

The West Indies made 195 in their first innings at Kensington Oval, and an even batting performance by Australia, with Taylor, Steve Waugh and Healy each passing 50, saw an Australian lead of 151. Batting again, the hosts succumbed to Australia's intensity, Lara nibbling at McGrath to fall to him for the first time in Tests, and Adams top-scoring with an unbeaten 39. McGrath took five wickets and Warne, whose first three balls of the match had gone to the boundary, took three. Taylor and Slater polished off the 39-run target in seven overs. Simpson had gone to hospital with a thrombosis in his leg, and when the team drove by in their bus after the game they shouted in unison, 'Simmo, we've done 'em!'

Rain ruined a potentially great Second Test at St John's, Antigua, the West Indies needing 177 more runs with eight wickets in hand. The match would be remembered for two outstanding catches. Boon, fielding at an unconventional short mid-on, leapt to his left to catch Lara for 88 off Steve Waugh in the West Indian first innings, celebrating with a statuesque stance before being swamped by his teammates. In Australia's second innings Richardson bettered it with a right-hander at third slip to remove Slater, continuing a frustrating run for the right-hander. Slater batted with purpose throughout the series, making starts nearly every innings, but was to finish with 139 runs at 23.16. He was one of 10 batsmen on both sides to average between 20 and 34. It was a bowlers' series. Statistically, there was only one difference between the teams when it came to batting – Steve Waugh's 429 runs at 107.25.

West Indian pitches had slowed dramatically since the mid-1980s, a symbol of the general neglect into which Caribbean cricket was falling. Sabina Park would, in 1998, suffer the ignominy of having its Test match called off after a few overs of Ambrose and Walsh peppering and wounding England's top order. The slowness of the Antigua Recreation Grounds wicket had vexed the West Indian team, who were wondering why their groundsmen were not preparing pitches that would offer more assistance to their own bowlers. Somebody was listening at Queen's Park Oval, the home of spin in the Caribbean, which was expected to be the slowest of the lot. Instead, when the Australians first walked on for a practice session, they could literally not tell the difference between the pitch and the rest of the oval. It was, Taylor said, 'one of the worst big-match wickets I ever saw in my career. To be fair to the groundsmen, there had been a lot of rain, but when they pulled the covers off, the grass was about three centimetres long! We presumed they would cut it but they didn't, merely running the roller up and down. If I ever needed to win a toss, this was it. I called tails, as I always did, and lost it.'

Australia's 128 was punctuated by a notorious confrontation between Steve Waugh and Ambrose. Coming in at 3/14, Waugh played one of his finest innings. Booed onto the ground by Lara's home crowd, he played his shots as the wickets fell around him, mostly to a rampant Ambrose and Walsh. At 3/37, he ducked an Ambrose bouncer. Ambrose followed through with what Waugh termed, in his West Indies Tour Diary, 'the regulation Clint Eastwood stare ... I thought he went on with the silent assassin style interrogation for longer than was necessary, so I came back with, "What the f--- are you looking at?"'

Unused to being addressed by a batsman, Ambrose bellowed: 'Don't cuss me, man!' Waugh told Ambrose to get back to his mark and bowl, which went down, in Waugh's words, 'as well as an anti-malaria tablet'. Ambrose made as if to charge into Waugh, but Richardson, rushing in from the field, held his bowler back. It was a significant moment in the iconography of West Indian – in particular, Antiguan – cricket, although the West Indies were to go on and win this low-scoring match. Richardson's authority in the team had weakened since his enforced lay-off. The usual inter-island jealousies were running stronger than usual, and team unity was also weakened by a number of sub-factions. Lara, the world record holder, wanted to be captain, and with Hooper's collusion was agitating among young players for Richardson's dismissal. Walsh, meanwhile, had led the team well in Richardson's absence, and some of the older players, particularly the Antiguan bowlers – Ambrose and Winston and Kenny Benjamin – wanted Walsh in charge. Richardson had minimal support from his players. Only the beleaguered coach, Andy Roberts, was on his side. All of this was to boil over on the 1995 England tour, when Lara and Hooper walked out for short periods and Ambrose and Kenny Benjamin were fined for minor disciplinary breaches, and in the 1996 World Cup, when Richardson and Roberts finally quit after the humiliating loss to Kenya at Pune. In the Caribbean in 1995, the Australians' feistiness seemed to widen the cracks in the West Indian team. Even though the West Indies won easily on the Port-of-Spain greentop, the Antiguans were outraged by Richardson's action in pulling Ambrose away from Waugh on the first day. It was seen as an embarrassment to Antiguan pride. While they lost the game, the Australians were able to sniff the disunity and move onto the final Test with their momentum intact.

Sabina Park was, if anything, a win for unity. The Australians competed with a death-defying singleness of purpose from the first day, when the West Indies won the toss and batted. Even when Richardson and Lara added 103 for the second wicket, the Australians were notably noisy and spirited in the field. Their constant pressure cracked Lara, Adams, Hooper and Keith Arthurton, only Richardson battling on for an even 100. It was the West Indies' only century for the series. On a flat, fast pitch of rolled mud, the West Indies' 265 was a missed opportunity.

The extent of that miss was revealed gradually. Walsh and Ambrose removed Taylor, Slater and Boon for 73 runs, and at lunch on day two Australia were 3/91 with the Waugh brothers at the crease. They added 101 in the next session, young Bajan keeper Courtney Browne committing the blooper of a lifetime when he dropped a straightforward edge from Steve Waugh on 42 off Kenny Benjamin. Waugh could well have turned to Browne and said, as he was fabled to have said to South Africa's Herschelle Gibbs at Headingley in the 1999 World Cup, that Browne had just dropped the Frank Worrell Trophy. Mark Waugh played his best Test innings to that point, in Taylor's judgment an even better innings than his twin's. Just before stumps, after a two-session partnership of 231 runs, Mark prodded Hooper to Adams at bat-pad. Australia were four down, 39 ahead.

Greg Blewett's crackling 69 on the third morning, dominating a 113-run stand with Steve Waugh, was the essential follow-up. When Mark Waugh fell, the West Indians could have hoped to limit Australia's lead to less than 100. But when Blewett strung together some masterly pull shots, Australia's lead was out to 152, and they could think about putting some serious pressure on the West Indian batsmen. Steve Waugh, last man out at 531 for his first Test double century, was the cornerstone. After a faltering early career, during which he had seemed destined never to fulfill his vast promise, he had reassessed his batting methods while out of the Test team in 1991–92. Much has been made of his decision to eschew the hook shot and other more flamboyant trappings, but the essential change was one of attitude. Waugh decided to face fast bowling as a challenge rather than a threat. In short, he started to believe that the art of dodging 'throat balls' was as much fun as hitting fours. He began to relish the fight, where in early years he had baulked at it. He now liked nothing better than the sight of bowlers trying to knock his head off. Never a vain batsman, he cared even less about how he looked as he jumped and twisted away from bouncers. Indeed, his ungainliness worked in his favour, because it encouraged bowlers, from Ambrose to Allan Donald, in their belief that he was uncomfortable or suspect against short-pitched bowling. They never learned their lesson. Instead, they were given false hope by balls such as the one Kenny Benjamin bowled to him on 200 at Sabina Park, at which he flinched and gave a catch to the hapless Browne. Waugh said it had nothing to do with weariness, or the fact that he had just been engulfed by a swarm of rum-soaked Australians, led by former Test batsman and full-time yobbo Greg Ritchie. No, Waugh said, that ball would have got him out if he'd received it on 0, 10, 42 or 200.

On a crumbling wicket, the West Indies were not up to the task. Finally, they had been broken. Reiffel's grubber trapped Lara – a career highlight for the Victorian – and only Winston Benjamin, as nightwatchman, passed 50. Warne took the last four wickets to complete a solid series. The final one, Kenny Benjamin, was caught, appropriately, by Taylor.

The Australians owed their win to meticulous planning, especially in the bowling department. As Reiffel recalled, 'We had a different plan of attack for every batsman we played. There are so many good, sharp brains around in cricket that it is not hard to work out a batsman's strengths and weaknesses ... Against Richie Richardson, we resolved to keep it tight on off stump, and not to give him any width because he is famous for sweating on balls that he can throw everything at. The length had to be pretty full because he is not renowned for using his feet. We figured that by keeping it up and on off stump, we were always a chance to bowl him or have him lbw. Above all – and we reiterated this in team meetings and among ourselves – we weren't to overdo the bouncers against him, because he had a very effective hook shot.'

The aftermath of the series was interesting. Richardson, besieged on all sides, said he 'couldn't believe' the West Indies had lost to an Australian team which he rated the weakest he had played against. On paper, perhaps it was. Certainly the 1991 Australian team appeared a better one. But, as most of the senior Australian players observed, it was a matter of timing. Players like the Waughs, Taylor, Warne and Healy were at or near the peak of their careers in 1995, and they were bolstered by fearless youngsters, such as McGrath, Slater and Blewett, who carried no scars from old beatings. Moreover, the West Indies were weakened by the retirement of their heroes Richards, Marshall, Dujon, Haynes and Greenidge, and riven with dissent through the plotting of Lara and Hooper and the ineffective leadership of Richardson. The planets were all aligned for Australia in 1995. To underline Australia's achievement, the West Indies remained unbeaten on home soil in the next four seasons, against all comers. The Australian win in 1995 was the only home loss for the West Indies between 1973 and the end of the century.

Views differed on whether the win made Australia nominally the best team in the world. Taylor thought it did: 'The West Indies have been the best side in world cricket for 12 to 15 years. Now I think we are the better cricketers. Pakistan play us next summer in three Test matches. If they beat us on our soil, they are the world champions.' Ian Healy, on the other hand, said: 'I don't believe this talk of us being world champions just yet. At the moment, I believe the title is in limbo.'

After a raucous celebration in Kingston, the Australians were joined by their wives and girlfriends for a short working holiday in Bermuda. They played and won three one-day matches, and set another record to cap off the tour. Tour manager and ACB director Jack Edwards threw a victory party for the team, the bill for which came to $AUD10,000. By all accounts, they drank nothing but Moet. Edwards had to explain the bill when he returned to Jolimont, but the incident was brushed aside in the euphoria of the win and the subsequent celebratory motorcade in Sydney. The board felt they owed that much to the players, anyway. What did not emerge for another three years was how much the players – especially Mark Waugh and Shane Warne – owed the board. The victory was a thorough-going team effort.

West Indies in Australia, 1996–97

Compared with West Indian teams of the past, this one had an unusual flavour. Its captain, Courtney Walsh, and coach, Malcolm Marshall, were both fast bowlers. It had no Richie Richardson, no Desmond Haynes and no opening-batting combination of any repute. Most of its batting order were grafters rather than flashy hitters. What was familiar about them was their reliance on fast bowling – they brought six pacemen and no spinners – and their overreliance on Brian Lara to lead their batting.

Tony Cozier has said of West Indian teams that they are always factionalised, always fighting, and it is only winning that has papered over their internal differences. After the West Indies lost the Frank Worrell Trophy to Australia in 1995, they fragmented. Richardson had never recovered his poise or stamina as a batsman since his year off, and on the 1995 tour of England he faced a full-scale mutiny, led by Lara, who thought he should have replaced Richardson as captain. Lara and Carl Hooper both walked out of that tour, for short periods, to visit friends elsewhere in England. They were fined, but to say that the fines were a disciplinary measure is to speak more in hope than fact. On the other side, Richardson was unable to control his fellow Antiguans, the perpetually unstable Kenny Benjamin, Stuart Williams and Curtly Ambrose. As coach, Andy Roberts was similarly unable to exert authority over the Antiguan clique. An unhappy team was able to draw the series with England, but their loss to Kenya at Pune in the 1996 World Cup spelt the end of the Richardson–Roberts leadership.

There were sound enough objections to Lara succeeding Richardson, so the captaincy was given to the phlegmatic but popular Walsh. He, at least, had a spotless record on and off the field. Under Walsh, the West Indies recorded a comfortable 1–0 win in two home Tests against New Zealand after the World Cup, and came to Australia with their customary confidence, sure of regaining the trophy.

Perhaps the first omen for the tour came in the first match, when, in the festive atmosphere at Lilac Hill, 41-year-old Allan Border came on to bowl and dismissed Lara with his first delivery. It was not unusual for a West Indian team to start an Australian tour sleepily – indeed, many of their most devastating raids on Australia had begun with a rash of losses to Sheffield Shield teams – but this squad lacked the class and depth to rest on its laurels. Their early games saw sporadic form from Lara, Hooper, Jimmy Adams and Shivnarine Chanderpaul, but little commitment from the fast bowlers to getting their games up to Test standard. In their final lead-up game in Hobart, against an Australian second XI, the West Indies were slaughtered by 10 wickets. Left-handers Matthew Elliott (158) and Matthew Hayden (224) batted through the first day and added 323. The Australian XI scored 4/544 and rolled through a shivering, sweater-laden West Indian team twice in two days. Marshall, accustomed to these sorts of performances in his time as a player, was full of bluster, saying: 'It will be a grave mistake if Australia take any significance out of this result.' But Marshall, it was soon apparent, derived his confidence from a past era. This West Indian team had come to Australia with a healthy advantage in preparation. While the Australian players had only had one Sheffield Shield match in which to recover form from their dismal spring 1996 Indian tour, the West Indians had enjoyed three weeks of solid acclimatisation and cricket. They wasted it.

Australia were not without problems of their own. During the Sheffield Shield match between NSW and Queensland at Bankstown Oval in mid-November, selector Steve Bernard called Michael Slater across to one of the empty grandstands for a chat. Slater could not believe his ears. Bernard was telling him that his shot selection, the keystone for a batsman with such aggressive tendencies, had deteriorated badly in the past two seasons. Slater's dismissal to David Johnson in the second innings of the Delhi Test match had left a deep impression (certainly far deeper than his disciplined top-scoring 44 in the first innings). Calmly, Bernard told Slater that he had been dropped. The little opener cannot be said to have taken the news well. He was, he later admitted, suffering a mixture of shock and rage when he stormed away from Bankstown after play. His Test average was still in the high forties, and three Tests back he had scored a career-high 219 against Sri Lanka. To his fans, also, his omission was unthinkable. Statistically, he and Taylor were the third most successful opening partnership in Test history, based on the number of century stands. They had 10 in 57 innings, compared with Greenidge/Haynes (16 in 148), Hobbs/Sutcliffe (15 in 38), Gavaskar/Chauhan (10 in 59), Lawry/Simpson (9 in 62). Taylor/Slater's average stand of 59.30 ranked behind only Hobbs/Sutcliffe (87.81), Hobbs/Rhodes (61.31), Lawry/Simpson (60.95) and Hutton/Washbrook (60.00). Greenidge/Haynes averaged 47.31.

Taylor's subsequent loss of form was blamed on the absence of his reliable partner of three years. But Taylor was party to Slater's omission. There was a feeling among some senior members of the team that Slater had risen too far too fast. His effervescent batting and personality had rocketed him, in a short period, to the top of the sponsorship and endorsement tree. He was earning more than all but one or two of his teammates, sparking some resentment among those who had been there longer and achieved more. It was felt that he would benefit from a kick in the pants.

The logic of this rite of passage, which had indeed worked very well with the likes of Steve and Mark Waugh, Boon and Taylor, was questionable in Slater's case. Devastated by his omission, he had a dreadful season for NSW, only lifting his average above 30 with a couple of late-season scores. His maturation as a batsman was set back by a year as he came, slowly and painfully, to terms with his fall. He retreated into himself and often presented a sour, resentful face to the world. He was enraged by what he saw as added pressure from the media, who referred more often than he would have liked to his recent purchase of a big house in Queens Park, Sydney, and his expected difficulties in maintaining his mortgage now that his cricket earnings were down by an estimated $80,000 a season. Slater's reaction to his newfound obscurity was viewed so dimly that one ACB insider remarked confidently and repeatedly that Slater would never play for Australia again.

In Slater's place, for the moment at least, was Matthew Elliott, the stylish and gifted Victorian. At 25, Elliott had built a reputation in Victoria as a magnificent batsman. He deserved his elevation, with scores of 187 against a full-strength NSW and 158 against the West Indies, but when he joined the Australian squad in Brisbane for the first Test he presented an idiosyncratic face. Elliott was not a product of the Adelaide finishing school, nor was he a member of the in-crowd of Australian cricket. Fiercely loyal to Warne, who took him under his wing, Elliott seemed troubled by the off-field pressures of the international arena. Two days before the Test, he argued with News Limited photographer Trent Parke over a simple request. Elliott said he had family coming up from Victoria and needed to clear his mind for cricket, and had no time for the photographer. Certainly there was no absolute requirement for Elliott to comply with Parke's request, but the signs were there, already, that Elliott was a highly strung character who was not going to slip into the stream of public life with any ease. His intensity – his almost paralysing desire to do well for Australia – was going to cause him great problems over the succeeding years. He was poorly advised at this stage of his career, too. It would have helped Elliott if someone like Taylor or Healy had counselled him and brought him into the fold. Instead, his role model was the non-conformist showman Warne, whose example encouraged Elliott to buck the system.

Champing At The Bit . . . Matthew Elliott eschewed a visor on his helmet for his first Test against the West Indies, Brisbane, 1996. Mark Ray

Warne, of course, was under a different kind of pressure. His Sheffield Shield form in his first games back from his 1996 finger surgery was unimpressive – but that was consistent with his career pattern. Warne said he was setting his sights on 300 and then 400 Test wickets, and claimed that, although he had wondered if he would play Test cricket again, he was going to bowl better than ever. It was to become a constant ritual for the next four years: Warne drawing attention to himself by voicing his self-doubts aloud, then putting on a show of undaunted confidence. The cricket public, he felt, was in the palm of his hand.

Yet it was Healy who suffered the most scrutiny in the lead-up to the Brisbane Test. In *The Australian*, Mike Coward reported that Healy's position had been discussed at the selection table. Coward wrote that the ACB and selectors were already toying with the notion of bringing in the talented Adam Gilchrist – who had just scored a superb unbeaten 108, off 101 balls, for Western Australia against the West Indian speedsters on the fiery Perth track – and passing the vice-captaincy to Warne, whom they then regarded as Taylor's natural successor. Coward wrote the piece as a speculative column, based on solid information but not suggesting that Healy was about to be dropped. Coward said simply that the matter had been discussed, as indeed it had. Yet his editors at *The Australian* decided to put the column on the front page of the newspaper, and Healy was besieged with television crews wanting to know his reaction.

It is not too much to say that Healy played the first Test, in front of his home crowd, in a mood of finely focused fury. He had had a poor tour of the subcontinent, disrupted by his captaincy experience in Sri Lanka and a hamstring injury in India. He knew he was under pressure. It is also not too much to say that the 'kick in the pants' theory was enough to propel Healy, over the next three years, to new heights as a cricketer, entrenching his status as one of the very best wicketkeeper-batsmen the game had seen.

He came to the wicket in Brisbane with Australia at 5/196 on the first afternoon. Elliott had made a 15-ball duck, caught behind off his shirt sleeve – yet was praised by most of the media for his style and composure, making his innings one of the most celebrated and promising ducks in history – but a 126-run stand between Taylor (43) and Ponting (88) had blunted the West Indies' new-ball burst on a humid morning. Ponting had had his share of luck, exasperating Ambrose with some edges over and through the slip cordon, but Australia seemed to have gained the advantage before Taylor chopped on, Ponting skied a catch to mid-on, Mark Waugh (38) was caught down the leg side, and Bevan seemed to confirm suspicions about his timidity before short-pitched bowling when, first ball, he fended a Walsh lifter to gully.

Healy joined Steve Waugh and could have been run out on 1 if Adrian Griffith had hit the stumps from mid-on. In a classic old-firm counterattack, Healy and Waugh responded to the crisis by smashing the West Indian bowlers around the Gabba. The West Indians' fitness and fielding proved inadequate as Healy and Waugh built a 127-run final session. They seized the moment on the second morning, too, slowing the pace after Waugh was out for 66, but compiling a matchwinning 479 by the time the innings ended after tea. With some lower-order help from Reiffel's 20 and Warne's 24, Healy finished with 161 not out, his highest score in all cricket. He had scored three Test centuries and none in other first-class cricket: a succinct indication of his ability to rise to the occasion. And a reply to his critics? Healy preferred to let his cricket do the talking, literally. He came to a press conference after the day's play and refused to answer questions except with surly monosyllables. If he wanted to show the press

Going to Plan ... The Australians felt they could cramp Brian Lara and get him flashing to slip. Here it works for the first time in the 1996-97 series, Mark Waugh catching him in Brisbane off Paul Reiffel. Jack Atley/Age

that he was unaffected by their reports, his contrived rudeness proved just the opposite.

Australia removed the two West Indian openers, Sherwin Campbell and Robert Samuels, before stumps, and McGrath picked off Lara early on the third morning. If Australia needed any convincing of how violently these West Indians could fluctuate, they gained solid proof of it in the next five hours. Hooper (102) and Chanderpaul (82) were absolutely untroubled for two sessions, adding 172 on a perfect wicket. Yet Hooper suddenly lost his rhythm in his nineties, and had to dive for his hundredth run, avoiding a run-out by centimetres. Sensing weakness, Taylor then pulled two rabbits from his hat. He gave Steve Waugh the ball, and Waugh had Hooper brilliantly caught by a diving Ponting at mid-wicket. Waugh promptly pulled his groin muscle, so Taylor gave the ball to Ponting for an over of dibbly-dobbly outswing. Immediately, Ponting trapped Adams in front. Reiffel came back for a three-wicket spell, Warne took his first two of the series, and the West Indies, having lost no wicket in four hours, had now lost 7/28 in less than one. Their 277 failed to meet even the follow-on target – by two runs.

Taylor did not enforce it, believing Australia would still need to score about 200 runs to make the match safe, and that those 200 would be easier to score now than on the fifth day. Elliott made his first Test runs, but apart from Mark Waugh's 57 and Healy's unbeaten 45, the Australians were unable to blast off and get the West Indians back in to bat. Bevan was again in a torment, relieved by Lara, who dropped a sitter at first slip when Bevan was still on his pair. Bevan made 20 in 74 minutes, and Ponting let himself down after his aggressive first innings, being caught down the leg side for nine.

Facing some criticism for not enforcing the follow-on, Taylor declared at 420 runs ahead and with 120 overs to play. Lara, with a quick 29 on the fourth evening, threatened the improbable, but he was out early on the last day and only Sherwin Campbell stood between Australia and a good win. He scored 113 in seven hours before being the second-last man out, late on day five. Bevan shone with three wickets – his first three in Test cricket – bowling a bouncy, fast version of left-arm unorthodox spin.

With the 123-run win under their belt, the Australians moved on to Sydney for the second back-to-back Test. English writer Scyld Berry has likened back-to-back Test matches to being served entree and main at the same time, and the West Indians were unhappy with the scheduling. Certainly Austalia felt they had some momentum to carry on from Brisbane, although a terrible Sydney pitch and outfield, Peter Leroy's last as curator, took the vigour out of their roll. Steve Waugh and Reiffel ruled themselves out with injuries, replaced by Greg Blewett and Jason Gillespie, the latter making his Test debut.

Walsh lifted, taking five wickets in Australia's 331, but the four-man pace battery was exposed on the sludgy SCG wicket. Ambrose looked particularly out-of-sorts, his bowling mechanical and his ground fielding sieve-like. Benjamin didn't seem to have his heart in the job, and Bishop was a poor replica of his past self. After Blewett's 69 and Healy's 44 had stapled together the Australian middle order, the West Indies pacemen were embarrassed by McGrath (a career top score of 24) and Gillespie (16), who lasted an hour for the tenth wicket. McGrath had special motivation. *Sydney Morning Herald* journalist Michael Koslowski had written a statistical analysis of McGrath's batting, showing that by most measures he was the worst batsman ever to play Test cricket. Steve Waugh had taped the offending article to McGrath's locker. Mark Waugh, meanwhile, had bet Shane Warne $1000 that McGrath would never score 50. For a while, his money looked unsafe. Even more humiliating for the West Indies was the fact that McGrath was finally dismissed - and contentiously, at that - leg-before wicket by Adams's loopy left-arm spin.

Campbell again thwarted the Australians in reply, scoring 77 and adding 92 with Samuels as the Australian fast bowlers found the same problems as their counterparts. But McGrath often thrived on just such unhelpful wickets, digging the ball in just short of a length and cramping the batsmen. He removed Samuels and Lara (for two), and the Australians ground down their opponents for 304. Gillespie, bowling fast, full outswing, impressed everyone, and earned two late wickets.

Cordoned In . . . The old firm on their toes, West Indies Test, Sydney, 1996. Tim Clayton/Sydney Morning Herald

Taylor's resumé of courageous, attacking captaincy was a long one, but never prouder than late on the third afternoon. In fast-fading light, at 0/18, the umpires invited him to leave the field. Wanting to show the West Indian pace bowlers that he held no fear, Taylor declined the offer. It was a great, symbolic moment. Australia thought they had more to gain from playing on. Taylor was right, though he himself was out soon after. Elliott hit some stirring cover drives and pulls, both that evening and the next morning, until he was involved in a bizarre incident with his partner, Mark Waugh.

At 2/143, Waugh hit Hooper into the deep. Coming for their second run, Elliott and Waugh changed direction at the same time and collided mid-pitch. Elliott – who had lost his wicket at Sydney in identical circumstances in a Sheffield Shield match a month earlier – instantly tore the cartilage in his right knee. The ball was returned to Hooper who, in a typical brain-fade, forgot to run out the stranded Elliott at his end and tossed the ball to keeper Courtney Browne at the other. Waugh was safe there, and by the time the ball got back to Hooper, Elliott had limped home. Elliott's survival mattered little. He was driven off the ground in a

We Have To Stop Meeting Like This ... Mark Waugh looks down on the wreckage of Matthew Elliott, Sydney, 1996. Tim Clayton/Sydney Morning Herald

drinks cart and played no further part in the series. Yet his unbeaten 78 was an innings of such authority that he was recalled, once fit again, to tour South Africa at the end of the summer.

Mark Waugh made 67 and Bevan 52 as Australia set up their declaration – at 339 runs ahead and with 102 overs to bowl. Campbell and Samuels couldn't last long into the fifth morning, and McGrath pinioned Lara yet again, coming around the wicket and having him caught behind. On his return to the dressing room, however, Lara was told that the ball had bounced before Healy scooped it up. On television, Michael Holding was saying the ball had not carried. Incensed and emboldened, Lara marched across the SCG Members' Bar to the Australian dressing room, and told Geoff Marsh that Healy would not be welcome in the West Indian rooms. It was not the first example, nor the last, of Lara's petulance. An embarrassed Clive Lloyd apologised for his player, who had broken a pre-series pact of friendship between the teams. The next day, Lara did not travel with his team, preferring to stay for a few extra hours with friends in Sydney.

Despite Chanderpaul's astonishing counterattack, hammering 71 in an hour, the West Indies never looked like surviving a whole day. Chanderpaul's was probably the innings of the series, and it took the ball of the series to dismiss him. Warne, whom Taylor recalled just before lunch, ripped one out of the rough that turned a full metre and bowled Chanderpaul off glove and pad. Taylor removed Hooper with a spectacular juggled catch, off stomach to boot to hand, when Hooper edged a Bevan wrong'un. The West Indies tail, again, showed little stomach for the fight.

The West Indians were in the midst of a losing run of seven straight matches. Their fielding was often laughable, particularly Courtney Browne's wicketkeeping and Lara's attempts at slips catching. Ambrose and Benjamin seemed sleepy, and Bishop could only lift himself in spurts. Team morale was low enough before it was punched harder by one-day losses to the Prime Minister's XI, Australia (twice) and Australia A. They rebounded by defeating Pakistan in a one-dayer in Adelaide, reserve keeper Junior Murray bursting back into the top team with a hard-hitting 86. Lara's ill-starred tour, however, was continuing. He hit 86 in 92 balls against Victoria in Wangaratta before being given out – probably wrongly – hit-wicket when he trod on his stumps after watching his shot fly over the slips. More runs from the consistent Campbell at least saw the West Indians record a win, their first in a first-class game since the opening week of the tour.

Ambrose and Lara promised their team big efforts in Melbourne on Boxing Day. Ambrose obliged, his five wickets wrecking Australia's first innings for 219. Giving his second interview in five years, he said after the first day's play that he had promised ten wickets for the match and Lara had promised a century. Ambrose, at least, was helped by an uneven MCG wicket and some surprisingly panicked Australian selections. Matthew Hayden, Justin Langer, Steve Waugh and Reiffel had come into this team to replace Elliott, the unlucky Ponting, Bevan and Michael Kasprowicz.

When the West Indies replied, McGrath's 5/50 matched Ambrose's 5/55. McGrath again frustrated Lara, who had backed off to No 4 behind the dependable Chanderpaul. He again failed at McGrath's hands. Hooper tried hardest to get himself out, lobbing an on-drive off Warne to McGrath. It dropped short, but Hooper had wandered far enough out of his ground to present an easy run-out. Australia looked set for a valuable lead until Gillespie broke down with a side strain and Adams and Murray added 90 for the sixth wicket. For once, Australia's support bowling was ineffective and the West Indians scrounged a lead of 36 early on day three.

Out Of The Rough ... A stunned Shivnarine Chanderpaul's counter attack ends, courtesy of a Shane Warne ripper, Sydney, 1996. Tim Clayton/Sydney Morning Herald

Nobody could have guessed that the game would be over later that day. But Ambrose, Benjamin and Walsh ripped through the Australians in less than four hours, for 122. Australia's top order (4/27 in the first innings, 4/47 in the second) looked weakened by the selection changes, and this time Blewett, Steve Waugh and Healy could not dig them out. With 87 to win in the last session, the West Indies threatened to botch it – McGrath got Lara again, making it 2, 1, 2 and 2 in four innings – but Chanderpaul and Hooper hit the requisite runs for a turnaround six-wicket win.

The teams broke up for their limited-overs break. The third team in the triangular series was Pakistan, who came with a mix of experienced players and exciting young newcomers. Australian crowds were familiar with Aamir Sohail, Inzamam-ul-Haq, Wasim Akram and Mushtaq Ahmed, but this tour introduced them to a new generation. Saqlain Mushtaq's 'doosra', the off-spinner that turned away from the right-handers, fascinated audiences and bamboozled batsmen. The big hitting and fast leg-spin of Shahid Afridi was an exotic cocktail, while Mohammed Wasim was a picture of textbook elegance in the middle order. Mohammed Zahid was another interesting starter. The fastest bowler seen in Australia since Jeff Thomson, Zahid terrorised Lara in Brisbane before breaking down with a back injury.

As the West Indies recovered strength and morale, Australia's one-day plan was disintegrating. Taylor's form was beginning to decline alarmingly. *The Age*'s Martin Blake had written during the Melbourne Test match that Taylor might soon be under threat. Blake's comments looked premature, but in the one-day series Taylor just could not get going. His slump started to affect the team, who struggled to regain ground from their customary slow starts. While Australia lost ground, the West Indies and Pakistan were playing some vibrant cricket. Lara finally blossomed, hitting match-winning innings against Australia in Brisbane and Perth and another century against Pakistan in Perth. After his awful early tour, Lara strung together innings of 48, 102, 103 not out and 90. This last one was possibly the best, achieving a seemingly impossible run rate of 10 an over for the last 10 overs to knock off Australia in the Perth thriller, and smashing Warne for 28 runs in two overs.

Even in the low-scoring games, Australia's one-day play was looking antediluvian. Dismissing Pakistan for 149 on an up-and-down Hobart pitch was not good enough, as Australia's response was a paltry 120. An amusing, if apocryphal, story was told two years after this Hobart match in a Tasmanian newspaper. According to unnamed sources, some of the Pakistanis had taken bribes to lose this game, and their mediocre batting was taken as proof. When Australia batted even worse, some of the Pakistanis were said to have been in a miserable funk, wondering how they would explain this result to their bookmakers. The story is probably untrue. Wasim Akram bowled beautifully, taking 3/13 in eight overs, and if he had to use as bowlers Ijaz Ahmed and Mujahid

Jamshed – whom Wasim had never seen bowl, even asking Moin Khan if Mujahid bowled fast or slow – it was only because Pakistan had taken a batting-heavy team into the match. More likely, it was a good story illustrating Australia's plight as the proverbial losers: if Pakistan had taken money to lose the match, try as they might, they still could not play worse than the Australians.

While most local attention was focused on Australia's – and increasingly Taylor's – one-day slump, the West Indies had reversed the momentum of their tour with remarkable grit and character. From losing seven games straight, they won eight straight up to the last preliminary one-day match. While much of this was owed to Lara's rediscovered form, Walsh and Ambrose could also take considerable credit. Ambrose, his own high standards offended by his indifferent play before Christmas, was a transformed character. He was running around helping the younger members of the team, and bending his back to pick up, rather than soccer-stopping, balls in the field. Walsh's leadership was similarly rousing. The West Indies had for so long been allowed to get away with looking as cool as they pleased, that many doubted their ability to dirty their knees and hands, to try as hard as debutants.

They could. But in the process their bodies broke. Ambrose's frame held up only until the one-day finals, when he strained his groin – adding to chronic knee and hamstring problems – in the first match, which Pakistan won comfortably at the SCG. Against physiotherapist Dennis Waight's advice, Ambrose picked himself up again to play in the second final, in Melbourne. He bowled 9.3 overs and took 2/17, but aggravated his groin injury when Waqar Younis hit it while Ambrose batted. The Pakistanis made only 165, but it was enough. The West Indies were 7/85 when the MCG lights failed, and the players huddled in the middle while the public address system played the Rolling Stones song 'Start Me Up'. Ambrose, with Adams as a runner, finished with an unbeaten 31 as Pakistan took the match by 62 runs, winning their first World Series trophy.

Ambrose's body-breaking effort emphasised the difference in priorities between the West Indians and their hosts. In the midst of Australia's slide to oblivion – failing to make the home one-day finals for the first time since 1979–80 – Taylor had commented, famously, that the Australian public didn't care much about one-day cricket as long as the Test team won. His sentiments were on the mark, reflecting a jaded attitude from players and public, although they did offend the ACB, who still derived a lion's share of its sponsorship and television income from the one-day series. Taylor would pay, in due course, for his candour.

The West Indians, on the other hand, were desperate to win a trophy – any trophy – to redeem what had started as such a gloomy tour. Ambrose and Walsh pushed themselves beyond their endurance to try and wrest the one-day title. They failed and, in the process, also ruined their team's chance of salvaging the Test series.

With Perth the West Indies' favourite ground in the world, the fourth Test in Adelaide shaped up as the decider. Steve Waugh viewed the Test, starting five days after the West Indies lost the one-day series, as 'the most important match in all our lives'. Haunted by their one-run loss, from a winning position, at this ground four years earlier, the Australians went into the game with desperate desire. Their preparation and motivation were superior to the West Indians', and perhaps this match was decided even before the first ball. On match morning, Ambrose pulled out – and his team responded like a bath with the plug pulled out. Their batting, on a glorious first morning, was as poor as had been seen from a West Indian team in 50 years. They were dismissed for a reckless, perplexing 130 in a tick over three hours. Australia were experimenting with Bevan at No 7 as an all-rounder, and he and Warne were bowling by drinks on the first morning. Les Burdett's pitch was not taking a great deal of spin, but that mattered little as the West Indians self-destructed. Lara was the worst offender, deciding to treat Warne as a park bowler by charging at his first ball. Lara managed only to swipe it to mid-on, making himself look like nothing so much as a park batsman. Bevan ran through the tail, helped by three magnificent Healy catches, and Australia underlined the lesson by batting for 11 hours in reply.

Taylor and Langer failed again, but Hayden struck his first Test century, a 354-minute 125. An interesting, thoughtful character, Hayden was trying to make the most of his third start in Australian colours. Asked what was different about his attitude this time, Hayden said:

> My brother told me to think about it as if you're driving your car, and the police are on your tail. If you spend all your time looking in the rear-vision mirror, you're not going to drive very well. You just have to be calm and think about what you're doing. That's been my problem in the past. I've been thinking too much about who might take my place, who else is making runs.

Mark Waugh helped out with 82, Blewett with 99 and Bevan with a valuable if painstaking unbeaten 85, batting for nearly as long as Hayden. Bevan said: 'I don't care if people think I'm batting slowly. All I care about is that they see I can face short-pitched bowling.'

Steve Waugh, always more at home in a vicious scrap than at the smorgasbord the West Indian bowlers were serving up, was out in the most embarrassing fashion. He had hit the ball sweetly for 26 runs when Walsh brought on Chanderpaul to try his quickish leg-spinners. Chanderpaul bowled one very, very short and very, very wide, which Waugh reached out for and clubbed to cover. Hooper pounced, taking a brilliant diving catch, the skill of which went unappreciated by Waugh. Malcolm Conn wrote in *The Australian*: 'It is unlikely a worse ball has ever dismissed a better batsman.'

The West Indies' bowling was tired without Ambrose, and their fielding was woeful. The burly Bajan quick Patterson Thompson, playing his first serious match in more than a month, looked as if he had spent his spare time eating, and Cameron Cuffy, called out to replace Nixon McLean and Kenny Benjamin, was not up to replacing one bowler, let alone two. Even Walsh flagged, grounding an easy catch off Blewett. Hayden was dropped three times, and the West Indies bowled 20 no-balls, three of which 'took' wickets. Cricket had seen greater days than this.

Australia made short work of the West Indies' second innings, Bevan capturing another six wickets, 10 for the match to go with his 85 runs. He still denied he was a genuine all-rounder, but these things are always relative: bowling to the West Indies in this match, he was unplayable.

Backed up by Healy's catches and Taylor's sprawling right-hander to dismiss Campbell, Bevan was as genuine an all-rounder as Keith Miller. Lara finally recorded a Test innings of note, cracking 78 when it was too late, and Thompson provided some entertainment, swinging Warne over the fence and saying to the close fieldsmen: 'I thought this guy was meant to be a legend!'

Crack Me Up, Curtly . . . Ambrose hits a fault line and bowls Greg Blewett, Perth 1997.
Patrick Eagar

It had been a long summer, and inevitably tempers were worn thin by its end. Australia's easy retention of the Frank Worrell Trophy in Adelaide was a blow which galvanised the visitors into one last act of revenge. The final Test match, in Perth, was played in unbearable heat and humidity. Unbearable, at least, for David Crane's pitch, which began to crack up on the first day. Hayden nicked the third ball of the match, from the returning Ambrose, and Taylor proved the rule that bad luck follows bad form when he was run out by a scintillating pick-and-throw from Chanderpaul in the gully. Mark Waugh (79) and Bevan (87 not out) were the only Australians to pass 17 runs as the home team made a moderate 243.

As if following the brooding weather, the series turned spiteful on the second day. Robert Samuels, recalled for the injured and inept-looking Adrian Griffith, frustrated the Australians by supporting Lara in a 208-run stand over nearly five hours. Warne was hardly used until after tea, and when he was, he taunted Samuels mercilessly. Samuels was the type of opponent who got under the Australians' skin. He strutted as if he were Viv Richards, but his moderate results failed to justify the posturing. Warne, in particular, held the belief that respect had to be earned, and he was particularly exacting on young players whom he saw as getting too big for their boots. Samuels had had a few words to say from third slip, and the Australians had replied in kind. They called him a 'loser' whenever they walked close by. But here, he was playing a matchwinning role with Lara. Together they lifted the score past Australia's. Warne finally dismissed Samuels for 76, but Lara made an overdue 132 and the West Indies led by 110 at stumps on the second day with three wickets still in hand.

This wasn't, however, the whole story. Lara, never one to miss an opportunity to defend himself or his teammates, used his post-century press conference on day two to blast the Australians for their sledging. 'They shouldn't talk like that to younger players,' he said. 'Calling the guy a loser – I can assure you, we won't be losers when they come to the West Indies in two years.'

Lara had a point. The Australians' sledging seemed to get out of hand when they were losing a game, and they targeted young players, particularly when they felt verbal abuse might get them a wicket. But from their point of view, all teams engaged in this from time to time, and Lara had violated the on-field code of silence by mouthing off to the press. Taylor later accused Lara of being an 'antagonist, in the same way as I use the term to describe Arjuna Ranatunga'. Taylor resented Lara not coming to him personally, and instead using the media to make his point. Would Taylor now go to Lara to sort the matter out? No, Taylor said. 'He started it, and I think it's up to him to come to us.' The water-fight had a sequel after the match, with Warne saying that his friendship with Lara was now finished. In truth, the friendship was a superficial celebrity-amour anyway, and Warne would bear few hard feelings towards Lara by the time Australia toured the Caribbean in 1999.

But Lara did plenty to earn his reputation as a squealer. On the third morning, he chose to come out as a runner for the injured Walsh. He wanted to renew the argument, and the umpires had to step in and separate Lara and Walsh from Warne and Steve Waugh, and tell the captains to cool their players down.

Darrell Hair, who was officiating with Peter Willey, wrote: 'A lot had been said and a large number of players had been "chatting" each other, which is and always has been impossible for umpires to hear, so I was surprised when Lara indicated that if the Australians did not shut up he was going to ram his bat down a couple of their throats.'

Undoubtedly, what was preying on the Australians' minds more than the verballing with Lara was the state of the pitch. The cracks were visible from the boundary. They even had a bizarre part to play in Ambrose's dismissal, run out, on the third morning. Ambrose scuffled the ball away and took a few steps down the pitch. Healy went after the ball to short square leg and flicked it behind his back speculatively. Ambrose would have made his ground except, sliding into his crease, his bat jammed in one of the cracks and stopped short. He could not extricate it before the ball hit the stumps.

All this was less than funny when the Australians batted. The ball jagged at crazy angles, both up and down and sideways, as the West Indians aimed at the widest cracks just short of a length. Taylor failed again, and Blewett, promoted to No 3, was bowled by one that ran along the ground. Mark Waugh received a ball from Walsh that came back like a big off-break. Still, the Australians had only trailed by 141 runs and were thinking that a lead of 100 might be a winning break. Hayden was playing a superb innings of 47, arguably a superior knock to his Adelaide century. What cut short Australia's hopes of winning the match was an amazing 20-over spell from Walsh, who had been carried off in the first innings and had batted with a runner. His thigh strapped, bowling off five paces, Walsh generated prodigious pace and movement. Later, I walked onto the ground and inspected the pitch. The worst crack, about half a ball's width, was at a very awkward length from the Lillee-Marsh Stand end Walsh had taken. The area around the crack was literally painted red, having been struck and marked repeatedly by Walsh's deliveries. His accuracy, already legendary, needed no further testimony. He took five wickets in the middle order as Australia crumbled to 8/133.

Things were not quite as pure at the other end. Ambrose wanted to carry on the previous day's fight, and when Warne and Andrew Bichel were staging a quasi-fightback for the ninth wicket, adding 56 runs, Ambrose decided to mark his last Test appearance in Australia with a spiteful, unethical spell. His last over, perhaps the longest in Test history, took 12 minutes. It contained 15 deliveries, nine of them no-balls. That does not tell the full story. He bowled the over around the wicket, overstepping by a full half-metre. He pitched the ball very short and aimed every one at Bichel's or Warne's head. There was little doubt the no-balling was deliberate and the tactics intimidatory. It was poor sportsmanship, obviously conducted for his own amusement, and unedifying for the game. Australia were out for 194 and Ambrose left the field with his arms raised to the crowd. He was man of the match – deservedly – and, what he probably never understood, left the country with an immense local following. He and Walsh warranted every bit of the public's admiration for their bowling, but only Walsh deserved the same for his grace and sportsmanship.

So ended a strange series. For the last three Tests, the teams resembled those sumo wrestlers who wage everything on a massive first effort – break the opponent in the opening move, or be broken. The third, fourth and fifth Tests lasted a cumulative 10 days. So convincingly did the West Indies win in Melbourne and Perth, and so shatteringly did they lose in Adelaide, that it was hard to gauge the difference between the teams. Perhaps the pre-Christmas spell had been the best guide, when Australia won two hard-fought Tests on the fifth day. Taylor had pride in 'winning the big points'; although the final margin was a narrow 3-2, the Australians could wave off their guests in full knowledge that they had retained their crown without a shadow of argument.

The Beginning of the End ... The conclusion of the West Indies series in 1996–97 was just the beginning of Mark Taylor's form slump. Trent Parke

What the Australians had done best of all was imitate the tactics of the best West Indian teams. David Boon, speaking of the West Indies in 1991, could as easily have been describing the Australians of 1996-97: 'This West Indies team was just so good, so professional. If they didn't get wickets, they'd drop back a cog and bowl beautiful line and length. Their strategy revolved around frustrating the batsmen out, and a key component of this part of their bowling plan was sending down as few overs as possible. But when they did break through, they'd automatically go full-on; the first 20 minutes after a wicket fell were invariably highly dangerous.'

Warne, whose series was profitable despite the recent finger operation, was reminding Taylor of a West Indian fast bowler. 'He might not strike immediately,' Taylor said, 'but when he does he's all over you.' The same could be said of his entire team.

Australia in the West Indies, 1999

The Asylum is a nightclub in Kingston, Jamaica, a city stigmatised as one of the crime capitals of the third world. Kingston throbs with hustlers, drug dealers, mobsters, robbers and muggers; when touring cricket teams come to Jamaica, they are warned not to leave the safety of the Wyndham or Pegasus Hotels, together on the northern side of the town, except with a local escort.

The Asylum is just around the corner from the hotels, however, and many visiting cricketers will venture past the sellers of ganja and souvenirs on the kerbside to spend an hour or two at Kingston's liveliest nightspot. Like most West Indian clubs, the Asylum only comes to life around midnight, when the sharp young men and women of the city rouse themselves to come and dance to the reggae, rap and dance hall music favoured in these parts. The Asylum hits its peak at around three or four in the morning, and most nights keeps humming until dawn.

In the early hours of 12 March 1999, Brian Lara was an unlikely face – or, perhaps, all too likely – as he slouched at the Asylum bar. The sun was beginning to break over the Caribbean, and the puffiness in Lara's smile was only partly attributable to the number of Jamaican rums he had drunk or the number of dances he had accepted or declined.

No other cricketers, West Indian or Australian, were in the Asylum at four o'clock that morning. Thirty hours later, they would be setting foot on Sabina Park, Kingston's run-down but intimidating cricket ground, for the all-important second Test of the series. All-important for the West Indies, that is, because they had just lost the first Test in Trinidad, being rolled for 51 in their second innings. All-important because they had come off a 0–5 thrashing in a Test series in South Africa, and a 1–6 loss in the one-dayers there. And all-important for Lara, because he had been placed on a two-match probationary term as West Indies captain. The humiliation of Port-of-Spain, his home town, was his first probationary match. Kingston would be his second.

Brian Lara partied on. He seemed in a good mood. Perhaps he was trying to forget South Africa, where he had been reported by his coach, Malcolm Marshall, and manager, Clive Lloyd, for a cavalier attitude to the captaincy. Lara had been playing golf rather than encouraging the youngsters; Lara had been consorting with the South African stars rather than his teammates; Lara had been fighting with some of the hotheads under his charge, and disrespecting his elders.

Perhaps he was trying to forget Port-of-Spain, where the Australians had been irresistible. On a wickedly uneven pitch, Matthew Elliott and Greg Blewett had ground down the West Indian pacemen, and then Glenn McGrath (39) and Jason Gillespie (28 not out) had embarrassed them with 66 runs for the last wicket, hauling the team score to 269. Lara had steeled himself for a big innings, and looked to be on his way when, on 62 and with his team 3/149, he had pushed a Shane Warne ball to bat-pad. Justin Langer had flicked it to Ian Healy, but Healy had seemed to spill it as he broke the stumps. The third umpire, Clyde Cumberbatch, a man of notoriously unreliable eyesight, had ruled against Lara. The West Indies fell 102 runs short, Michael Slater scored a marvellous century for Australia, and the demolition crew of McGrath (5/28) and Gillespie (4/18) bowled the hosts into submission.

Or perhaps Lara was trying to forget the events of the previous day, 11 March, when he had gone to practise at the dusty, bumpy Kensington ground in suburban Kingston and been booed by the locals. Jamaicans are a hard bunch, and they had not forgiven Lara for taking the West Indies captaincy away from their hero, Courtney Walsh, in 1998. To make matters worse for Lara, Walsh had performed honourably in South Africa and in Trinidad, where he had become the third bowler to pass the 400-Test-wicket mark. The day the locals booed Lara at practice, the mayor of Kingston presented Walsh with the keys to the city.

Lara still partied on. He had promised to mend his ways. He had promised to be responsible. He had made so many promises, and apologies, and pleas for one last chance, that even sober he would have been hard-pressed to remember them all.

He left the Asylum at around five o'clock and was 40 minutes late for practice that morning. Clive Lloyd said Lara was doing radio interviews. The newly appointed team psychologist, Rudi Webster, a veteran of the World Series Cricket years, had a twinkle in his eye when he said Lara had better bring his money, as he'd be paying a fine. When Lara showed, he said he had been at the doctor's.

At practice, Lara was booed again. Locals collected around the fringes of the ground, smoked reefers, and lambasted the Trinidadian. He had a short centre-wicket bat, and spent the rest of the practice lounging in the cool of the changing rooms.

Next day, the Australians batted lazily for 256. The wicket was flat and fast, yet only Steve Waugh, with 100, seemed to recognise the seriousness of the situation. This was a Test match, these were the West Indians, and the series was not yet won. Mark Waugh was bowled by a mullygrubber for 67, but the next best Australian was Warne with 24. Still, it didn't seem to matter much. By stumps the West Indies were 4/37. Would they make 51? Would they get that far? Lara, on seven, was their only hope. One more good day, and the Australians would have retained the Frank Worrell Trophy. It seemed inevitable.

Next day, Lara scored 205 runs. The West Indies didn't lose a wicket. For all his errors, for all his self-centred unorthodoxy, Lara was still Lara. He hammered the Australian bowlers, absolutely hammered them. McGrath and Gillespie bowled superbly but didn't take a wicket all day. Warne was tight but innocuous; Lara was able to sit on him and punish the bad ball. Steve Waugh protected Stuart MacGill, but when he risked him MacGill was savaged worst of all. At the other end, the West Indies didn't lose a wicket either; nightwatchman Pedro Collins retired hurt after an hour, but Jimmy Adams, who as a deputy could not be more unlike his captain, stayed with Lara all day. When he made his hundred, Lara was swamped by a crowd of around 200. The Jamaicans were dancing in the stands all afternoon. When Lara made his double century, he ran to the dressing room to escape the invasion, and then emerged triumphant, bat and arms raised. Adams was ecstatic. By stumps, the West Indies were 4/377 and in total control of the match and the series.

Notionally, cricket is a team game. In 99 of 100 matches at Test level, victory is achieved by an ensemble effort. Lara changed that mindset in Kingston, and in doing so he put a virus into the mental program by which Australia had achieved their position over the previous five years. Australia's dominance was all about applying pressure, waiting for the mistake, and flooding in to capitalise. It was about backing their own ability to win the big points. It was about manufacturing situations where luck would flow their way.

But this time, one individual had turned the universe on its head. Lara was resistant to all forms of pressure. The Australians became obsessed with him that day, focusing their energies entirely on him, allowing Adams to pad the ball benignly away. Warne, only half-recovered from shoulder surgery, could not break through, and Steve Waugh placed most of his eggs in the basket of McGrath and Gillespie. MacGill, given limited opportunities, was flayed by Lara. There was no plan B, and the Australians grew impatient. To that point, they had been conditioned to think the West Indian batsmen would self-destruct sooner or later. When it didn't happen, the Australians became agitated. This mood spread into their batting, and by the time they replied to the West Indies' 431, they were mentally spent. Australia capitulated for 177 as some of their senior players, notably Healy and Mark Waugh, gave their wickets away softly. It was, indeed, the softest Australian performance in years.

Two weeks later, they regrouped in Bridgetown, Barbados. Unlike the bustling, edgily tough Jamaican capital, Bridgetown is a charming town, full of narrow rickety streets with an unmatched love of cricket. In the interim, Australia had beaten a West Indies A team with a solid performance in Antigua, Elliott and Langer recording much-needed centuries. The day before the Test, Steve Waugh had a hit-out with some local and visiting schoolboys. Happy and relaxed, the Australians were content to view the Jamaican result as an aberration. 'We still have to win one Test to keep the trophy,' Waugh said. 'Nothing's changed.'

Lightning struck a second time in Bridgetown. This time, Australia surrendered an incomparably strong position to lose a Test which will be ranked among the greatest of all. On the first and second days, Steve Waugh (199) and Ricky Ponting (104) took Australia from 4/144 to 4/425, setting up an innings total of 490. It hadn't been easy; on the first morning, Waugh said, he had played and missed more than he could remember in one innings. Ambrose and Walsh peppered him with good balls, short and full, and it was all he could do to survive.

On the second evening, normalcy seemed restored as the West Indies collapsed. Lara fended a Gillespie lifter, and on the third morning defeat seemed only a matter of time when they slid to 6/98 – and no Lara in sight. But again, Australia's reliance on McGrath and Gillespie was unhealthy. As soon as they left the attack, the West Indies were able to fight back. Sherwin Campbell and Ridley Jacobs relaxed against Warne and MacGill, and counter-punched with a stand of 153. Still, the hosts only made 329 and Australia's old formula seemed on track. All they needed was declare at about 150 in the second innings, to add to their 161 first-innings lead, and surely they were safe.

They staggered to 146 – and no declaration was possible, as Walsh's five wickets, and two each to Ambrose and left-armer Pedro Collins, made a mess of the Australian batting. On the fourth afternoon, the West Indians made it to stumps at 3/85, their target reduced to 225 in a day. Out were Campbell, Dave Joseph and Collins. Lara, on two, was at the crease. He had been booed on arrival, for the seeming cowardice of his choice, for a third time in three innings, to send in the tailender Collins ahead of himself.

McGrath and Gillespie took two early wickets on day five, and at 5/105 the West Indies were given little chance. Except that Lara was still there. The bad news was, he'd been staying up late and partying in Bridgetown, too. The other bad news was that Adams had joined him. Once again, though, they blunted Waugh's pacemen and profited from the spinners. It was the job of MacGill and, particularly, Warne to remove the West Indies on the last day, on a wearing pitch; but the opposite happened. When the leg-spinners came on, the pressure lifted. Adams stayed with Lara adding 133 until 71 were needed. McGrath, who was to bowl 77 overs in the match, bowled Adams and removed Jacobs and Nehemiah Perry 10 runs later. Eight for 248 – Australia's match? Lara was still there. Ambrose, of all people, who never practised his batting, stuck around. Gillespie suffered a back spasm and Waugh kept tossing the ball to Warne. MacGill brooded in the outfield. A shattered Elliott, his presence of mind gone, kept misfielding. And Lara kept batting.

With seven needed, Ambrose gave Elliott a catch off the brave Gillespie. Elliott held it at fourth slip. Walsh, a world-class bunny, came to the wicket and nearly caused a riot in the packed ground with his flourish and twirl as he let the ball go by. Then he jammed out a yorker. About 25,000 packed Kensington Oval; all were on their feet. One run later, Lara edged Gillespie to Healy behind the wicket, but the wicketkeeper, whose form had declined on the tour, dropped it. Walsh bunted McGrath away for an over, and then Lara smashed the winning drive through cover. His teammates converged on him, and the crowd erupted in unadulterated ecstasy. West Indies by one wicket; series score 2–1.

Now it was Steve Waugh who looked devastated. The teams moved to Antigua for the deciding Test match, and Waugh was facing, in his first series as captain, a symbolic undoing of everything Mark Taylor had achieved. The capture of the Frank Worrell Trophy in 1995 remained the signature achievement of the Taylor years. Seven weeks after Taylor's retirement, was Waugh going to hand it back?

After the mighty Test matches in Jamaica and Barbados, Waugh was pale and drained as he recovered in Antigua. He confessed to not knowing how he could inspire his team. It was, he said, all up to the individuals around him to realise what was at stake.

One individual would not take part. Waugh and Geoff Marsh had decided that Warne was no longer worth his place in the side. They met in a room in the Rex Halcyon Cove Hotel, on Antigua's north coast, and told Warne they would outvote him if he challenged their selection. He argued in his own defence, but the die was cast. He had taken two wickets in the series, and four in four Tests since his return from the shoulder operation. He had been tidy but unpenetrative. Warne believed he was a better bowler than MacGill, evidenced by Lara's greater respect for Warne's servings in Barbados and Jamaica. But MacGill was still averaging five wickets per Test match, and had picked up 12 in a game against a local selection in Trinidad. Gillespie would not play in Antigua, giving Warne more ammunition. He argued that experience was needed in such a crucial game. But Waugh and Marsh had made their minds up. They had entrusted Warne with a job on that last day in Bridgetown, and he had failed to take a wicket.

Their attack in Antigua, then, consisted of McGrath, Adam Dale, MacGill and Colin Miller. Both teams were exhausted, and Australia's greater depth was eventually to see them through. Steve Waugh, Langer and Miller made the soundest contributions to a first innings of 303, and then it was down to Lara. He had only – only! – the strength to last 88 balls, off which he hit 100 runs exactly. His innings was either pure indulgence, or the last ravings of a man on the brink of psychological and physical breakdown. He managed to avoid McGrath for most of his second fifty, which took him just 23 balls. When McGrath finally got another go at him, he had him caught down the leg side.

The West Indies trailed by 81 runs, and Langer's excellent 127 gave Australia their winning lead. Lara's captaincy bordered on the absurd, as he gave Adams and Carl Hooper extended stints with the ball, as if to lull the Australians into a false sense of security. Lara's strikeforce of Walsh and Ambrose was ground down after four Tests in five weeks, and he had insufficient faith in his backups, debutant Corey Collymore and spinner Nehemiah Perry. Australia made 306 and bowled out the hosts, Lara falling to McGrath again, to win by 176 runs and save the Worrell with a draw.

This was the strangest of series, because it was ruled by so few individuals. For Australia, Waugh scored 409 runs, way ahead of Langer (291) and Slater (277). In their bowling, McGrath took 30 wickets at 16.93, compared with the next men, MacGill (12 at 29.33) and Gillespie (11 at 21.91). Warne was dropped after taking two wickets for 268 runs. For the hosts, Lara scored one-third of their runs, 546 at 91.00 compared with the next man, Campbell, 197 at 28.14. In their bowling, Walsh (26) and

Ambrose (19) duopolised the wickets. Rarely has a series been so gladiatorial in nature. Supremacy between Australia and the West Indies is the most keenly fought over, and the Worrell is the most prestigious trophy in Test cricket; that goes without saying, but this time it all came down to a battle of wills among five men: Waugh, McGrath, Lara, Walsh and Ambrose.

The subsequent seven-match one-day series was notable for two things. The indiscipline of West Indian crowds vitiated the results in Guyana and Barbados, leaving a sour taste over a series nominally shared 3–3. Secondly, the titans of the Test series were all but bystanders. McGrath bowled a solitary over in the series before injuring his ankle, and Waugh only played one notable innings – a very good one – to steal the tie in Guyana. Lara faded away after four games, as did Ambrose and Walsh. As it often had been in the past between these two great teams, one-day cricket was a mere afterthought after the unforgettable spectacle of Test cricket at its best.

South Africa: The Throat Ball

SOUTH AFRICA WERE the great pretenders of the 1990s: the team which should have climbed to the top of the Test and one-day ladders, but which was held back by flaws within its own structure. Notably, as individuals and a team, the South Africans buckled at crucial moments against this one opponent. They defeated all other nations around the world in all forms of the game, leaving aside a devastating 'choke' in a series against England in 1998, and regarded themselves as Australia's heir-apparents. Yet, like Allan Border's teams against the West Indies in 1991 and 1992–93, South Africa could not translate their on-paper strength to Test match wins. Like Australia in Border's last days, the South African team consisted of a conservative captain (Hansie Cronje); a number of veterans who could not quite overcome the scars of past battles (Brian McMillan, David Richardson, Gary Kirsten); a heroic, athletic fast bowler who could never quite finish the job when it counted against this opponent (Allan Donald was the Proteas' Craig McDermott); a mercurial but unreliable champion batsman (Daryll Cullinan); and several youngsters (Shaun Pollock, Mark Boucher, Lance Klusener, Jacques Kallis) who were held back by the fearful negativity of their seniors. At time of writing, at the turn of the century, it seemed certain that South Africa's time would come, as the Australians' time had come six years earlier. But perhaps that time would be stalled until a new leader could take over and release the attacking instincts of the talented juniors.

Australia in South Africa, 1997

No team, not even the dominant West Indian outfit of 1977–95, could enjoy its best form match in, match out. Taylor's team of 1994–99 will be remembered as one of Australia's best, thanks to their overall record and their ability to 'win the big points', yet Test cricket had evolved beyond the days when one team could expect to rule any opposition for long periods. With the improvement of the minor nations – *pace* Sri Lanka's World Cup win – and the increasingly heavy scheduling of international cricket, every team's form was bound to ebb and flow.

In the Taylor years, the Australian team hit and sustained its very best form on few occasions. One of those high-water marks was in the first stanza of their tour to South Africa in 1997. There were no warnings that Australia was about to hit such a rich ore. Indeed, they had finished the 1996–97 West Indies series with a three-day, 10-wicket defeat in Perth, and the speculation over Taylor's batting form was starting to have an erosive effect on team morale. Moreover, the programming was so tight that the team only enjoyed five days at home with their families between the fifth Test in Perth and their departure for South Africa – travelling, annoyingly, via Hong Kong. Had the fifth Test against the West Indies proceeded to a fifth day, the rest period would have been just three days.

The South African tour was not, initially, meant to be shoe-horned between a heavy home season and an Ashes tour. By its end, players wanted assurances that this would not happen again. The reasons were somewhat complex, and had to do with political arrangements and shifting alliances between the various boards of control. In short, India wanted Australia to tour there in early 1998 – the intended slot for Australia's tour of South Africa – and Australia, having not played India in a full series since 1991–92, and having not played one in India since 1986, were keen to accept the Indian invitation. Consequently, the tour of South Africa was brought forward a year.

It is a mystery – part of the natural flow – why the Australians suddenly played so well once they arrived in South Africa. Steve Waugh felt that they lifted themselves for what was acknowledged as the world

334 Precisely ... two views of Mark Taylor on top at Peshawar.
BEN RADFORD/ALLSPORT

Hear No Evil, Speak No Evil, See No Evil ... Javed Miandad, Ijaz Ahmed, and Mushtaq Ahmed in one of those Pakistani hotel rooms, Lahore 1999. AP/AAP

Too Fast By Half? ... Shoaib Akhtar rips into it, Perth 2000.   *AFP/AAP*

Lean On Me ... Glenn McGrath and Steve Waugh test their courage, Kaieteur Falls, Guyana, 1999.
Ben Radford/Allsport

Out all night, in all day ... In a haze of ganja smoke, Brian Lara redeemed himself to Sabina Park in 213 ways, 1999. Here the faithful Jimmy Adams again holds him up.
Trent Parke

The Record-Holder ... On one leg, Courtney Walsh produced one of the most astonishing spells of modern times to win the Perth Test in 1996-97. He was 34. Four years later he was still at it. *Trent Parke*

Hungry Eyes ... Well into his thirties, Curtly Ambrose continued to haunt the Australians. When he pulled out of the decisive Test in 1996-97, the West Indies lost their soul. TRENT PARKE

Limited Appeal ... Allan Donald was his country's Craig McDermott: athletic, tireless, big-hearted, but somehow just short of the mark in the big moments. TRENT PARKE

Allan Donald wonders why he forgot to run. Steve Waugh, Adam Gilchrist, and Glenn McGrath don't care.
AP/AAP

Pity You Didn't...Hansie Cronje in happier times ALLSPORT

Frog in a Blender ... Paul Adams ties himself up. Allan Mullally ponders whether it's a new wrong'un or not, Johannesburg 1999. *Juda Ngwenya/Reuters*

The Wizard ... Shane Warne's body strength and wrist torsion are perfectly illustrated against England, Sydney, 1995. Steve Bucknor looks on in admiration. PATRICK EAGAR

championship of Test cricket. South Africa had not been tested against Pakistan or the West Indies, but on paper they looked a very good, emerging team, and they had just beaten India in a three-Test series at home.

Much of the focus from outside the Australian team remained on Taylor. On arrival, the Australians settled at the Sandton Sun Hotel in the rich, mostly fortified white area in the northern suburbs of Johannesburg. This cavernous gilded cage was to be their home for 5 of the next 10 weeks. While Johannesburg was nobody's idea of the friendliest city in the world, at least this part of the schedule ensured a certain comfort and continuity for the players.

In the opening game of the tour, Taylor came immediately under more scrutiny. Against an invitational XI in grounds owned by the diamond-mining Oppenheimer family, just north of Johannesburg, Taylor showed that the flight from Australia had not broken his downward spiral. Batting at No 4, he struggled to make 18 runs while the recalled Elliott, Hayden and Steve Waugh enjoyed a low-pressure hit-out.

The first ominous signs of Australia's form came in the next match, a four-dayer against Western Province in Cape Town. They scored 4/439 against an attack including Test players Brett Schultz, Craig Matthews, Meyrick Pringle, Jacques Kallis and Brian McMillan. Even Taylor made 85, sparking relief and celebration from his team and supporters – not to mention from the travelling press, who were bored and frustrated with writing the same story, again and again, about Taylor's form. Elliott was looking settled at No 3 behind Taylor and Hayden, and Blewett was continuing his fine home summer at No 6. The South African selectors decided to 'hide' Chinaman bowler Paul Adams from the Australians – as they did with Shaun Pollock and Lance Klusener in the next game, against Natal in Durban – but the Australians were in irresistible form. They beat Western Province by 32 runs. Test players Herschelle Gibbs and John Commins scored useful runs for the hosts. Australia thrashed the provincial champions, Natal, by eight wickets the next week. Their only hiccups were a hamstring injury to Reiffel and a virulent stomach complaint that passed through the team in Durban. Even local boy Jonty Rhodes got it, spending a day during the Natal match in hospital. The Australians were, understandably, keen to get back to their digs in Johannesburg to prepare for a crucial first Test.

A final exhibition match in Soweto, played before hundreds of schoolchildren bussed in by South Africa's indefatigable cricket boss Ali Bacher, was Australia's last tune-up. Geoff Marsh had brought a friend of his from Perth, Steve Smith, into the fold as a fitness advisor, and the team's general physical state was good. The jockey-sized Smith's lack of cricket knowledge was a constant source of amusement to the team, some of whom felt they had a personal axe to grind with him after the rigorous regime he put them through.

The South Africans, however, seemed equally confident on Test eve. Allan Donald was a picture of athleticism as he tore into nets training, and Hansie Cronje put his men through a series of slick fielding routines. If any two opponents looked like world title contenders, it was these two.

It came as something of a shock, then, when South Africa were so overwhelmed in Johannesburg. The Wanderers Ground, known as the 'bull ring' because of its high, claustrophobic, noisy stands, was uncharacteristically subdued as the Australians dominated the match from the first morning. The talismanic McGrath removed Andrew Hudson with the fourth ball of the series, and by tea South Africa were 6/182. Cronje's hit-and-hope 76 and Dave Richardson's punishing 72 (off 87 balls at No 9) pumped the hosts up for a respectable 302, but most observers agreed it was a 400-run pitch. The impish Adams made light work of it, daring a reverse-sweep at Warne before getting himself out trying a repeat.

Taylor missed out, but Elliott's 85 prompted Graeme Pollock to predict that the Australian would 'have an average of 50 by the time he finishes Test cricket'. In gloomy light, Elliott, hooked and drove the South African pacemen at will. He played a pull shot off Donald – flying head-high from the wicket to the boundary – that still sticks in the mind as one of the greatest single shots of the Taylor era.

At 4/191 after a rain-interrupted day two, it only remained for Australia to press home their advantage. The pitch was playing extremely well, and the situation called for the type of batsmen who would not give their wickets away. Steve Waugh and Blewett were the pair who best fitted that description, and they demonstrated their powers of concentration by becoming the 10th pair to bat through an entire day in Test cricket. Their 385 runs was Australia's highest partnership against South Africa, and the 11th highest in all Tests. Statistics make dull reading; and the partnership made dull watching. The crowd dwindled, deprived of any real contest, as Waugh and Blewett piled it on. Waugh had the temerity to compliment South Africa's fielding, saying 'they saved at least 50 runs', but exact numbers were irrelevant in the end. Australia declared at 8/628, Waugh making 160, Blewett 214. The South Africans looked shattered by the time they took the crease, and capitulated for 130 runs in four hours. Warne, playing his 50th Test, took four wickets and Bevan four in his last two overs. What was, for the standard of Australia's cricket, something of a climax – they never played a better Test match under Taylor – was a hollow spectacle. Puffed up with arrogance and confidence before the game, Cronje's team had been exposed.

Or so it seemed. Top gear is hard to maintain for long in any sport, at any level, and it was only a few days before the Australians were back in the gutter, engaged in the sort of fight they liked best. It could be argued – and was, by some players – that Taylor's team was never entirely comfortable snuffing out an opponent as thoroughly as they did at the Wanderers. Many would rate the next match, at Port Elizabeth, which they won by two wickets in the most desperate circumstances, as the greatest of their careers.

It was played on a pitch maligned by most, if not all, the participants. The Australian team suspected that the Eastern Province Cricket Association had been ordered by the South African board to leave the wicket underprepared. The South Africans had learnt at the Wanderers, if not before, that Australia's preferred pattern of attack in Test cricket was to set up a situation, with a heavy-scoring first innings, whereby McGrath and Warne could bowl their opponents out on the last day. South Africa's answer was to aim for a low-scoring game, and favour pace bowlers, of which they felt they held a strong hand in Donald and Pollock.

So much for the theory. The politics were a different matter. On each morning of the Test, Taylor dispatched the team manager, Col Egar, to St George's Park to supervise the pitch preparation. The Australians believed that the hessian mat customarily laid over a pitch at night, to soak up excess moisture, was not being used. Egar was sent with the simple brief: to make sure the hessian was there. Dr Ali Bacher, incensed, accused the Australians of ungentlemanly conduct. The curator denied he had been placed under any pressure, contradicting his own disgruntled pre-Test remarks that 'we'll get what the Doctor ordered'.

Be that as it may, the teams found an unevenly grassed, unpredictable strip. On the first day, Taylor won the toss and sent an opposition in for the first time in 26 Tests as captain. Australia dismissed South Africa for 209, Gillespie making his first deep impact on Test cricket with 5 for 54. South Africa had been 7/95 until the veterans, McMillan and Richardson, staged a feisty counterattack.

The score seemed inadequate until Australia batted. Hayden couldn't last the first evening, and Taylor was out early on day two, caught behind off Pollock, who strained his hamstring with that ball and did not bowl or field again in the match, retiring from the scene with 2/6 in six overs. Mark Waugh looked as fluent as Daryll Cullinan had in the South African innings but suffered the same fate, losing his wicket when he was set. Elliott hung around for nearly three hours to make 23, and the Australian run rate trod water at around one an over. In the end, with no South African bowler taking more than two wickets, Australia were dismissed for 108 in 70.4 overs.

Finally, when Adam Bacher and Gary Kirsten opened for South Africa, the pitch seemed to settle. In two hours, they wrested control of the match away from Australia, posting 83 runs by stumps. Port Elizabeth is a huge industrial port with a strong black proletarian population – it is one of the birthplaces of the African National Congress – and an advanced multiracial cricketing set-up. The stands filled with black choirs and bands, and St George's Park heaved with their triumphal music as South Africa took charge. The hosts' lead by the end of the day was 184, with all 10 second-innings wickets in hand. It was impossible to imagine them losing – certainly for this writer, who sought the wisdom of history in that night compiling a chart showing how Australia had under Taylor found it almost impossible to win low-scoring matches of this kind.

Still, what happened in the next two days left deeper scars on the South Africans than on any prematurely speculatiorrespondent. It is hard, even looking back, to imagine how such a hard-bitten, motivated team let such a lead slip.

Gillespie bowled Kirsten early, and then Blewett performed a blinding piece of fielding, running from square leg to mid-wicket and throwing without looking, scoring a direct hit at the bowler's end to account for Kallis. Bacher, unsettled by the run-out, top-edged a hook to fine leg, and Cullinan was trapped in front. Four wickets had fallen for 13 runs, three to Gillespie and the run-out off his bowling. Just as Elliott and Blewett were making their mark, so was the young fast bowler. He had another role to play in this match later, with the bat.

Cronje tried to steady, but Taylor swung Bevan and Warne into action after McGrath removed Gibbs. At 5/137, with a lead of 238, the South Africans were still in the box seat. But Bevan and Warne worked at their minds, conceding only a run or two an over, and the wickets kept falling. Bevan got Cronje, McMillan and Donald, and Warne dismissed Pollock and Adams, celebrating the latter wicket with an unsavoury mock-belly laugh in Adams's direction. It was another example of Warne's petulance when challenged by someone he considered unworthy of occupying the same stretch of turf.

Incredibly, then, South Africa had lost all 10 of their wickets for 81 runs on the third morning. Bacher suffered an inordinate crucifixion in the press and on television for his involvement in the Kallis run-out, which was, in all objectivity, solely due to Blewett's athletic fielding, and for his own dismissal. Even so, a lead of 269 seemed more than enough for South Africa. Australia had a poor fourth-innings chasing record, as South Africa knew from Sydney in 1994, and the innings scores in this match had been 209, 108 and 168, confirming the improbability of a successful pursuit.

It started poorly when Taylor failed yet again and Hayden was involved in such a terrible mix-up with Elliott that both batsmen raced each other to the one end, each man stretching to save his skin. Elliott won.

Elliott had a let-off next ball, when Adams dropped him at fine leg. South African coach Bob Woolmer quipped drily that 'the sky must have been too blue' for Adams to pick up the ball. Anyone watching Adams knew that he was talking with members of the crowd and enjoying the music rather than concentrating on the match. He at least redeemed himself by dismissing Elliott late in the day, but only after Australia had advanced from 2/30 to 3/113. From 3/30, it is impossible to imagine Australia's success.

At stumps, Australia's hopes lay with the Waugh brothers. Steve's record against the Proteas made him the more feared, but he cut Kallis to Cronje at deep point early on day four to leave Australia four down for 167 – still 103 to win. It was an especially satisfying dismissal for the South Africans. Before the match, Waugh had told the press: 'I can't see us being beaten.' Throughout his two innings, McMillan taunted Waugh with the question: 'Any more statements, Steve?' Waugh's scores were eight and 18, rare failures in the pressure-cooker.

His brother was playing the innings of his life. Blewett went for seven, but Mark Waugh held strong with Bevan for another 64 runs. With Pollock injured, Donald bowled over after over of classy, straight pace bowling. The battle between Donald and Mark Waugh decided the match. As so often in these situations, Donald was unlucky. When South Africa needed him most, he went wicketless.

So at 5/258, needing 12 to win, Australia were coasting. This riveting match had one more twist, however. Mark Waugh played around a ball from Kallis, and next over Bevan was caught off Cronje. Healy and Warne inched along to 265 – five to win – before Kallis trapped Warne. Gillespie, riding a high after his match-turning bowling effort, blocked out an excruciatingly tense over from Kallis. Only McGrath remained, and each ball could have been the second-last of the match. Australia, bowing under the tension, had lost three wickets for seven runs. Next over Healy faced Cronje. Healy backed away from the second ball, complaining to the umpires that South African fielders were changing position – running backwards – as the bowler came in. One of those offending fieldsmen was at square leg. Next ball, with cheek and flourish, Healy scooped over square leg's head into the midst of the singing, dancing crowd for a matchwinning six.

Premature Emasculation ... Hansie Cronje thought he'd done the Aussies when he trapped Mark Waugh in the first innings at Port Elizabeth. How wrong he was.
Mike Hewitt/Allsport

The series decided in two Tests, Taylor's team enjoyed one of their real highs. They had put their hosts away with a mix of efficiency and heart. Some luck had gone their way, especially with Pollock's injury in Port Elizabeth, but few could argue that they were not markedly the better team.

'It's undoubtedly the biggest Test win I've played in by an absolute mile,' Taylor said. 'I just can't think of a win which rates with it. To climb off the canvas like we did was very special. There is no better Australian side I've played in than this one. I think we are a better side than we were in 1995. I can't think of a win which tops this. No side in the world could have chased like we did and won.'

Yet the win, great as it was, could not help being overshadowed by

Taylor's ever-deepening slump (see next chapter). When they travelled from Port Elizabeth back to Johannesburg, staying at Sandton again to commute each day to Pretoria for the third Test match, the Australians' celebrations were still shrouded by concerns over whether the captain should stay in the team.

Taylor was nothing if not a trier. He picked himself again, and batted 197 minutes on the first morning at Centurion Park. It was agonising – he only scored 38 runs – but at every moment he looked as if he might be playing the innings that would turn his form inside out. He saw off Hayden, Elliott and Mark Waugh, who fell to South Africa's rejuvenated new-ball attack of Donald and the recalled left-armer Brett Schultz. But Taylor's dismissal, caught behind off Lance Klusener, stunted the Australian innings. While Steve Waugh made a flawless 67, given out dubiously caught behind off Schultz, Australia could only score 227.

The highs and lows were in close proximity for Healy, too. He had enjoyed the rare distinction of hitting a six to win the Test match in Port Elizabeth, and on the second day at Centurion Park he became the second wicketkeeper after Rod Marsh to effect 300 dismissals in Test cricket. Yet at Centurion the task was completed amid a trying atmosphere. In the heart of Boer country, Centurion (formerly Verwoerdburg) is an unforgiving rustic community. Braais, or barbecues, were set up around the grassy mounds, and the smoke of roasting meat suffused play. The Northern Transvaalers taunted the Australian team, one man repeatedly shouting 'Shane Warne, your mother is a goat!' for the duration of the second day. Adam Bacher and Brian McMillan (with a heel injury, promoted to No 3 as a specialist batsmen) put on 102 in two hours for the second wicket, giving South Africa some overdue stability at the top. Bacher was unluckily dismissed for a 444-minute 96, though he had spent so long in the nineties that some said the umpires had merely got bored with him. The umpires, Mervyn Kitchen and Cyril Mitchley, came under increasing pressure with some poor decisions, frustrating the Australians. More frustrating was the obdurate South African batting, which built a lead of 157 despite McGrath's sterling 6/86 in 40.4 overs, carrying a foot injury which was to send him home after the match.

Australia stumbled badly in the second innings, Taylor reverting to form with five runs and Hayden given out padding up to Schultz, umpire Mitchley taking an eternity to make what was, admittedly, a correct-seeming decision. Hayden strode up the stairs and, once he had entered the glass-fronted dressing room, speared his bat against a wall.

Healy's timing was not so clever. After Mark Waugh (42) had played an airy shot at Pat Symcox and embarrassed himself, and Blewett and Bevan both succumbed, Healy was trying with Steve Waugh to mount an improbable fightback. The veteran pair had added 31 runs when Mitchley gave Healy out, caught down the leg side off Schultz. The poor luck was too much for the Australian wicketkeeper. Halfway up the stairs to the dressing room, he launched his bat underarm into the room. The difference between Healy's behaviour and Hayden's was simply that Healy's had been public. Referee Raman Subba Row suspended him for the first two one-day matches, jeopardising Healy's grip on the vice-captaincy. As had happened so often, it was Healy who paid the price for being the one to show the team's frustration. In an exasperating Test match for the Australians, Healy had been the man trying his best to keep them enthused in the field, often taking a light-hearted stance during their misfortune. They were all complaining about the umpiring, many worse than Healy was. But he lost his temper at just the wrong moment.

Australia were out 54 runs later, Donald mopping up with 5/36. Chasing 32, South Africa lost Bacher and Kirsten but achieved a face-saving if anti-climactic win.

For the one-day series, Elliott, Hayden, the injured McGrath and Justin Langer flew home. Langer, whose wife was expecting a child any day, had to travel the comparatively short distance from Johannesburg to Perth via Hong Kong, Sydney and Melbourne, courtesy of the ACB's contract with Cathay Pacific. It was ludicrous that the board did not buy him a direct Qantas ticket. In their place flew out Adam Gilchrist (as cover for the suspended Healy), Brendon Julian, Adam Dale and Michael Di Venuto.

The seven-match one-day series was dominated by two themes. One was the Taylor issue, and the other was Australia's experiment with selecting a team of 'one-day specialists' for the first time. These issues did overlap, as Taylor was eventually to fall victim to the 'two teams' selection policy.

Australia and South Africa traded wins in the first three matches. South Africa won convincingly at Buffalo Park in East London, Australia hit back at St George's Park (Mark Waugh returning to the scene of his greatest moment with another century), and South Africa cruised home at Newlands, where Healy returned to captain the side, Taylor sitting it out with a back injury, and Mark Waugh split the webbing in his finger, ruling himself out for two matches.

The Australians were in a state of some chaos off the field, but they showed some of the spirit that was to take them to a World Cup victory two years later by winning the next three matches and the series. In Durban, after a dreadful start, Gilchrist's unbeaten 77 off 88 balls gave them a defendable total, and Dale and Andy Bichel ran through the South African middle order to achieve a 15-run win. In Johannesburg, Di Venuto's 89 off 115 balls pointed to a new era at the top of the order, after which Bichel, Warne and Gillespie did the job with the ball, ensuring a win by eight runs. In Pretoria, Australia had their finest hour, after letting the hosts score a mountainous 284 runs thanks to eighties from Cronje and Cullinan. The returning Mark Waugh was out to the third ball, and the series looked certain to go to a decider when Australia slipped to 3/58. But Steve Waugh (89) and Bevan (103) added 189 runs in 174 balls, a masterful escape act. Conditions were difficult for both teams, the poor floodlighting hampering the batsmen's sight and the heavy slippery dew frustrating the bowlers and fieldsmen. Gilchrist came in and hit two boundaries off the 49th over to get Australia home with six balls free. It was their best one-day win in some years, and capped a remarkable turnaround from their disastrous home summer. The win also helped them keep some psychological 'wood' on the South Africans, on which they were to capitalise in 1998 and 1999. Steve Waugh led Australia for his first international in the meaningless seventh fixture at Bloemfontein, and hit a blistering 91 off 81 balls to become the fourth Australian, after Allan Border, David Boon and Dean Jones, to pass 5000 runs in one-day cricket. It was not enough, as Australia went down by 109 runs – not the first nor the last time they would produce a sub-par performance in a dead rubber. Shaun Pollock, with 152 runs at 38 and 12 wickets at 21.4, was a deserving if narrow man-of-the-series award winner ahead of Steve Waugh, Bevan and Cullinan.

The Taylor Slump

To his undying credit, in his dark days of early 1997 Mark Taylor remained capable of separating the team's imperatives from his personal horrors. At times, however, he was not able to achieve this 'compartmentalisation' as easily as it appeared. At the end of the one-day series in South Africa, Taylor went onto Springbok Park at Bloemfontein to accept the trophy. It was an awkward, incongruous moment. He had only played the first two matches, and had failed badly. The series had been a triumph for Healy's stand-in leadership. Taylor had been dissuaded from playing in the latter games, and his team knew it. They wanted Gilchrist, not Taylor, to play. The captain, who had been advised to go home with the other Test-only players, had stayed on and done what he had promised not to do: taken up a seat that could have gone to a more deserving youngster. Daily, he was receiving unsolicited advice from home, both encouraging and damning, by telephone and fax. He was under pressure from his board to head off any mutinous tendencies in his team. The pressure from the media distilled and concentrated all these other pressures, and was unremitting. When Taylor came onto the field at Bloemfontein, he was wearing casual clothes, whereas his teammates stood in their playing gear. Almost shamefacedly, he took possession of the trophy. Never had he looked more like a non-playing captain.

Taylor's technique, it was true, had never allowed for a great margin of error. Even at his best, in the years 1989-91 and 1993-96, he was one of those batsmen who left a large number of observers unimpressed. He was legendary for his apparent 'luck' – his capacity to play and miss good balls, to edge the ball onto his pad or wide of the stumps, and to loft it just clear of fieldsmen. Of course, it is hard to believe that luck alone could account for 7000 Test runs. Even at the depth of his slump, Taylor had still scored about 400 more Test runs than Steve Waugh while playing 11 fewer matches. Yet the style – or non-style – of his best innings had left him with a dwindling store of 'brownie points', of general admiration, for when the lean times came.

Out Of Touch, Out Of Luck ... Mark Taylor goes again, to Curtly Ambrose this time, and tries not to think of slumps, Melbourne 1996. Trent Parke

Most of his critics came from Queensland and Victoria. One was *The Age*'s Martin Blake, who gained the 'honour' of being the first observer to write about Taylor's 'slump', during the Boxing Day Test against the West Indies in 1996. It seemed premature for Blake to be writing that Taylor's place was in question. He had been Australia's best batsman on the ill-starred Indian tour, and his Test scores against the West Indians had been 43, 36, 27 and 16. He did look clay-footed in Melbourne, making seven and 10 on a bowlers' wicket, but what was new about that? Even at his very best, Taylor could look out of form. The key was, he could clear the poor shots and sloppy footwork from his mind and concentrate on the next ball, not the previous one. He came under pressure in the one-day arena first. This was unsurprising, as he had come to the Australian captaincy as a non-automatic selection in the one-day – he had insisted on selection in both codes if he were to accept the job. By the lead-up to the 1996–97 season, though, he had prospered in India, leading Austalia's one-day aggregates and averages in the Titan Cup. At Bangalore, he had scored his first one-day century. He had had a good World Cup. There were few signs of what was to come.

The mixing up of one-day and Test seasons in Australia did him no favours. His Test form seemed good enough early in the summer of 1996–97, but he found it difficult to adjust to the pace of one-day cricket when those matches came along to interrupt the season. In the early matches, he scored 29 (from 67 balls), 17 (off 35) and 28 (off 55). After the Melbourne Test, he scored 11 (off 16) before being run out while looking good, 26 (off 52) and then six off 23 in the loss to Pakistan at Hobart. His scores, in themselves, were not too bad. They were to look quite respectable a couple of months later, when every single run was cause for relief, but his slow strike rate was placing the middle order under stress, and Australia were starting to lose games. The Hobart match, which Australia lost badly, was on 7 January, just a week after the Boxing Day Test, which they had also lost. Taylor's survival was for the first time being linked to the team's results. At a press conference after the Hobart game, News Limited's Robert 'Crash' Craddock wanted to ask Taylor about his future. Embarrassed and somewhat ashamed to be asking the question, Craddock stumbled along nervously, unable to put the inquiry into words.

'Come on, Crash,' Taylor interrupted. 'You can ask me the question. Am I going to drop myself?'

It was Taylor's first acknowledgment of his situation. He said his position was in the selectors' hands, but personally he favoured retaining himself. The caravan travelled to Perth, and Taylor scored a laborious 18 off 55, the team's loss forcing Australia out of the finals for the first time in two decades. Much of the blame was slated to Taylor. In the final 'dead' match against Pakistan in Melbourne, Anthony Stuart took a hat-trick and Australia saved face with an ugly three-wicket win. But Taylor could only make eight from 22.

By the Australia Day Test – the most important of their lives, according to Steve Waugh – Australia's attention was fixed on the captain. Surely, it was felt, a return to Test cricket's more studied rhythms would revive Taylor's footwork and eye. Technical explanations were being offered by discriminating judges: he was angling his bat, he was stepping across the crease rather than to the ball, he was playing the ball too square of the wicket. Greg Chappell and Dennis Lillee said Taylor should not be an automatic choice for the South African tour. Ian Healy made a veiled criticism of Taylor's style, saying other captains tended to consult more than Taylor did with senior players. Taylor argued, publicly, that he should be seen as a captain–batsman–all-rounder, with the weighting about 90 per cent on the captaincy and the team's results. Healy countered that Taylor, as good a captain as he was, deserved less favourable weighting and should still be judged first and foremost as a batsman.

Thanks to the West Indies' capitulation, Australia won the Frank Worrell Trophy convincingly in Adelaide. On a belter of a pitch and against a demoralised attack, Taylor missed his chance, scoring only 11. A week later in Perth, he was no match for the West Indian fielding (run out for two in the first innings) or their bowling (caught behind for one in the second).

Suddenly, his statistics were looking as bad as his timing. His Test figures for the series were 153 runs at 17.00. Eight one-day innings had yielded 143 runs at 17.87, made at fewer than 50 runs per hundred balls. In the Sheffield Shield, six innings for NSW brought him only 99 runs at 16.5.

Still, there was never any real likelihood of his missing the South African tour. It still seemed a matter of time before he played the one innings that revived his unconscious memories of how to bat. He struggled horribly in the exhibition match at the Oppenheimer ground, but it seemed that he made that turnaround innings with his 85, off

140 balls, against a Test-strength Western Province attack at Cape Town. In the press box, each new edition of the Australian papers was being updated with a new story of Taylor's success: when he passed 40, 50, 60 and 70, new introductions were written along the lines of 'He's back.'

Yet it proved a false dawn. He scored 20 and one against Natal, 16 (another of his confessed missed opportunities) in the first Test at the Wanderers, and then suffered a muscle spasm in his back on the first morning of the first-class match against Border at East London. It was commonly thought, both inside the team and out, that the inevitable stress of his personal situation had contributed to the return of his old back complaint.

He recovered in time for the second Test at Port Elizabeth, where, amid Australia's great comeback, he made a minimal batting contribution of eight and 13.

His last seven Tests had now given him 190 runs at 15.8. It was 18 innings since his last half-century (against Sri Lanka at Perth in 1995) and 21 since his last century. No other Australian batsman had ever survived in Test cricket with such a lean spell. In world cricket, only two others had. His situation might have been relieved had he scored runs in other forms of cricket, but his first-class record in the same period was equally poor, with the 85 at Cape Town and a 53 for NSW contributing 138 of his 205 runs in nine innings. Taylor's slump has, in retrospect, been discounted by some as a natural ebb in any batsman's career; yet this was a very unnatural ebb, and it was only prolonged by Taylor's ability to maintain a winning percentage as captain, and convince the powers in Australian cricket that that winning record could only be maintained under his leadership.

Privately, however, the pressure was mounting. Some of Taylor's teammates were saying, in their hotel rooms and at bars throughout South Africa, that the team's success was being jeopardised by the captain's self-selection. The thread of this argument was that Michael Bevan was being selected as an all-rounder at No 7 to cover for the weakness at the top of the order. As a consequence, Australia were one bowler short. McGrath, Gillespie and Warne were having to shoulder an unreasonable burden. This was especially apparent at Port Elizabeth, where the uneven wicket would have suited Paul Reiffel perfectly, and at Centurion, where McGrath was bowled into the ground and the spinners were ineffective. Had Australia lost both of those Tests, instead of one, Taylor would almost certainly have been dropped.

In fact, it looked imminent after they collapsed for 108 in their first innings at Port Elizabeth. The absence of Reiffel and of a useful opening batsman looked to be costing Australia the series. Asked how close Taylor was to omitting himself, Geoff Marsh paused for a long time, sighed, and said, staring aimlessly at the floor: 'Well, Mark's a stronger man than you or me.'

Reiffel recalls: 'When we arrived at Port Elizabeth, we found a pitch so green that I thought, "I've got to play; they've got to go with three seamers on this." But they didn't, which was a crushing disappointment. A couple of teammates said words to the effect that they could not understand why I was not playing. I bit my tongue; it is not wise to become known as a malcontent on a tour. But I'm convinced to this day that they made the wrong decision.'

Mark Waugh's great century saved Taylor at Port Elizabeth. That evening, the team celebrated hard. Taylor and Healy, as well as Steve Waugh, wore their beer-soaked baggy green caps out to the local bars. Healy accompanied Taylor for much of the night, perhaps to supervise the captain, and make sure he did not lose his cool again as he had earlier that night, when he confronted *The Australian*'s Malcolm Conn in the lobby of the Holiday Inn in Port Elizabeth.

Taylor's relationship with the press had remained astonishingly good to that point. Astonishing, because it was unprecedented for a player who was so out of form to have to field questions on his batting almost every single day, and certainly after every innings. The press follow an unwritten rule: when seeking comment from players, they seek it from the captain plus any player who has done exceptionally well on the field. Players who have failed are left to their own devices. But because of Taylor's captaincy duties, he found himself answering questions about his form every time he presented himself to talk about the team. In South Africa, and later in England, nearly every significant press conference ended up as an examination of Taylor's form.

He was certainly inventive with his explanations for why he should keep his place. At various times, he owed his retention to (a) the preparation of green pitches by overseas groundsmen intent on blunting Warne; (b) the fact that openers were suffering all around the world; (c) the fact that captains were struggling for runs all around the world; (d) his poor luck in running into the West Indies and South Africa, who had the best bowling attacks; (e) the fact that no other Australian opener was scoring many more runs than he was; (f) the fact that there was no other Australian opener who had played sufficient recent cricket to come into the Test team, an especially spurious claim on the 1997 Ashes tour, because reserve opener Michael Slater was only underprepared because Taylor had been omitting Slater for himself in the tour games; and, most importantly, (g) the team's winning record proved that they needed Taylor's captaincy.

At times, Taylor's ways of rationalising his continued retention smacked of desperation. Looking at it another way, however, they can be seen as a direct result of his constant exposure to media questioning. He knew very well that he couldn't continue getting away with making the same excuse, so he had to keep thinking up new ones to shake the media off his back. It could be argued that his attempts to explain away his bad form in fact contributed to its continuance, and to what Greg Chappell described as Taylor's 'denial' phase.

Denial or not, Taylor maintained his cool until Conn wrote in *The Australian* that Taylor's teammates were muttering behind his back. Taylor could accept criticism from outside the team, but would not acknowledge that it had been happening inside. In Port Elizabeth, he told Conn that this was the most harmonious team he had toured with. Conn replied that harmonious or not, certain members were quite freely questioning Taylor's continued selection. Their sorest point was the omission of Reiffel in Port Elizabeth, where Australia literally put the series on the line by allowing Taylor to pick himself.

At the same time, as Judi Taylor later revealed, the Australian captain was ringing home and suggesting that he should quit. 'He rang me one night from South Africa at the time of the Second Test and told me he was thinking of standing down. I was thinking, "Shit!" but I was trying to keep it calm. "You must do whatever you want to do," I said. Mark's mum and dad were away, and I didn't know who to talk to. I rang Neil Marks, and told him what Mark had said. "No, no!" said Neil. "Get a piece of paper!" He then proceeded to give me all these reasons why Mark shouldn't stand down. "Ring him back this afternoon with some sort of excuse and just run through these things with him." I did just that.

'Mark went through such a stage that he can't even remember talking to me much about it. I can recall one thing he said to me: "Jude, I'm sick of being a passenger in the side." I kept telling him: "Mark, you are not a passenger – you are the pilot."'

After a heated argument that night in the Port Elizabeth Holiday Inn, Conn and Taylor agreed to disagree, but the supposed harmony of the team was shaken again the following week, when Elliott, Langer and Hayden were told their services were not needed for the one-day tournament. None was known as a top one-day batsman, but what rankled was that Taylor was chosen, despite having said 'I don't want to be taking up space; I don't want to be taking some younger bloke's seat on the plane.' Elliott was in outstanding form, Langer had not played a Test but had sparkled on his few opportunities, and Hayden had his claims, and was certainly in better form than Taylor. Some discontent lingered in the team over the 'two teams' policy now emerging – not because they disagreed with the policy per se, but because they believed Taylor should be as subject to its dictates as every other player was.

Said Reiffel: 'Three players – Matthew Elliott, Matt Hayden and Glenn McGrath – were sent home, but Tubby, who plainly wasn't in much form, stayed. The three guys who went home were pretty disappointed, and I think matters came to a head a bit then.'

In fact, Trevor Hohns had asked Taylor if he wanted to go home and rest before the Ashes tour, which was to start three weeks after the team was to return from South Africa. Taylor resisted this sensible offer, believing he could regain his form during the one-dayers against possibly the best bowling attack in the world. He also believed that the captain should remain in charge of his team, especially as vice-captain Healy was suspended for the first two one-dayers after his bat-throwing at Centurion Park.

ACB chairman Denis Rogers flew to South Africa for the first one-dayer, in East London. When Rogers arrived, he was disturbed to learn of the mutterings in the team. Warne, Healy and Steve Waugh – three of Taylor's most senior teammates – were cautious about offering Taylor their full support. None said directly that he should have dropped himself, but there was a consensus that he needed to 'see things the way they are', in the words of one. It was frustrating the team that Taylor remained so oppressively upbeat about his situation.

Rogers threw his ample influence behind the captain. In East London, he assured Taylor that he had the board's full support. The ACB felt it owed Taylor for the team's run of success, and there was a belief at board level that only Taylor could hold together the fragile balance of personalities and egos in the team. It was a fair response from Rogers, and one that Taylor would pay back during the players' pay dispute later in the year.

Taylor failed again in East London, and hit one of his lowest points in the second one-dayer, in Port Elizabeth. His batting was desperate – and desperately bad. He charged the bowling, lifted his head and swung at everything. He could manage neither to lay much bat on ball nor get himself out. As Australian Associated Press's Cole Hitchcock wrote, Taylor batted 'like a schoolboy in the last over before the lunch bell'. Craddock wrote: 'It's sad and it's silly.' There was an air of silliness about it. Taylor was out for 17 in 45 balls, and said afterwards that by now he considered himself 'a free wicket'. It was a humiliating admission, and a far cry from saying, a week earlier, that he didn't want to take someone else's seat on the plane.

When Healy returned, for the third game in Cape Town, Taylor stood aside, claiming a recurrence of his back injury. Healy had been happy for Taylor to play in the first two matches, because he felt that either the captain or the vice-captain should be part of the team and if the third man in line, Steve Waugh, had taken the captaincy, this would only have highlighted Healy's own unfortunate absence.

Healy, in fact, was exhibiting several changes in behaviour. Back in 1994, he was appointed vice-captain largely to counterbalance the NSW influence in the team. Steve Waugh was acknowledged to be the second-best captaincy candidate, but Healy was given the job as Taylor's deputy. Time and again, Healy had deferred to Waugh, his best friend in cricket, when it came to speculating on the next captain after Taylor. Healy's response was: 'If there's a bloke standing over there in the gully who can do the job as well as or better than I can, then I think he should do it. I've got enough on my hands.' Healy had even reiterated this view after the tour match against Border in which he led Australia, when Taylor's back injury first flared.

But in Cape Town for the third one-day international, Healy had a change of heart. Now, he said, he would like to be considered Taylor's successor. He claimed, quite nonsensically, that he had been misquoted on the earlier occasions. Healy said: 'I'm not saying it will be an issue, but if it does happen, after Mark has retired, I'd like to have my hat in the ring. I could do the job as well as anybody.'

There was no visible falling-out between Healy and Steve Waugh, but it did seem strange that Healy should now withdraw three years of support for his friend. There was no doubt, however, that Healy was exercising his prerogatives as stand-in captain and third tour selector. Mark Waugh split the webbing in his hand at Cape Town, and by the fourth match in Durban, Australia only had 12 fit players to consider for selection. In a meeting with Marsh and Healy on the Kingsmead ground after practice, Taylor suggested that he come back and play. Healy and Marsh suggested that Adam Gilchrist might be a better option. Taylor pressed. As Healy said later, Taylor 'really wanted to play'. But Marsh and Healy persuaded him to continue 'resting'. As he came off the field, Taylor ran into ABC Radio's Tim Lane, who asked him if he was going to play the next day. Taylor said, tightly, 'You'd better ask the captain.'

A dressing room coup? Not quite, but Healy's behaviour had taken an authoritarian turn. He and Marsh later denied that they had 'outvoted' Taylor – no formal vote had been taken. Yet the facts could not be denied: Taylor had wanted to play, but his coach and his deputy had talked him out of it. The captain had been overruled.

Australia won the next three games and, under Healy, their first significant one-day tournament in two years. Taylor was a shadowy, forlorn figure. Consigned to an enforced 'rest', he was neither a captain nor a batsman. His one-day international career, if not his Test career, seemed over. There was intense speculation about whether he would be retained for the Ashes tour, the team for which would be picked a few days after the return from South Africa. Secretly, however, Hohns had assured Taylor, while the South African tour was still going on, of his Ashes selection. In a press conference at Durban, I asked Taylor if he had received such assurances. He said: 'I can't really answer that.' A few days later, in Pretoria, Cole Hitchcock repeated the question. Taylor said: 'No. Nobody has been given any assurances about the Ashes tour.'

It was, no doubt, a necessary fib. The atmosphere in the team was brittle enough over the Taylor issue without him coming out and saying that he, above all others, had been guaranteed a place for the England tour. Some semblance of fairness had to be maintained.

And so, as a non-playing captain, wearing his civilian clothes, Taylor received the one-day trophy in Bloemfontein. The team flew home, and he was picked as captain for the four-month Ashes tour. Slater was brought back, at Hayden's expense, and Elliott was chosen as a No 3 or opener. Ricky Ponting was also brought back from the wilderness, Michael Kasprowicz was reinstated, but, surprisingly, Reiffel, whose career suffered most of the collateral damage from Taylor's poor form, was left out.

The bombshell was Healy's dumping as vice-captain. By now, Taylor's position was so tenuous that the selectors felt they needed to elevate Steve Waugh, as alternative captain, to step in at any moment. Asked if he was paying the price for his suspension in South Africa, Healy said: 'No, I think the decision on me was made a long time ago.'

In the three weeks between tours, Taylor accepted his long-time mentor Neil Marks's advice to 'go away and not touch a cricket bat'. The advice was issued during the South African tour, but Taylor had opted to persevere through the increasingly humiliating one-day leg. He, Judi, and sons Jack and William took a holiday together to recover from the ordeal. It had reached the stage where well-wishers were faxing Taylor diagrams of the position of his feet while he was batting – suggesting improvements, of course; newspapers, on the other hand, were being bombarded with letters calling on Taylor to quit.

A tour to England would only concentrate the questioning. Not only was England's cricket media the largest and most trenchant in the world, but playing England brought focus to the real issue, as many Australians saw it. England had a tradition of choosing a captain, and building a Test team around that man. Australia had always scorned that approach; Australia picked a team of the best players, and chose its captain from them. It was embarrassing to many former Test players, especially those of the Chappell era, that Australia was now sliding towards the English model. Taylor was being retained as a captain, Mike Brearley-style. It was too much for Greg Chappell, who said Taylor had become 'mentally unfit' for the captaincy. Chappell, as good a judge as any, believed Taylor's discrimination in his tactics and team selections was impaired because of his form. Chappell had seen this first-hand. When he tried to offer Taylor advice, Taylor had denied that there was anything wrong with his batting. In Taylor's view, he was hitting the ball well enough, but just getting out. Chappell felt that unless Taylor acknowledged how poorly he was batting, he would never come out of his slump.

On the way to England, Australia played a match at the Kowloon Cricket Club in Hong Kong. Taylor was first out for the visitors, caught behind off one Mohsin Kamal. When the Australians arrived at the airport in London, he handed his passport to a customs officer, who said: 'Mark Taylor, eh? Captain of the Australian cricket team?' Taylor said: 'Yes, that's right.' The officer said: 'Ah, but for how long?'

In the Arundel Castle match to kick off the England tour, Taylor survived a confident caught-behind appeal before eking out 45 runs, from 87 balls, against an attack of retired bowlers including Neal Radford, Neil Foster, David Capel and John Emburey. Two days later, signs of return: a top-scoring 76 off 126 balls against Northamptonshire in a limited-overs match. It was the first time Taylor had top-scored for his country, in any kind of fixture, in nearly two years. The following day, at Worcester, he made 14 out of Australia's 121. They lost by five wickets.

Losing matches, of course, placed most pressure on Taylor. His one-day position became absolutely untenable as the team lost the three-match series against England 0-3. Taylor made seven (16 balls) and 11 (35 balls) before omitting himself for the third match at Lord's. He was never to play one-day cricket for Australia again. He had only played in this series, in fact, because the scheduling had made it impossible to bring out Di Venuto to take his place before the Test series.

In the next county game, against Gloucestershire at Bristol, Taylor missed out again, with a first-innings duck and 30 in the second innings. When he arrived at the ground for the third day's play, he stepped out of the team bus to be met by a *Daily Mirror* employee who tried to have himself photographed presenting Taylor with a foot-wide bat. Team manager Alan Crompton seized a camera from the *Mirror* photographer and insisted on having the film taken out. With some satisfaction, Crompton achieved his aim, only to discover later that he had taken the film from the wrong camera. The pictures were duly published. Possibly more humiliating than this, to Taylor (who refused to pose with the bat, saying later: 'I can laugh at myself, but I don't think I need to stand next to a three-foot wide bat to prove it'), was that while he was failing, Elliott (124) and Langer (152 not out) were able to treat the Gloucestershire game as a fun hit-out.

There was no fun for Taylor – and even less at home, where Judi was exposed to the constant stream of reports on and condemnations of her husband's situation. It is often harder for the spouse than for the player himself, for she is absolutely powerless over affairs, whereas he can at least make plans to arrest his slide in his next innings. Rather than listen to the endless advice from known and unknown sources, Taylor confided in Judi. She joked about how hard he was making life for his children, saying: 'Are you going to score runs today, so we don't have to drop William off around the corner from school?'

Judi was living by the stoic's motto – Whatever doesn't kill me makes me stronger. Taylor was later to tell *Sports Illustrated*: 'She used that saying a lot. When you have a win or you make a good 100, at the end of the Test you get all the blokes around you and you have a beer and tell each other how bloody good you are. She doesn't get to experience all that. At home she's reading the newspapers and it's "Taylor has got to be dropped, he's a failure." Judi gets the lows. It was tough for her.'

One week before the first Test, Australia were playing Derbyshire at the Racecourse Ground in Derby. Taylor again picked himself ahead of Slater, thus ruling his young NSW partner out of consideration for the Test match. It was another self-preserving manoeuvre by the captain, for he could now say that whatever happened to him in this game, Slater was not match-hardened enough to replace him in the Test team.

Taylor made five in the first innings, and the *Daily Telegraph* in Sydney ran a front-page story saying Taylor had dropped himself from the Test team. It was untrue, but the newspaper was only trying to take the lead in a story it felt was inevitable, if not that day, then the day after. The London *Daily Telegraph* wrote: 'The signs are that he is not simply out of form but past his peak ... England will be happy if he stays in the Australian side beyond the first Test.' Australia made 6/362 in its first innings, Blewett top-scoring with 121. Derbyshire replied with 9/257.

When Taylor walked out to bat with Elliott for the second innings, press photographers followed him most of the way to the wicket. 'They all wanted the picture of me going out to bat for the last time,' he told *Sports Illustrated*. 'Why I didn't belt someone, I don't know.'

Elliott was out for four, and Langer joined Taylor. The score was 1/5 when Taylor, on one, chased a wide ball and attempted a big cover drive. It was typical of the addled shot selection brought on by his poor form. He edged it straight to first slip, manned by none other than Dean Jones, playing as Derby's professional for a short time (before leaving in acrimonious circumstances). Jones dropped the sitter.

Taylor walked down the wicket and said to Langer: 'That's it. I can't play. I'm gone. I can't bat. I've lost it.'

Langer, who knew the meaning of self-doubt, and knew how to overcome it, replied: 'That's bloody rubbish. Watch the bloody ball, and play the bloody ball.'

Taylor made 63 – just enough to regain a shred of confidence before the Test – and called Langer to his room later to thank him.

It was ironic that, as a captain saved by his team's ability to win matches, Taylor saved his place in a game which they lost badly. Electing to bat first on a green Edgbaston wicket, Taylor lost Elliott early. But next over, Taylor crashed Devon Malcolm through cover to go to seven and felt a minor flow of ease running through his limbs. He took guard, and Malcolm bowled a similar widish half-volley. Taylor tried to repeat the shot, hesitated a fraction, and nicked it to Mark Butcher at slip. Australia collapsed to 8/54 before Warne (47) and Kasprowicz (17) engineered a face-saving ninth-wicket stand to get the score to 118.

McGrath, Gillespie and Kasprowicz each took an early wicket, and Australia seemed back in the game when Graham Thorpe joined Nasser Hussain on the first afternoon. By the time they were separated, 290 minutes later, England's lead was 220. The Australian bowling lost its consistency, McGrath, Gillespie (who strained a hamstring) and Warne posing no sustained threat as Hussain and Thorpe flayed them. England declared at 9/478. Throughout, Taylor watched grimly from first slip. His parents, Tony and Judy, were there, watching what seemed likely to be their son's last Test match. 'I told them that maybe I should go,' Taylor said. 'The team was getting upset.

Every question was, "Should the captain be sacked?"'

To make bad matters worse, Mark Waugh suffered acute stomach pains and was taken to hospital with suspected appendicitis. Taylor went out to bat with Elliott shortly after England's declaration on the third morning. Elliott faced Darren Gough's first over, leaving Taylor to deal with the fast but errant Malcolm. Taylor faced up, and Malcolm turned at the top of his mark. As he came in, Taylor backed away – something was in his eye. The tension was unbearable. Finally, Malcolm came in and Taylor let the first ball through.

His innings was a streaky one. He top-edged a hook off Malcolm that flew into the crowd just over fine leg's head. But he persisted, watching the ball with visible intensity. It helped him that Elliott also batted well for 66 and then Blewett stayed with him for more than four hours, adding 194. Just before stumps, Taylor pushed one wide of mid-off and took off for his hundredth run. It was a typical Taylor innings: resilient, stilted, characterised by his concentration and capacity to forget the previous ball's play-and-miss. He allowed himself a left-handed punch at the air as he ran the single, then removed his helmet and saluted his teammates. He resisted the urge to give any kind of signal to the press box.

'It would be lowering my standards. It would have given them a headline,' he told *Sports Illustrated*. 'And a few of them would have sat down with their gin and tonics at night and said, "We got Tubby. We finally got him to crack."'

Taylor and Blewett lasted until stumps, reviving hopes of a draw or a miraculous win. They added another 71 on the fourth morning before Taylor chipped a drive back down the pitch to off-spinner Robert Croft. Australia lost their next eight wickets for 150, and the match by nine wickets.

Yet Taylor had survived. He said, diplomatically, at the post-match press conference that he would 'prefer to make nought and win the game – it's nicer to sit here as a winning captain', but, win or lose, another failure would have ended his Test career.

And there was no doubt that the team had been affected. When

Reiffel arrived to replace Andy Bichel, he was shocked by the team's low morale: 'It was obvious to me that Tubby's string of failures and the huge publicity around them had created a negative atmosphere in the team. They were very low. These things can run through a team like a virus, and it seemed that everyone was looking at themselves and believing or at least imagining that they were also out of form.'

When Taylor survived, the team regained its life. The drama of the moment – one last shot, one last chance at redemption – still rings in the air. Edgbaston was to be the scene of another great Australian moment in 1999, the tie with South Africa that qualified them for the World Cup final, but no innings resounded so deeply for the future than Taylor's in 1997. Had he dropped himself then, Steve Waugh would have become captain for the rest of the Ashes series. An alternative universe pans out: one in which the players' dispute takes a different course, in which Australia might have lost to New Zealand or South Africa at home, or perhaps beaten India in India. Certainly, we would have lost the romance of Taylor's 334 not out in Peshawar in 1998. Perhaps Matthew Hayden would have gone there and scored 335.

No other Australian cricketer has survived such a lengthy period of failure. It is hard to imagine any cricketer, or sportsman, being able to. Taylor admitted that he owed his survival to keeping the game in perspective. I recall one night in South Africa, after the two-wicket win in Port Elizabeth, returning to the Holiday Inn at around two o'clock in the morning and talking to Taylor. At that point, of course, he was near his nadir. He said that the next morning he had to be up at six o'clock to film a live interview with Ray Martin. I groaned in sympathy. Taylor said, 'Yeah, it's hard. But the hardest thing is when they tell me I've got the next most important job in the country apart from the Prime Minister's. I reckon that's bullshit. This is only a game. I can't believe people think it's that important.'

There was no reason to disbelieve him. He had enjoyed nine years as one of the game's premier opening batsmen, and three as leader of the premier team. He never lost his perspective, even if others did. Two years later, when he spoke to *Sports Illustrated* after retiring, Taylor had the same simple insight:

'I was getting hammered, but I knew I was still travelling a lot better than a lot of other people are, in Australia and around the world. I might have been having a nightmare in this game of cricket, I couldn't make a run to save myself, but if that's the worst thing that can happen to me in this life, that isn't going to be too bad.'

South Africa in Australia 1997–98

Avenging their 2–1 series loss to Australia at home had become something of an obsession among the Proteas' hierarchy. The captain, Hansie Cronje, and coach, Bob Woolmer, had been devastated by the defeat from a winning position in Port Elizabeth, and spent the intervening 10 months planning their campaign. Their spearhead, Allan Donald, said on the eve of the Australian tour that winning this series was his greatest desire in cricket. When the South Africans won their series in Pakistan, 1–0, on their way to Australia, they again forced comparisons between themselves and Australia as the best Test cricket team in the world.

They had some reason for confidence when they arrived in Perth in November. Australia were in disarray. Coincidentally, the South Africans were in Perth when the Australian players were discussing whether or not to strike. While Australia defeated New Zealand, almost desultorily, on the WACA ground, the South Africans practised in the WACA nets. Cronje and Woolmer stole away for long periods to sit in the stands and watch Australia in action.

Woolmer, the most scientific of cricket coaches, relied on a number of computerised models based on painstaking collection of data on his own and opposing players. As so often, the former England opener was a pioneer in coaching technology. He also employed Paddy Upton, a bio-mechanicist, to advise the team on the arcane-seeming mysteries of their own bodies. Cronje, meanwhile, brooded.

After the New Zealand–Australia Test series finished, it was time for a quick burst of one-day cricket. South Africa gained a psychological leap over Australia by winning their first two encounters convincingly. Their first meeting, in Sydney, was a tempestuous affair, the crowd on Yabba's Hill bombarding Pat Symcox with matter ranging from half-full beer cups to a whole roasted chicken. Cronje gathered his players in the centre and threatened to walk off. When they resumed playing, Symcox and surprise off-spinner Daryll Cullinan went through the Australians, Cullinan especially enjoying his dismissal of Shane Warne, trapped leg-before wicket. As Gary Kirsten recorded in his diary, Cullinan and Warne resumed their old verbal battle. According to Kirsten, Warne said to Cullinan: 'I've been waiting 10 months to bowl at you again, Daryll.' To which Cullinan replied: 'You look as if you've spent all that time eating.' The story may be apocryphal – the South African's quip has more the flavour of Kirsten's sense of humour than Cullinan's.

The running battle with Cullinan was a highlight of the South Africa–Australia encounters in the 1990s. It started under Allan Border. Cullinan, the Proteas' most gifted batsman, had scored a triple century in first-class cricket as a teenager, and came to Australia in 1993–94 with a towering reputation. But it all went wrong from the start. David Boon said:

> Cullinan had come to Australia with a reputation as a good player, but while we were batting he dropped four catches at second slip – while continuing to sledge our players. His mistakes were, of course, like the proverbial red rag to a bull. When South Africa batted, Cullinan finally came to the wicket. First ball, Cullinan, caught Border, bowled McDermott. From that moment on, as Warney cast his spell around him, Cullinan would be greeted with: 'Is the shower already running, Daryll?' More than most, Cullinan suffered from Shane's flipper. 'It's going to be the third ball, Daryll,' we'd tell him. 'Make sure you come forward. Oh, you're out!'

In 1997 in South Africa, Warne had bowled beautifully in the first Test at the Wanderers, but couldn't help adding the provocative post-match remark: 'I didn't care how many I got, so long as I got Cullinan.' Cullinan continued to struggle against the Australians' verbal barrage. A shy, brusque customer, he was not particularly popular in his own team, either. If he was going to succeed on the 1997-98 tour of Australia, he would have to concentrate all his mental resources and shut out the negative feelings around him. His start to the tour, with runs and wickets in Sydney, boded well for his summer.

That match was to have an unfortunate consequence for the South Africans, however. A week later, as South Africa played Tasmania in a four-day match in Devonport, the Nine Network released videotape of Cronje apparently tampering with the ball during the Sydney day-night match. During the interruption caused by the crowd's misbehaviour, Cronje was caught rolling the ball on the ground under his foot, driving his spikes into the ball and roughing it up so as to increase its chances of reverse-swinging late in the game. Although the videotape seemed conclusive, Cronje denied he had broken Law 42 (5), which says: 'No-one shall rub the ball on the ground or use any artificial substance or take any other action to alter the condition of the ball.'

Cronje said: 'The last thing on my mind was trying to alter the state of the ball. Often you stand there messing with the ball, waiting for things to happen, thinking of other things, so whatever I did, it was certainly not to alter the state of the ball. It was more to mess around, or wait, or think, or try to get other things off my mind.'

Inadvertently, however, he showed a flawed grasp of the laws when he admitted that the South Africans deliberately skidded the ageing ball onto rough areas of the field while returning it to the bowler.

'Umpire Terry Prue asked me why we do that,' Cronje said. 'I said that's the way we pass the ball from one player to another. Sometimes we do it out of fun, and sometimes we do it to get the ball a little bit rough on the one side.'

At the time when he gave that press conference – immediately after the Devonport match in which he scored 165, his first century in any form of cricket in two years – Cronje had not seen the videotape, so could not have been aware of how damning it was. When he did see it, he and Woolmer changed their defence to a conspiracy theory counterattack on Kerry Packer's Nine Network.

'I haven't been found guilty by the ICC, and I didn't know that Channel 9 was now the ICC,' Cronje said. 'Channel 9 has not come up to me and said I've done anything wrong. Until I'm proven guilty, or asked by the match referee to look at something, I haven't done anything. I am also very disappointed that there is an insinuation that we tried to gain unfair advantage, which is totally contrary to the way in which we play the game.'

Cronje and Woolmer tried to use the incident to knit the team together against a 'siege' by the hostile Australian media and public they felt was surrounding them. It was typical of their leadership style, and similar, in its obsessive, defensive mindset, to the alliance of Allan Border and Bob Simpson which had overseen Australia's rise from the depths of the 1980s. Few of the younger South Africans cared a whit about the Cronje incident. They simply wanted to get on and play cricket. Yet Cronje and Woolmer built the incident up, reflecting only their intense paranoia.

The first fracture came in their next match, their third draw in three first-class games, against Australia A in Brisbane. Cullinan, batting well on 43 in the first innings, pushed forward to a Stuart MacGill leg-spinner that pitched outside off-stump and turned away. Umpire Steve Davis gave Cullinan out. To the batsman's chagrin, the other umpire, Peter Parker, gave him out in identical fashion, also to a ball that would clearly have missed the off-stump, when he was on 83 in the second innings. Enraged, Cullinan protested the decision and earned a reprimand from his own team management. Never a popular figure in his own dressing room, Cullinan felt victimised by Woolmer and Cronje. His confidence shattered, Cullinan fell prey to Warne in both innings of the first Test and played little part in the remainder of the tour. It was perplexing management by the South Africans. They had defended Cronje, with unreasonable paranoia, when he had been caught tampering with the ball. Yet they condemned Cullinan to obscurity for the relatively minor matter of dissenting on two patently poor umpiring decisions. They could little afford to destroy their best batsman on such a tour.

Australia's cricket fans were roused in great numbers for the Test series. With the pay dispute and a low-key series against New Zealand behind them, the public was hungry for some competitive cricket against a South African team they liked and respected. A crowd of 73,000 attended on Boxing Day at the MCG, the biggest crowd at a single day's Test cricket in Australia since the 1975–76 series against the West Indies. They saw a fascinating, if slow, opening stanza. Jacques Kallis dropped Matthew Elliott early, but the Australians still slumped to 3/44 in the first two hours. Elliott, distracted by the Christmas birth of his first child and some ongoing personal problems, was not the batsman he had been in South Africa earlier in the year, and Donald exploited his heavy footwork. Taylor cut Brian McMillan hard, but was caught brilliantly by Kirsten at cover, and Mark Waugh edged Donald for a painful 18-ball duck. Yet Australia's pugnacity again retrieved the situation, Ricky Ponting (105) and Steve Waugh (96) adding 145 in four hours for a first innings total of 309.

Not for the last time in this series, the South African batting appeared paralysed by a fear of failure. They scored 186 in 416 minutes, Kirsten fighting for nearly a day-long 83 and the veteran McMillan, whose touch had deserted him, eking out 48 in 227 minutes. The Australian bowling was competent, but far from dangerous. McGrath had been rushed back into the team despite a half-healed stomach muscle injury, and was well below his best. Kasprowicz stepped in with three wickets, his best return in Australia. Warne took three and Mark Waugh two as Australia seized a 123-run lead.

Elliott, Greg Blewett and Mark Waugh all failed again as Donald lifted himself in the second innings. Taylor scored a steady 59 before being given out caught off a big-turning Symcox off-break that spun so much that umpire Steve Randell could not believe it had not hit the bat. Donald (six) and Shaun Pollock (three) took nine Australian wickets, but Paul Reiffel's unbeaten 79 at No 8, with good support from the tail, helped Australia double their score from 7/128 to 257 all out, a lead of 380.

With 125 overs to force a result, the Australians had reason for confidence. But McGrath was clearly hampered by his injury, and the wicket improved on the last day to help South Africa's survival effort. Kallis (101) defended stoutly for his first Test century, and despite Warne's two-over surge to remove Adam Bacher and Cullinan, each of the South African lower-order batsmen chipped in to help Kallis force the draw. McGrath did not take a wicket until the 118th over, his ineffectiveness illustrating how Australia had come to rely on him, rather than Warne, to bowl out opposing teams on the fifth day.

While they should have been inspired and invigorated by their sturdy survival effort in Melbourne, the South Africans' analysis paralysis only deepened when the series moved on to Sydney. Winning the toss and having the best of the batting on day one, South Africa limped to a mere 5/197 that day, despite an Australian attack so threadbare, with McGrath barely functional, that Taylor employed no fewer than eight bowlers.

The second morning brought the first hint that this was to be Warne's match. The leg-spinner had undergone a trying season, as he had lost his sense of humour in the face of relentless public ridicule of his weight. Cullinan and the other South Africans had ribbed him about his expanding girth, and on the 1997 Ashes tour spectators had taunted him with a chant of 'Who ate all the pies?' Perhaps it was when the teasing came from Australians, from people he had believed to be his unquestioning admirers, that Warne lost his sangfroid. In fact, the criticism came from closer than he was aware. His coach, Geoff Marsh, and the Australian team physiotherapist, Errol Alcott, had been dissatisfied with Warne's weight for some months. They felt he had not been training hard enough to sustain his fitness. Warne countered that he was 'cricket-fit' and able to bowl to his captain's requirements. In early December, *The Australian*'s Malcolm Conn took the bait from management and phoned Marsh for an on-the-record opinion of Warne's weight. Conn wrote the story as a report of what Marsh had said, and *The Australian* ran it with an amusing photograph of Warne stuffing his face with confectionery snakes during a drinks break in the Test match in Perth. Warne refused to speak again to Conn, but it was not Conn who had launched the personal taunts. Tabloid and television media turned the affair into a joke at Warne's expense. For him, the breaking point came when he was unveiling a wax statue of himself at a Madame Tussaud's exhibition at Crown Casino in Melbourne. A (rotund) television reporter asked Warne, early in the press conference, if he thought his figure had changed shape since the somewhat slimmer statue had been designed. Warne walked out, accusing the reporter of 'spoiling it for everybody'. The next time Warne played, he was greeted with placards as inventively humorous as the one in Sydney which said: 'Don't worry, Warney, only ... Minutes to Lunchtime.' In the space, a handmade clock counted down the minutes.

Warne's sense of humour might have remained intact if he were more secure about his bowling. While he had contributed solidly since his finger operation in 1996, it was now two years and 16 Test matches since he had taken five wickets in an innings. He was also troubled, personally, by the disastrous World Cup final in Lahore, where he had lost his grip on the ball in the heavy dew and allowed the Sri Lankans to vindicate their boasts at his expense. There was no question over his place in the team; but there were questions about whether he had returned from the operation as good a bowler as he had been before. He was still a wonderfully tight, gifted leg-spin bowler; but had he lost the ability to run through opposing teams the way he had between 1993 and 1995?

Whatever his travails against other batsmen, Warne could still rely on his psychological edge over the South Africans. His six wickets in 86 overs in Melbourne suggested a blunting of that edge, and he was wicketless on the first day in Sydney. On the second, however, he roared back with a five-wicket spell. Ripping the ball across the right-handers, he accounted for Cronje, Pollock, Richardson, Symcox and Paul Adams as South Africa lost 5/49 and their foothold on the series.

Cronje, their best player of spin, had said of Warne in 1994: 'My stock shot is the sweep ... I'm quite prepared to slog-sweep over mid-wicket. You can't allow him to dictate terms – rather, you must look to dominate him. By sweeping or using your feet to go down the wicket to him, you also increase the chances of him bowling bad balls; then you look to cut or pull.'

Warne countered by pitching the ball on Cronje's legs, too full for him to get down and sweep. Cronje liked to clip the ball off his toes, but Warne had noticed the South African captain's tendency to play across his pad, leaning towards the off side, which caused him to lift the ball in the air. In Melbourne and Sydney, Warne dismissed Cronje this way, having him caught in close on the leg side. It was a wonderful tactical battle between two expert practitioners. Just like the old West Indian fast bowlers, Warne was at his best bowling to the opposition captains.

In Sydney, Australia replied with a strong 421, Mark Waugh stealing his brother's thunder – it was Steve's 100th Test match – with a century. The Waughs' 116-run partnership in 131 minutes, only their fourth century stand in Test cricket, was the counterattacking key to Australia's innings. Between them the Waughs hit 21 fours and a six. They resisted a fierce spell in the overcast from Pollock and especially Donald, who covered both Waughs with welts and bruises. Part of their innings was played under lights, under the agreement between Australia and South Africa that time lost to bad light should be minimised by any means. Donald tore through Steve Waugh eventually with a superb leg-cutter, but Cronje gave the less-dangerous Symcox and Adams a combined 77 overs, allowing Australia to pace out a 134-run lead.

It was more than enough. Reiffel and McGrath chipped in to remove the openers early, and in a stormy, humid afternoon Warne turned the match on its head, running through the South African middle order with his best spell in three years. Only Kallis, with 45 in 155 minutes, showed the necessary technique to resist him. South Africa's old hands – Cronje, McMillan and Richardson – were visibly demoralised and disoriented. Warne's dismissal of Richardson, a lame pat-back for a return catch, was his 299th in Test cricket. Sadly for Warne, a thunderstorm halted play for more than three hours, clearing the SCG of all but a few thousand patient spectators. Remarkably, the ground was ready for play again at 6.20pm, Australia needing three wickets to win. In Sydney's tropical midsummer, there was no certainty that rain would not wipe out the fifth day's play, so there was some urgency. Warne complied, bowling Kallis from around the wicket for his 300th. He became the second Australian to pass that mark after Dennis Lillee.

Warne said later: 'As a kid I was like any other youngster. I wanted to be Dennis Lillee, or Rod Marsh, or Ian Chappell. When I played backyard cricket with my brother, we had Rod Marsh behind the stumps, and [we'd] charge up and imitate Dennis Lillee, or be Ian Chappell with the collar up, playing with your protector and all that sort of stuff. To be up in that company is an honour. I feel very proud to be in that company.'

While not a 'stats man', Warne raised his arms with manifest jubilation when he dismissed Kallis. 'I don't play the game for those milestones, but when they come along you give yourself a pat on the back and say, "Well done",' he said.

Happy 300th Shane ... Jacques Kallis was the victim as Warne joined Dennis Lillee in Australia's 300 Club, Sydney 1998. Trent Parke

As the darkness and rain closed in, South Africa tried to hold out. Symcox crashed the ball around for 38 but was bowled by Reiffel. Still, it began to rain again and umpire Peter Willey told Taylor that Reiffel's next ball, the last of his 12th over, would be the last of the day. The hapless Donald edged it to Healy, and Australia had won by an innings and 21 runs.

'This is a very bad defeat for us,' Cronje reflected. 'We came here very positive after beating Pakistan, and riding a high, and then we got knocked over by Warney today and in this whole Test match. It certainly hurts very much. I can only speak for myself at this stage, but it certainly hurts me.'

A return to one-day cricket gave the South Africans a chance to restore their morale in a form of the game in which they were more confident. They continued their dominance over Australia, defeating them in Brisbane by five wickets and in Perth by seven wickets. South Africa had more trouble defeating the New Zealanders, who pushed them to a two-run margin in the best game of the series, in Brisbane. The Australians, meanwhile, covered New Zealand with wins in Melbourne and Sydney, leaving Australia and South Africa as finalists with two preliminary games still to be played.

The captains' positions were reversed after the Test series. The beleaguered Cronje led with less inhibition in the compressed game, while Steve Waugh, taking over the reins from Taylor, was in terrible form with the bat. Waugh's first six scores in the one-day series were 1, 7, 0, 0, 4 and 0. Mindful of the team's agony in 1997 over Taylor's slump, Waugh approached Trevor Hohns and offered him his head. Waugh said he did not want a repeat of the Taylor situation, where the team had had to carry its captain, and gave Hohns carte blanche to omit him. It is likely that only Australia's win over New Zealand in Sydney on January 14 - ironically, the first game in 12 years in which neither Waugh brother played for Australia and Shane Warne was captain - saved Waugh's position by qualifying them for the finals. In the 'dead' game against New Zealand in Melbourne on 21 January, which New Zealand won, Waugh showed a return to form with an unbeaten run-a-ball 45.

His confidence back, Waugh set about eroding South Africa's. In the lead-up to the finals, to be played over the Australia Day long weekend in Melbourne and Sydney, Waugh did not exactly use the word 'chokers', but he alluded to it in his assessment of South Africa's recent record. In the 1996 World Cup, in the 1996 Titan Cup, and in 1997 in South Africa, the Proteas had played irresistibly in preliminary matches but seized up in the crucial ones. Despite being probably the best team in each tournament, South Africa had won none of them. They hit back at Waugh's comments with a last-over win in the first final, but the win only postponed their purgatory, a state of mind that was to continue at least through the 1999 World Cup, when Waugh was to apply the same kind of verbal pressure with the same effect.

Rain and poor drainage at the SCG delayed the second final for a day, and South Africa's 228, with Cronje scoring 73 and Jonty Rhodes 82 not out, was a competitive target. But Gilchrist chose that moment to play his finest one-day innings so far, stroking 100 in 104 balls to give Australia a comfortable win. Geoff Marsh, an enthusiastic patron of Gilchrist, was so excited when the left-hander reached his century that he leapt into the air and cracked his knee against a table. The injury hobbled Marsh for several days. He watched the third final on crutches as Australia, led by Ponting (76) and Steve Waugh (71), rolled inexorably over the South Africans. Waugh and Cronje argued toe-to-toe when Cronje brought the athletic Herschelle Gibbs onto the field to replace 38-year-old Symcox after the veteran had bowled his 10 overs – it was a pre-planned substitution to which Waugh took understandable offence.

Adam Bacher (45) hit a string of fours early in South Africa's chase for 248, but the team staggered when Reiffel had Bacher caught and pushed Kallis back for a hit-wicket dismissal, and Cronje charged Warne and missed. (Again, the dismissal was prophetic of Cronje's pair of ducks, both to Warne, in the epic final stages of the 1999 World Cup.) Lance Klusener returned from his lean series by slugging 46 at the end, but McMillan ran out Symcox and then himself in another sign of South Africa's malaise: their senior players were unable to cope with the pressure of a series-deciding match against Australia.

Both teams' physical exhaustion was palpable when they arrived in Adelaide a few days later to resume the Test series. Donald, McGrath, Reiffel and Jason Gillespie were all missing from the fast-bowling ranks. Australia's bowling attack consisted of Michael Kasprowicz, playing his 10th Test, Andy Bichel (second), Stuart MacGill (debut) and Warne. Healy, playing his 100th Test, had to deal with the sadness of having lost his father, Neville, to cancer on match eve.

The match was notable for a handful of great individual performances. Gary Kirsten scored 77 and 108 not out, yet hardly picked up a vote in the 3-2-1 man-of-the-match tally. Taylor carried his bat through the Australian first innings (scoring 169 not out), becoming the first to do so since David Boon against New Zealand in 1985-86. Taylor was on the field without a break from the start of play on day one until late on day four, when Klusener bowled him in the second innings. After South Africa had opened up with 517 – not one player making a century, remarkably enough – the match degenerated into an arm-wrestle between Taylor and Shaun Pollock, who stepped into Donald's boots with one of the most courageous and accurate fast-bowling performances seen in Australia for many years. In 41 overs, Pollock took 7/87 and joined his father, Peter, on the Adelaide Oval's honour board. At times he pounded away at Taylor, moving the ball in the air and off the seam, over after over, only to watch the ball slide past a groping outside edge.

Pollock had received inspiration from two sources. His board chief, Ali Bacher, had called him on Test eve to remind him of Glenn McGrath's efforts in the West Indies three years previously, replacing Craig

Gladiators ... Mark Taylor and Shaun Pollock turned the Adelaide Test in 1998 into their personal battle. Trent Parke

McDermott and taking 25 wickets after the Australian spearhead had broken down.

'He phoned to tell me this was the time for me to come to the party,' Pollock said.

His other inspiration, he said, was seeing the name of Malcolm Marshall on the Adelaide Oval honour board.

'Malcolm played at Natal for four years and he was a mentor for me,' Pollock said. 'He took five wickets in each innings here. I wanted to be up on the board with my mentor.'

Australia made 350, occupying the crease for 122.5 overs thanks to Taylor, but still the South Africans were able to attack in their second innings and declare with an unassailable lead and 109 overs to bowl at Australia. Cronje admitted that this match meant everything to him; having come to Australia with high and realistic hopes of winning both the Test and one-day series, the Proteas were in danger of leaving empty-handed.

They believed they had shaken their bogey when they dismissed Taylor and a hopelessly out of form Matthew Elliott early on. Shortly before stumps, Cronje introduced Symcox to bowl at Mark Waugh. This pair had an interesting history. Waugh's contempt for off-spinners was well documented, and Symcox's record had the Australian right-hander salivating. Yet the ebullient South African had the personality to get under Waugh's skin; his relentless verbal posturing galled Waugh into an over-aggressive frame of mind which cost him his wicket more often than seemed credible.

Symcox stirred Waugh up with some choice words, challenging him to come down the pitch. His first ball was a kicking off-break which Waugh turned straight to Bacher at short leg. Bacher dropped it. His blunder was to foreshadow an agonising fifth day for the Proteas. With some help from each of his partners, Waugh managed to survive with an unbeaten 115 to save the match and the 1-0 series win for Australia. He was dropped four times. South Africa put down 10 catches in a game they had to win. Pollock and Klusener laboured hard, but were denied catching support.

Dropping Their Bundle . . . The South Africans would blame the umpires for their failure to win in Adelaide, 1998, but they grassed 10 catches. Here Adam Bacher gives Mark Waugh the first of many lives. Bryan Charlton/Fairfax

Yet the South Africans were in no mood to lash themselves. Instead, they seethed after an incident shortly before the end of play. In the seventh-last over, when Australia still hung by a thread, Pollock bowled a rearing delivery at Waugh's elbow. Waugh reeled away in pain, shaking his bat. Unwittingly, as he did so, he brushed his stumps and knocked off the bails. Cronje, fielding at mid-wicket, rushed up to Waugh and said: 'You've trodden on your stumps.' Waugh turned to umpire Steve Randell and said that he must have hit the stumps after finishing his shot.

The decision was referred to South Australia's Steve Davis, manning the video booth. To all appearances, Waugh was clearly not out. Law 35 of cricket states that a batsman can only be out hit-wicket if he disturbs the stumps while preparing for or playing his shot, or while setting off on his first run. He cannot be out after he has completed his shot. Waugh knocked the stumps on his third step after the ball hit him.

'The ball hit me just above the elbow,' Waugh said. 'I completed my shot and thought I was walking away. It must have hit a nerve in my arm, because I couldn't control my arm. It went floppy, and my bat hit the stumps. I thought I'd completed the shot, and after that it doesn't really matter what happens.

I felt like my arm was broken, actually, but obviously it wasn't. It was just a nerve. I knew I hit the stumps, but I couldn't control where the bat went. But I'd finished my shot.'

Cronje's version of the story was: 'If somebody gets hit on the head, and he's a bit wobbly, and he walks on his stumps, he's out. That's all I want to say.'

The matter did not end there. Three balls later, Waugh prodded yet another catch into Bacher's midriff. Bacher dropped it. Not one of his teammates approached him with consolation. When the match finished, about 40 minutes later, Cronje refused to shake hands with the umpires. Instead, he removed a stump from the wicket, walked up the stairs to the dressing rooms, and rammed the stump through the door to the umpires' room. His frustration was understandable, given the collapse of an ambition he had chased with almost frightening intensity. It was because he understood Cronje's frustration that Ranjan Madugalle, the match referee, decided not to fine Cronje under the ICC's code of conduct.

Dave Richardson retired later, after a distinguished 42-Test career. No South African had played more Test matches since their return from exile in 1991–92.

For Australia, the most notable outcome of the series was the performance of the spin bowlers. Warne's 11-wicket feat in Sydney formed a peak to an otherwise sound summer. In late January and early February, the wear on his shoulder had become noticeable. The debutant, MacGill, outperformed him in the Adelaide Test, and immediately after stumps Taylor called on the selectors to rest Warne from the four-match limited-overs tour of New Zealand that the ACB had sandwiched between the South African series and the upcoming tour of India. Warne's eclipse by MacGill was to take another year, culminating in Warne's being dropped, in favour of MacGill, during the 1999 tour of the West Indies. Such a prospect was still unthinkable in 1998, even as Steve Waugh led his one-day team without Warne to New Zealand. But the overuse of Australia's key bowlers was beginning to bite. McGrath's abdominal injury was worse than first thought, and he was to miss India. Gillespie had hurt himself again in Sheffield Shield cricket. Warne was clearly fatigued, yet he was to lead the attack on the flattest wickets and the most formidable batting line-up in the world. It was to prove too much. Taylor's lucky streak was about to come down with a crash.

World Cup, 1999

If any games crystallised the mental grip the Australians, Steve Waugh and Shane Warne in particular, had over South Africa, they were the two encounters in the 1999 World Cup. Australia had no right to win either of these games, yet, at the crucial moment, South Africa choked. Or, as Waugh put it, both teams choked but South Africa choked harder.

Both games were knockout situations for Australia; only the second was for South Africa. This was due to Australia's mediocre start to the tournament. Appearing stale after their interminable 1998-99 season – Malaysia, Pakistan, Bangladesh, the Ashes at home, then 10 punishing weeks in the Caribbean preceded the Cup – the Australians had put themselves in the position where they needed to win, or avoid losing, seven games in a row to win the Cup. In their first three matches they played poorly; they beat Scotland, and lost to New Zealand and Pakistan. Yet it was probably the clear definition of their task at this point, the simple fact that a loss would send them home, that focused their minds. They lifted their run rate by beating Bangladesh heavily, then dismissed the West Indies for 111 at Old Trafford, knocking out the old enemy. In the Super Six phase, Australia lifted a gear and beat India and Zimbabwe with relative comfort. Everything was falling into place before the last Super Six game at Headingley against tournament favourites South Africa – except the worrying form of Warne. The leg-spinner had been belted by India and Zimbabwe, and was suffering problems of a personal nature. He had still to recover from the humiliation, as he saw it, of being dropped for the fourth Test in the West Indies, and while his one-day form had been good in the Caribbean, the loss of his Test place was still troubling him. In Antigua, he had said he would consider retirement if he did not perform to his standards in the World Cup. Now that that time was here, his form was falling away. He was, without a doubt, facing the possible end of his international career, at age 30. Moreover, an English tabloid newspaper had paid a woman to tape conversations between herself and Warne, leading to a story, which was never reported in Australia, about Warne's relationship with the woman. At a time when Warne's wife, Simone, was expecting their second child back in Melbourne, this was the last straw – Warne told Steve Waugh he was ready to quit the game.

At Headingley, however, Warne was the only Australian bowler to perform at his best as the South Africans raced away to 271. Herschelle Gibbs scored a sweet 101 on an uneven pitch and Daryll Cullinan a half-century. At 1/141, the South Africans had been looking at a 300-plus score, which would probably be unbeatable, when Warne turned the tide by dismissing Cullinan, and then Hansie Cronje for a duck. Jonty Rhodes and Lance Klusener lifted the tempo again late in the innings, and the South Africans' win seemed assured when Mark Waugh, Gilchrist and Damien Martyn were out with only 48 on the board.

Steve Waugh was to write later: 'I'd be lying if I didn't admit I had doubts about our chances at this point.' He walked out to join Ponting in a desperate situation, saying to himself: 'You've played one-day cricket for 14 years and this is not the time to end it. There's some unfinished business to be done.'

It all would, truly, have ended had Australia lost that day. Trevor Hohns had told Waugh that a poor World Cup would lead to a second spring-cleaning of Australia's one-day outfit, to follow the purge of Taylor and Healy in 1997. Had they lost in Headingley, the Waugh brothers and Tom Moody at least would have played their last game in the canary yellow. And, after drawn Test and one-day series in the Caribbean, the pressure on Waugh's Test captaincy would have increased.

He and Ponting scored 22 in their first 10 overs together. Yet they had a supreme confidence, based on the events of 1997 and 1998, that South Africa would crack if sufficient pressure could be applied. South

Africa, Waugh believed, 'are a regimented side. I think we are better than they are in stressful situations – a psychological thing that has evolved over time. When things are going well, they look ultra-intimidating but when you put it back in their face, give them a bit of stick and go hard at them, they can unravel like any other side. The most obvious sign of their distress came from their captain, who normally doesn't say much on the field. But there he was, quite animated and agitated as the game began to turn.'

Waugh and Ponting added 82 from the next 10 overs, during which Gibbs dropped the famous catch. Waugh chipped a ball to the on side, and Gibbs, one of the best fieldsmen in cricket, intercepted it at mid-wicket. During his short international career, Gibbs had enjoyed a stunt of tossing the ball in the air the instant he caught it – a mere show-off trick which had been indulged by his coach and captain. Trying to execute this trick, Gibbs dropped the catch. Waugh said: 'I hope you realise you've just lost the game for your team.' It was not quite the 'You've dropped the World Cup, sunshine' that was quoted in the press, but it typified the robust verbal exchanges between the teams, a running battle resumed every time they played one another. Later, Cronje was to cast doubt on the umpires' decision, insinuating that Gibbs had had control of the ball. Clearly, he hadn't. This inability to face facts was another sign of the poverty of Cronje's leadership. Cronje was happy to work at the margins of the laws, roughing up the ball in Sydney and allowing coach Woolmer to speak to him via remote control radio until the device was banned early in the World Cup. Yet when it came to straightforward captaincy – either telling Gibbs, as soon as he started playing international cricket, to desist from the stunt, or, after the awful blunder happened, accepting responsibility – Cronje's deficiencies were painfully obvious.

When Ponting was out for 69, Australia needed 98, at a run a ball. Waugh played some risky but intelligent slogs, taking the ball from the stumps and lifting it over mid-wicket. Bevan helped with a quick 27, and on the third-last ball, Waugh edged a Pollock yorker past the wicketkeeper and Australia were in the semi-final – to play South

Africa again. Waugh had scored 120 not out, the keynote innings of the whole World Cup and only his second century in 14 years of playing for Australia in limited-overs cricket.

Significantly, the win in Headingley lifted Australia above South Africa on the Super Six table. This meant that if they should tie their semi-final, Australia would proceed to the final against Pakistan, who thrashed New Zealand in the other semi. Waugh observed that for South Africa, 'the psychological damage may be hard to turn around'. They were carrying not only the weight of their lost opportunity at Headingley, but the memory of all those other lost opportunities, dating back to Port Elizabeth in 1997, which had stopped South Africa winning a series of any kind against this opponent. Waugh sensed a particular personal advantage over his counterpart. 'I have a handy track record against them and I definitely enjoy playing them. I also get plenty of satisfaction from the fact they don't respond too well to our style of cricket, especially the way we get in their faces. This is especially true of Cronje, whom I have the greatest respect for. However, I also believe I have a bit of an edge over him, similar to the advantage I have over the West Indies' Carl Hooper. As a player, there are opponents you enjoy locking horns with and others who sense they have it over you; the key to it is to try to exploit the former and suppress the latter.'

At their team meeting in Birmingham, the Australians emphasised intensity, decisiveness and, most importantly, the belief that South Africa would crack first. They discussed placing extra pressure on those players they considered mentally vulnerable: Cronje, Cullinan, and, since Headingley, the unfortunate Gibbs.

Australia did not, in fact, play especially well at Edgbaston. Their top order failed, leaving them 4/68. Only a salvage job from Steve Waugh (56) and Bevan (65) got them to a moderate 213. Gibbs and Gary Kirsten raced away to 0/45 in nine overs, and again Australia looked beaten. Waugh threw the ball prematurely to Warne, and the leg-spinner turned what could have been a panic for Australia into one for South Africa. His leg-break across Gibbs, taking the top of the off stump, sent a ripple of fear through the South African room. Warne then took Kirsten, playing a wild slash, and Cronje – unluckily, caught off his toe, for his second duck in the two encounters – in his first three overs. Cullinan ran himself out to cap a 4/15 collapse. Jacques Kallis and Jonty Rhodes added 84, however, to bring South Africa back into it, until Reiffel had Rhodes caught by Bevan. When Pollock joined Kallis, South Africa needed 69 in nine overs. With six overs remaining, Pollock lifted Warne out of the ground, but on the leg-spinner's second-last ball of the day, Kallis miscued a drive to Steve Waugh at short cover.

Lance Klusener would be named man of the World Cup for his late-order bludgeoning raids. He went to work on the Australian bowlers for a second time, looking likely to rescue his team when Moody failed to get near enough to a lob to the deep to lay hand on ball. McGrath dismissed Mark Boucher in the second-last over, and good fielding from Reiffel ran out Steve Elworthy with eight balls left. A ball later, Reiffel was villain, not only dropping Klusener at long-on but palming the ball inadvertently over the rope. A single off McGrath's last ball left Klusener on strike. With last man Allan Donald at the other end, Klusener needed nine runs off the final over, to be bowled by Fleming.

The first ball, from around the wicket to the left-hander, was a near yorker. Klusener slashed it through mid-off for four. Second ball, much the same, both in delivery and result. Fleming changed to over the wicket. Klusener and Donald did not confer. Klusener miscued the next, an attempted drive, to short mid-on. There were still four balls left to score one run, but Donald panicked and ran. Lehmann scooped the ball up and underarmed from point-blank range, but missed running out the retreating Donald. As Waugh wrote, 'We couldn't believe it. Our one last chance was gone.'

But they could never underestimate the senior South African players' capacity to falter at the crucial moment. Donald, still thinking of the last ball, was determined to stay in his ground. So when Klusener jammed the next one down the ground and ran, Donald was planted in his crease at the non-striker's end. In the confusion – Klusener running, Donald staying, Mark Waugh fielding – the ball was transferred through Fleming to Gilchrist at the striker's end. Donald dropped his bat and ran halfway before giving up. Klusener kept running, towards a dressing room in which the South African captain sat with head in hands.

Unsurprisingly, the Australians' mood was that of the thief who had pulled off a breathtaking heist. 'We really could not believe,' Waugh wrote, 'that we had sneaked through to the final, that we'd got away with the game.' Their score of 213 had never quite seemed adequate, but their bowling and fielding turned each of those runs into the Crown Jewels. It was for South Africa to breach Australia's defence. That they could not do so probably reflected more on themselves than on the Australians. Only one of the two sides had a deap, tigerish sense that it was better than the other. Cronje's South Africans needed a win like this, as they had for three years, to believe they were good enough. It was a vicious circle: tying, effectively losing, this match would further entrench in the South Africans the idea that they were an inferior team. In the end, the feeling was that if Australia had scored 270, or 190, or 300, South Africa would always have fallen just short. Soon after the game, Woolmer left the South African coaching job, his quest unfulfilled. Cronje stayed captain on probation, and threatened to quit until he was assured of the position on a longer-term basis.

England: The Ashes of the Ashes

BEFORE MARK TAYLOR became captain, Australia had won three successive series over England and established the pattern of psychological dominance that would last until the end of the century. While reclaiming the Ashes had been the apogee of Allan Border's tenure, under Taylor, beating England was business as usual. By the end of the Taylor years, the prestige of the Ashes had declined to the point where questions were being asked over whether England-Australia series were worth five-Test status.

England in Australia 1994-95

Of the four and a half years of Taylor's captaincy, the first year and a half saw the Australian team at its absolute peak.

Certainly there were other brief peaks – Adelaide in 1996-7, Johannesburg in 1997, Rawalpindi and Sydney in 1998 – when the Taylor teams performed at such a level that it is difficult to imagine their being beaten by any team in history. But consider the strength of Taylor's first trimester. In fast bowling, he enjoyed a remarkably seamless transition from McDermott at peak form to McGrath at peak form. McDermott was international cricketer of the year against England in 1994-95, injured himself in the West Indies in 1995, and came back for another dangerous summer in 1995-96. McGrath stepped into McDermott's shoes in the West Indies, and the two great fast bowlers had a short-lived partnership in 1995-96 before McDermott broke down, this time finally, in the World Cup in early 1996.

Meet Mr Right ... Mark Taylor gets an approving eye from media manager Ian McDonald at his first press conference as captain. Mark Ray

In spin bowling, Warne's peak years were from 1993 to early 1996. His career average, strike rate and economy rate all hit their best figures in 1995–96, by the end of which he had taken 207 wickets in 45 Test matches. In contrast, his next 26 Tests yielded 110 wickets, more expensively, and more widely spaced. His first operation, on his spinning finger, was in 1996, his shoulder operation in 1998. Both were consequences of the wear and tear of his best years.

Just as Australia's bowling was at its most potent in Taylor's first year in charge, so was their batting. The middle-order strength, based around the Waughs and Healy, was a constant throughout Taylor's reign. But the top three would never again be the force they were in 1994–95. Taylor, Slater and Boon formed an unstoppable combination at the top. Of the ten century partnerships between Taylor and Slater, four were in the 1994–95 summer and three in 1995–96. While Boon's form faded as he approached retirement in early 1996, he was still, even in his twilight, a more effective No 3 than Australia could find for the next three years. Once Slater was dropped in late 1996, the top three became a festering sore, and it did not heal after Taylor's retirement either. The opening and No 3 positions became a turnstile. Indeed, it was quite incredible that Australia were able to maintain their world rating through 1996–99 without a stable or dominant top order.

In confirmation of this rating, when Taylor named the best XII he had played with during his decade in Test cricket, all but the recently retired Border and Merv Hughes were from the XII who played England in Taylor's first home season.

They were a team of personality, too, as Gideon Haigh remarked in his diary of the summer:

> The national team contains box-office appeal unmatched since the Circus Maximus twenty years ago. Shane Warne has children aspiring to spin as once they pined for pace. In the Waughs, Steve and Mark, Australia have a fraternal fulcrum to rank with the Chappells. Mooching to the middle or inscrutable behind his Bolles, David Boon lacks only the accompaniment of an Ennio Morricone anthem. Michael Slater is one of those rare talents who acts his age and his average. And balls disappear into the gloves of the integral Ian Healy, never to return.

If Australia hit the richest ore of their golden age in 1994–95, England's nadir coincided with it. It is deceptive to judge the closeness of a series by its final scoreline, as England were wont to do from 1995 to 1997, pointing to ever-narrowing series margins. The more accurate guide is how early in the series did Australia retain the Ashes. How many 'dead rubbers' were there in each series? In their record six straight wins from 1989 to 1998-99, Australia won or retained the Ashes with two dead rubbers in every series except 1997, when there was one dead rubber. England won five Test matches during that period, but only one – the first Test in 1997 – was a live rubber. In each of the three series in Australia, the Ashes were decided before Christmas.

Still, England's optimists continued to draw hope from their consolation wins. When they arrived in Australia in October 1994, Michael Atherton blustered about the fear Devon Malcolm had struck into the Australians, notably Steve Waugh, during his six-wicket burst in the sixth (dead) Test at the end of the 1993 series. This was a new tack from England, marking the beginning of their mimicry of Australia's success. For years, they had tried to emulate the West Indian model of stacking their bowling with fast bowlers, often West Indian-born, such as Malcolm, David Lawrence, Phil DeFreitas, Joey Benjamin and Chris Lewis. This time, as if in recognition of Australia's rise, England were trying to counter Australia's robust psychological game. They picked two Australians, bowler Martin McCague and all-rounder Craig White, for the 1994-95 tour, and were soon to embark on the disastrous experiment with Australian brothers Adam and Ben Hollioake. So-called 'Australian' values, emphasising aggression bordering on hatred for the opposition, were suddenly the most desirable; Haigh paraphrased English essayist David Stove in divining the Australian secret: 'Australians actively hated their opponents, while the English merely despised their rivals.'

Australian players reinforced the message. Warne said of the young fast bowler Darren Gough, 'His approach to the game is more like ours.' The last great English cricketer, Ian Botham, was likened to an Australian. An Australian friend of Haigh's remarked admiringly of Alec Stewart, 'He's got a bit of the bastard about him.' All this was nothing more than empty stereotyping, but it played into the Australians' hands by building a healthy sense of inferiority among the English, as if they had to deny their national characteristics (weak, fatalistic, defensive) in order to succeed.

So DeFreitas clashed with Taylor during England's lead-up game against

NSW in Newcastle, and in that same match the Englishmen targeted Michael Bevan with a personal campaign of sledging, based on what an English journalist had heard coming from Bevan's hotel room at the Newcastle Radisson. Having so often borne the brunt of Australian sledging, England felt it was their turn – and the tactic did seem to have an effect on Bevan, who fared poorly in the first three Ashes Test matches and was dropped for the fourth. Yet it still seemed that England wanted to follow the latest trend rather than exploit their own strengths. Indeed, the mild-mannered Atherton appeared scarcely to believe his own words when he arrived in Perth boasting about Malcolm having had Waugh 'wetting his pants' at The Oval in 1993.

In any case, Malcolm did not make it to the first Test in Brisbane, falling ill with chickenpox after taking six wickets against NSW in Newcastle. England had performed creditably in their lead-up games, beating South Australia and losing by not too much to NSW. Yet this Ashes series was decided, symbolically at least, from the first ball. After losing the toss in Brisbane, Atherton gave the new ball to DeFreitas, then on one of the last of his (world-record) 16 recalls into the England team. DeFreitas served up a long hop outside Slater's off stump, which the batsman cut to the fence. Slater put away another four in that over, and Australia were on their way. Taylor chalked up 50 by lunch, and after he and Boon fell close together after the break, Slater and Mark Waugh tucked into the English bowling. Slater scored 37 before lunch, 68 between lunch and tea, and was on his way to a century inside the last session when he was caught smashing Graham Gooch's gentle outswinger to mid-off for 176. It was a wonderful century, comparable to Allan Border's 63 at Headingley in 1989 for its role in setting the tone for a whole series. Taylor took Slater aside afterwards and rebuked him for letting a huge innings go begging. It was a piece of advice that showed the transfer of wisdom through Australian cricket's generations; Border had done the same when Taylor got himself out on 219 at Trent Bridge in 1989, telling him that he had let a triple-century go. When Taylor was in the same position, in Peshawar in 1998, Border's words echoed in his mind and he pressed on.

Mark Waugh's 140 helped Australia to 426 in quick time, and McDermott barrelled into the Englishmen on the second afternoon, taking 6/53 in their collapse for 167, including the diabolical (with bat and ball) McCague on the last ball of the day. Having seen Salim Malik torture his tired bowlers after following-on in Rawalpindi, Taylor declined to ask England to bat again in Brisbane, despite a lead of 259. He became the first Australian captain not to enforce a follow-on since Bob Simpson in 1977–78. It was neither the first nor last time Taylor was to flout convention successfully. In batting for three sessions, extending their lead past 500, the Australians were able to give their bowlers a rest and allow the wicket to wear sufficiently for Warne. Taylor's reasoning was that he would rely on Warne more than McDermott in the second innings, so why not give the leg-spinner the best possible conditions? He was also able to surprise the Englishmen, particularly the openers, Atherton and Stewart, who were already padded up for a second trip to the crease.

Taylor's choice was vindicated, ultimately, by events. Australia built a mountainous lead, and, after Graeme Hick and Graham Thorpe had guided England to a competitive 2/211 on the fourth evening, Warne went to work on the fifth morning, capturing a career-best 8/71 as England folded quickly after lunch.

Taylor had, in fact, exercised the same option in his very first match as captain of NSW, in the Sheffield Shield final of the 1989–90 season. He had been elevated at the last moment – NSW did not have a designated vice-captain – when captain Geoff Lawson pulled out injured. NSW made 360, Taylor scoring a century, and Queensland replied with 103. Chairman of selectors Neil Marks counselled an undecided Taylor to bat again, saying: 'You can't lose if you bat now. The only way you could lose is if they knocked you over for hardly any, then had a target to chase on the last day with someone like Border there. Don't put yourself in the position of having to bat last under pressure, even if you've only got to get 100.'

Coach Steve Rixon had disagreed, advising the conventional kick-them-while-they're-down policy, while Steve Waugh had recommended batting again. That was what Taylor did, and NSW won easily. He repeated the move, to some criticism, several times in his Test captaincy, and more often than not it worked. The flip side, however, was that it entrenched a feeling of defensiveness, almost of fear, about batting last and chasing small totals. That fear exists in all cricket teams, and Australia had fallen prey to it before Taylor's time, most recently when unable to score 117 to win against South Africa in Sydney in 1993-94. It was to resurface again under Taylor, against England at Adelaide in 1994-95, Pakistan in Sydney in 1995-96, England at The Oval in 1997, and England at Melbourne in 1998-99. That habit of collapsing in the face of small fourth-innings chases was probably the only recurrent on-field frailty of Taylor's Australian teams.

Aside from their poor bowling, the main question being asked of England was whether they had brought ex-captains Gooch and Mike Gatting on one tour too many. Certainly they were still heavy scorers in county cricket, and demanded selection on form. But there is a particular mental edge a competitor gains from seeing men in their late 30s on an opposing team. This was no more evident than when England played two games against Australian Cricket Academy teams at North Sydney Oval between the first and second Tests. On the first ball of the first game, Gatting was bowled by Mark Harrity. The Australian teenagers won both games, by five and six wickets respectively. Australian media manager Ian McDonald had upset the visitors with his cocky pronouncement during the first encounter that 'The kids will probably finish it off early', but the English could not respond on the field. Malcolm and DeFreitas were savaged on both days. After the second – the Academy team winning with 6.5 overs to spare – England manager Keith Fletcher said: 'There's a deathly hush in the dressing room. They are all sitting there feeling ashamed, and as an international team, so they should.'

Much was made of the young Australians' brilliance, and of the local system's ability to produce international-standard players at a young age, in pointed contrast England's 'old men'. Haigh remarked tersely: 'Atherton can snuggle up in his eiderdown and consider that (chief selector Ray Illingworth) is the fourteenth ex-captain of England to hit Australia this season: Gooch, Gatting, Stewart, Fletcher, (Mike) Smith; commentators Bob Willis, David Gower, Geoff Boycott, Tony Greig and Allan Lamb, with package tour leaders Mike Denness, John Edrich and Tom Graveney besides. So much experience. So much experience of being sacked.' But it should also be pointed out that of the eleven Australian Academy players in those 1994–95 games, not one was to graduate to national Test honours in the succeeding five years. Only Ian Harvey was to play senior one-day international cricket in that time. For all Australia's boasts and England's despair, the Academy system was not a production line of Test champions.

Australia were able to rely on their existing champions instead. In the second Test in Melbourne, starting on Christmas Eve – a short-lived experiment by the ACB – Australia won by 295 runs, Warne icing the cake with a hat-trick on the fifth morning. Darren Gough, emerging as a feisty and skilled low-arm skidding fast bowler, took seven wickets for England, but Thorpe's 51 in the first innings was their highest score for the match as McDermott, with eight wickets, and Warne, with nine, closed in. At the end, Warne pushed one through to trap DeFreitas, had Gough caught off his gloves, and then lined up Malcolm for the hat-trick ball. As the Australians huddled, Taylor recalls that the flipper was a popular suggestion, but that he himself proposed a leg-break. Warne – bucking authority as a matter of principle – sent down a top-spinner with a touch of leg-spin. It popped off Malcolm's forward-pressing glove for Boon, on his 34th birthday, to lunge with right hand and complete the first hat-trick in Ashes cricket for 92 years.

Taylor's Australians were beginning to dominate England in the same way Clive Lloyd's and Viv Richards's West Indians had dominated Australia. They would go all out in the opening Test matches, establishing total psychological mastery, and then ease back. In the third Test, in Sydney, Australia had England 3/20 but let them get away to 309, McDermott taking another five, but the hosts collapsed on a humid third morning for 116. England's shaky team spirit was demonstrated on the fourth day, when Atherton gave Hick the chance to make a morale-boosting century but then took it away from him. Hick had batted streakily, offering three catches, being out off a no-ball and bunting a Tim May delivery onto his stumps without dislodging the bail. Atherton was growing impatient. Taylor slowed the over rate in the time-honoured West Indian style, taking a full minute to re-set his field between overs, and at the mid-afternoon drinks break Hick's partner, Alec Stewart, urged him to score the eight remaining runs for his century and let the captain declare. Fourteen minutes later, Hick had scored another six runs and was on 98. He faced Damien Fleming and played out a maiden. Atherton called the batsmen in. There was little doubt that Atherton did the best thing at that moment, but Hick and some of his teammates felt the captain had shown a lack of feel for team spirit. Gideon Haigh recalled that in 1982–83, 'Greg Chappell had been 94 not out with four runs separating his team from victory. Ian Botham, in one of those forgotten gestures, hopped in off a few paces to offer the Australian captain a slow half-volley that he could hit for six. It went for four, but my Australian friends to a man applauded Botham as he left the field. "Bloody good bloke," they agreed, for they knew how much a milestone meant even to one such as Chappell, who'd done it fifteen times before. On Atherton declaring on Hick at 98: "I made 98 not out in the backyard at Mum's." No, it still doesn't sound right.'

With a Hick century to celebrate, perhaps the bowlers would have gone out with an extra spring in their step. In any case, they made no impression on Taylor and Slater, who cracked 139 runs off the 38 overs to stumps and ended the day 310 runs from an improbable win.

Tight English bowling on the last morning held the Australian openers down, and although they both made centuries, Slater and Taylor were out after lunch, forcing the pace. Drizzle and humidity started to aid the ball movement of Gough and Angus Fraser, recalled from local district cricket, and in the end it was Warne and May, batting for 77 minutes in the gloom, who saved Australia and ensured that the Ashes were retained.

England's limited-overs campaign was, if anything, worse than their Test series. The ACB experimented with a four-cornered series, involving an Australia 'A' team, due to the low profile of the third team, Zimbabwe. It was a summer of experimentation for the ACB, who had taken over the series' marketing from Kerry Packer's PBL for the first time in 15 years. Sheffield Shield games were played under lights, domestic one-day teams

I Know, The Skipper's A @•$%&°... Graham Thorpe consoles Graeme Hick on skipper, Michael Atherton's, declaration – 'It's not as if you look back and say, "I got 98 not out in the backyard at Mum's..."'. Patrick Eagar

played in short pants, and State teams started to adopt monikers – Queensland became the Bulls, Western Australia the Warriors, and so on. In the international one-day series, Zimbabwe beat England once, but it was the junior Australians who caused the shock, beating England by 29 runs in the last qualifying match to secure a place in the finals against the senior Australian team. The Australia 'A' concept was widely condemned, in part because it was perceived as an insult to England – it certainly was when England couldn't beat them – but also because Australian crowds, being what they are, cheered for the underdogs when the two Australian teams met. Taylor was censured by the board for criticising the 'A' concept, saying 'I don't like playing against my own players and I don't like it when the crowd does not support us when we're playing at home.'

The senior men were on a hiding to nothing, expected to win but facing ridicule if they lost. The finals series had a farcical note when Australia 'A' bowler Paul Reiffel was poached by the main team, only to be designated twelfth man. They also had an aggressive note when Matthew Hayden clashed with McGrath, earning both a reprimand from ICC referee John Reid, during the first final in Sydney. Australia won both matches narrowly. David Boon, for one, supported the Australia 'A' concept, calling it 'a sensational idea, as it gives young players around the country an opportunity to play at international level, without having to wait to reach the real Australian team'. Boon was, however, biased – in the second final, against Australia 'A', he took his first international wicket, dismissing Phil Emery.

If the competition had any lasting benefits, it revealed the talents of several young players who were ultimately to force their way into the senior team. 'A' players Bevan, who showed his breathtaking skills in the shorter format, plus Damien Martyn and Ricky Ponting, who were to play in Australia's 1999 World Cup win. Greg Blewett, meanwhile, who was not even in the 'A' team at the start of the series, was later called up and charged into top-level cricket with a century and two fifties that earned him Test selection, at Bevan's expense, for the final two Ashes Tests.

At his home-town debut in Adelaide over the Australia Day weekend, Blewett celebrated with a first-innings hundred. He had to farm the strike at the end, batting with fellow South Australian debutant Peter McIntyre, elevated from his rightful No 11 while McDermott was in hospital being X-rayed. McDermott raced back to the Adelaide Oval in a taxi, but Blewett made his ton just before McIntyre fell. McDermott still went out to bat, continuing to dress himself as he walked from the pavilion. Gatting salvaged a poor summer with his first Test century in seven years, and Australia led by 66 runs on the first innings. In the second, Mark Waugh took a career-high 5/40 as England staggered to 6/181, effectively 6/115, late on day four. Day five was a typical dead-rubber day. Without any pressure, DeFreitas carved the Australian bowling for 88 in 95 balls and extended the lead to 262. The Australians, feeling there was nothing to lose (except a Test match), decided to chase the target in cavalier, perhaps reckless, fashion, and fell 106 runs short. Phil Tufnell caught Slater superbly at fine leg, and Devon Malcolm and Chris Lewis shared eight wickets. It was another of those silly days when a desperate England and a jubilant Barmy Army could raise their fists and claim better times had arrived. But, if a win was based on the efforts of DeFreitas, Malcolm and Lewis, it was never going to be of enduring value.

Haigh called it:

A victory of a team to whom winning was the only thing over one to whom winning was the main thing. 'I'd like to know why we don't perform so well at the beginning of a series,' Atherton muses. 'The Ashes are gone, but the series is still alive. A draw was no good for us the way the series is. From our point of view we might as well have gone 3–0 down as 2–0 because the series would have been dead.

... I'm struck at how little it probably means. Even the West Indies are prone to losing impetus during 'dead Tests', having lost three to Australia in the last four Worrell Trophies. In retrospect, Australia was a team playing from memory on the first four days. It was the first time in the series they genuinely waited for things to happen – for something to turn up, for someone to pitch in – and they're such gifted individuals that the tactic almost worked ... The home side was roused on the last morning by England's insurrection, and its response was mistakenly bold. The batting was like watching a rugby team charge deliberately into a series of tackles, when a sidestep would have been shrewder. Such errors aren't uncommon. So often teams are harangued to 'fight fire with fire' when, generally speaking, one fights fire with water.

As it turned out, Australia rebounded with a clinical 329-run win in Perth. Slater and Blewett scored centuries for Australia, Thorpe for England.

Steve Waugh should have scored one as well, but the injured McDermott's runner – Mark Waugh, no less – was run out when his brother was on 99. Only Geoff Boycott, in Test history, had been left 99 not out. England were left with 453 to make in seven sessions to square the series 2–2. Their final effort was a good indication of the difference between the teams. Gooch and Gatting, playing their last Test innings, went cheaply – Gooch dollying a rather sad caught-and-bowled to McDermott – and England were 5/27 at stumps on day four. A late revival got them to 123 on the fifth morning.

By this stage, the ubiquitous Barmy Army displayed a banner asking: 'Who are these cricketers who keep following us around?'

Haigh opined:

This was a series between an Australian team and a group of cricketers from England. Adding only three individuals to its Brisbane Test XII, the home side was a mutually reinforcing group greater than its parts. Tripping over each other as twenty-two men came and went, the tourists were like the changing cast of a long-running soap. Sometimes they activated round individuals like Gough and Malcolm. Otherwise they waited for lunch.

As transcendent as were the feats of Craig McDermott, Shane Warne and Michael Slater, it was in basic areas that Australia excelled and England lagged: on the park, between the wickets, behind the stumps, just turning up fit, the tourists were always catching up.

Taylor had won his first series as captain, a relief to him and a moment for the team to chart its course over the next five years. The West Indies, having just defeated India in India, were still true world champions, despite the retirement of their old guard. After a short, successful one-day series in New Zealand, the Australians would be on their way to the Caribbean again. In that regard, possibly the most long-lasting development from the Ashes series had come at the very end, when McGrath came quietly back into the Test team in Perth and picked up six English wickets.

McGrath had entered the Ashes series determined to change himself into a swing bowler. In the first Ashes Test he went wicketless, bowling wide of the off-stump and too full. The Englishmen did not rate him highly; nor, for the moment, did the Australian selectors. Back in Shield cricket, McGrath returned to his basic method – bang it in short of a length and work the ball off the seam. It was the last time he was to try converting himself into Dennis Lillee or Craig McDermott. From this point on, he would be Glenn McGrath. His change had profound consequences. He left for the Caribbean as McDermott's understudy, but returned as a series-winning, world-class fast bowler.

Australia in England, 1997

This was a tour which had, independently of Mark Taylor's woes but somehow entwined with them, started disastrously for Australia. Taylor's revival lifted a cloud, but there were other factors contributing to Australia's strangely diffident beginning. The squeezing-in of a nine-week South African tour between a hard home season against the West Indies and an Ashes tour allowed only nine scheduled days' play against the counties before the first Test match, compared with 17 on the previous Ashes tour, in 1993. Some of those precious few days were curtailed, or cancelled, due to rain. The entire match against Durham was rained out and often, as Tim de Lisle wrote in *Wisden*, 'if it was not actually raining, it was grey and dank'.

There was an element of fatigue among the Australians. Players who had been on every tour since Sri Lanka in August 1996, such as the Waugh brothers and Healy, had flown about 120,000 kilometres in seven months. Injuries affected the preparation, with Andy Bichel, Shane Warne, Adam Gilchrist, Brendon Julian and Jason Gillespie suffering ailments in the lead-up and McGrath still recovering from a badly bruised foot he incurred in South Africa. McGrath always needed plenty of bowling before he could work up to his best, and he went into the first Test at Edgbaston underdone. As usual in those circumstances, he pitched too short. The day after the Test match – in fact, due to England's easy win it was the fifth scheduled day – Geoff Marsh had McGrath, Kasprowicz and Gillespie out on the Edgbaston centre square aiming at a space between two witches' hats, set up at a fuller, 'English' length. For McGrath, that day – and the

The New Guard ... Geoff 'Swampy' Marsh took over as practice captain from Bob Simpson in 1996. By 1997, he was relaxed enough in the job to wear shorts in England. Patrick Eagar

self-appraisal that he needed to go back to his basic tenets and push himself through the crease – was a turning point in the tour.

There was no doubt that the Australians were stung by the English crowing after the first Test. Their 'Football's Coming Home' theme song for the 1996 European soccer championships was adapted into 'Ashes

Coming Home'. The low, sustained roar of the crowd at Edgbaston was, in Scyld Berry's view, the sound of the most influential crowd on an England Test match since 1981. Perhaps aware of the possible evanescence of their triumph, the English tabloids taunted the Australians mercilessly while they had the chance.

The other turning point, not to be underestimated, was the arrival of Paul Reiffel. Bichel having succumbed to his back injury, Reiffel was called in to fill the place that most good judges felt he should have had from the outset. He was a proven campaigner in England, and his batting would be useful in the lower order. He was rested, and determined to show Marsh and Taylor that he was a better bowler than they had given him credit for in South Africa, where he had languished without being picked.

We deal with Taylor's form slump, and his revival at Edgbaston, elsewhere. When Reiffel arrived with the team, he noticed the dampening effect of the captain's crisis: 'When I arrived, the guys were lower in spirits than I had been accustomed to in Australian teams. They were trying as hard as ever, but they lacked their usual zest. Perhaps my arrival triggered memories of cheerier times.'

Immediately, Reiffel had an impact, taking 3 for 15 in 10 overs against Nottinghamshire four days after the end of the Test match. McGrath, who later said Reiffel's very presence had lifted him, responded by taking four wickets of his own. The match was ruined by rain, but Australia moved on to Leicester on an updraft of confidence. That game, another to be rain-damaged, ended with an Australian victory by 84 runs. Reiffel took three wickets in each innings to amble straight back into the Test team.

Rain stopped a result at Lord's, but the Australians did enough in the second Test match to know they were back on track. The first day was washed out, and only an hour and a half was possible on the second after Taylor had sent England in. McGrath went through Butcher, Atherton and Stewart - a foretaste of the next day, when England could only just double their overnight 3/38 and were all out for 77, McGrath taking a career-best 8/38. On his way back to the dressing room, he noticed in the pavilion that someone (Marsh) had put a piece of tape on the Lord's honour board, recording great batting and bowling feats in Test cricket, and written on it: 'G.D. McGrath, eight wickets for 38 runs, Australia, 21 June 1997'. Reiffel was paralysing England at the other end, conceding a mere 17 runs from his 15 overs and taking the wickets of Thorpe and Mark Ealham.

Casting Off The Demons ... Mark Taylor celebrates a century and his future, Edgbaston, 1997. Patrick Eagar

Only nine times had England made a lower score against Australia, and most of those were in the era of uncovered pitches. If their confidence was deflated by their batting, it was stamped flat by their fielding, which was pitiful. Taylor went early, but Elliott, Blewett and Mark Waugh guided the tourists to 2/131 by stumps. Along the way, Elliott was missed three times – twice by Butcher at slip, once by Malcolm at fine leg – Blewett ballooned an edge between the immobile Thorpe and Butcher in the cordon, and Waugh was missed by Hussain at slip and John Crawley behind the stumps. Crawley was deputising for Stewart, who had one of his worrying back spasms.

On the fourth day, only 17.4 overs were bowled, but even so Australia put themselves into a potentially winning position. Elliott hit 20 fours in his maiden Test hundred, a streaky but punishing 112. Trying to smash it around one-day style, Australia got to 7/213 before Taylor declared, 136 ahead and a day to play. They might have forced an unlikely victory if Taylor had snapped up Butcher when the opener was on two. The Australian captain dropped it, however, and England survived on a 162-run opening stand between Butcher and Atherton.

Significantly, Warne had bowled better in the second innings at Lord's. Warne's tour had been a quiet one, a far cry from his emergence in England four years earlier. He was bowling without energy, and there were reports that he would have an operation on his right shoulder at the end of the tour. After being a glamour child in 1993, he was now a ridiculed and despised figure among the English crowds. Justin Langer wrote of the crowd's treatment of Warne at Taunton: 'I would shudder if my daughter, my wife, my mum or my grandmother had to listen to the disgusting and thoughtless rubbish coming from the stands.'

Sometimes, Warne was unaware of the actual extent of the abuse. At one ground, a soccer-style mob was calling him a name he could not quite catch. He asked an English journalist: 'What are those guys chanting? I think it's "Shane Warne is a real bloke" or something.' The journalist shook his head. 'No, they're calling you a rent boy.' 'Oh,' Warne replied, puzzled. 'Is that good or bad?'

Australia arrived at Old Trafford for the third Test having improved their mood with a strong win against Hampshire (Warne and Gillespie among the wickets, Taylor and Mark Waugh scoring hundreds), and an old-fashioned Manchester wicket gave them a further lift. It was dry and patchy in parts, green and damp in others – unfriendly to batsmen but, Taylor deduced, a timely platform for Warne. Accordingly, Taylor decided to bat when he won the toss, dismaying some of his top-order colleagues but giving his leg-spinner reason to smile.

All Australia's top order needed was to survive the first session. They couldn't. Taylor fell to Dean Headley (whose debut made him the first third-generation Test player, after grandfather George and father Ron, who represented the West Indies); Blewett couldn't keep Darren Gough out; and Mark Waugh feathered an Ealham ball to Stewart.

Steve Waugh's tour had been a quiet one to this point. He was disappointed with his failure to give England a fourth-innings target at Edgbaston, and was out first ball at Lord's. He chose this moment, characteristically, on the worst pitch of the series, to announce his presence. He lost Elliott for 40, and Bevan, Healy and Warne cheaply, before finding his ally in the lucky-charm Reiffel. They came together at 7/160 and separated at 8/230. Reiffel's attacking 31 was, as is so often the case with bowling all-rounders, a sign of his general happiness and confidence. Waugh had pressed on to his century – one he acknowledged as among the best three or four innings of his life – by the time Reiffel was out.

Atherton could not keep out McGrath's terrors, and Bevan's leg-side full toss to Butcher gave Healy his 100th dismissal against England – a blink-of-the-eye stumping – but the rest of the day belonged to Warne. Finally getting his shoulder into the right position and working the ball with immense force, Warne bowled better than at any time since before his 1996 finger operation. His six wickets, spinning England out for 162, were the final piece in Australia's jigsaw. For the next month they would be irresistible. In their second innings, the top order crumbled again but Steve Waugh made another century, becoming the first Australian since Arthur Morris 50 years earlier to make twin hundreds in an Ashes Test match. Some useful work from the lower order helped Australia to a lead of 468 before Taylor's declaration. McGrath and Gillespie, the latter back and bowling at fearsome pace after his hamstring injury, took seven second-innings wickets between them, but the bowling star remained Warne, who collected another three wickets, including the last of the match. Ironically, though, given Taylor's decision to bat first and allow Warne to exploit the pitch in the fourth innings, the leg-spinner had done most damage on day two.

A sense of inevitability, echoing past Ashes series, began to overtake the tour. Australia had squared up for their loss at Edgbaston and their ill fortune at Lord's. Their key players were in form. The Taylor saga was behind them. The captain's form was not great, but his first-Test century had at least forestalled questions of him dropping himself.

They rolled through a mid-tour clutch of county matches and came to Headingley, Leeds, without any fear. England could lay down their worst pitch, even worse than Old Trafford, and the Australians felt they could win. (This did not stop them lodging an unsuccessful protest, however, against England's chairman of selectors David Graveney, who they believed had been instructing curators on how to prepare – or un-prepare – the Test wickets so as to minimise Warne's effect.)

England were damned if they did and damned if they didn't. A dry pitch would risk opening the door to Warne. A greentop left them with the menace of McGrath and Gillespie. They went green in Leeds, and Taylor duly sent them in. They lasted fewer than 60 overs through a rain-interrupted first two days, scoring 172. McGrath (who dismissed Atherton again) and Reiffel did most of the bowling, but it was Gillespie's sheer pace that blasted the Englishmen out. He took wickets at a rate of one every 11 balls as he stormed through the England order like a hyperactive child in a toyshop.

As previously, the hosts had their chances. Bold opening spells from Gough and Headley removed Taylor, Blewett and the Waughs for a combined 13 runs. At 4/50, Elliott was joined by Ponting, recalled in place of Bevan, whose hesitancy before short-pitched bowling was again exposed by this opponent. Elliott had just edged England's debutant left-armer, Mike Smith, straight to Thorpe at first slip. Much has been made of Thorpe's gaffe, as if it cost England the series. But at that moment, Steve Waugh was still batting at the other end. Had Elliott been dismissed, who is to doubt Waugh's fighting focus? As it happened, Elliott was dropped and Waugh was out the next over. Whichever batsman was out seemed to matter little, because Ponting came to the crease in flamboyant mood, immediately striking the ball with great force and inspiring Elliott to do likewise. They added 268 runs in 261 minutes for the fifth wicket, but it was their manner as much as their statistics that demoralised England. They played as if they had come together at 4/300, not 4/50, hitting a combined 42 fours and four sixes. Comparing the fluency and class of Australia's least experienced players with the shy, stumbling efforts of England's newcomer Smith provided an unflattering comparative portrait of cricket in the two countries. Ponting made 127, his maiden Test century, and Elliott was one short of 200 when Gough beat him with a late (in both senses of the word) inswinging yorker. It mattered little. Australia had a huge lead by this point and all thoughts were on England's second innings.

Atherton had been thinking about it too much, evidently. He was McGrath's victim for the fifth time in seven innings, Butcher and Stewart following soon after. Hussain, whom Ponting had at his mercy with a run-out shy before he had scored, went on to make a dashing century, England's only one in the last five Tests of the series. With Crawley (72), he gave England a mirage of a chance. But Taylor introduced Warne early on the fifth morning. Warne beat Hussain, and Mark Waugh's brilliant catching at slip completed another convincing win. The last man, Smith, was out to the first ball after lunch on the fifth day – enraging Australian television viewers back at home, who had been unable to see the first session due to Channel 9's decision to keep faith with their non-sports evening audience. Australia now led 2–1 with two Tests to play. England could have seized back the initiative had they grasped one of three chances offered by Elliott, but it was clear that the teams were playing with different levels of self-belief.

Little had changed since 1994–95, when Gideon Haigh had observed: 'When Boon camped at short leg in Perth, he was there to catch; when Crawley took the helmet there for England, it was to hide. It was nothing to see two Australians turn one into three, and two Englishmen turn three into one.'

Australia's next match, against Somerset at Taunton, was marred by rain and the abuse showered upon Warne. The latter prompted former Somerset hero Steve Waugh, standing in for the injured Taylor, to complain to the umpires. Two men were ejected from the ground, and Warne gave them the finger after taking one of his five wickets, but the incident highlighted both the decline in behaviour among English crowds – at some grounds, they were almost as bad as Australians – and the end of Warne's love affair with England. He tried to respond with good-natured rudeness to the crowd's taunts, feeling, no doubt, that if he showed he understood their language, they would understand his. But his mock-boorish replies only inflamed them and embarrassed some of his countrymen. He couldn't win. Four years had been a long time in Warne's career.

Having fallen behind in the series, England's selectors succumbed to a familiar desperation. They dropped Butcher, Smith and Ealham, and brought in Andrew Caddick and the Australian-born brothers Adam and Ben Hollioake. Neither had the figures or the appearance of being up to this level, but they rode into the team on a wave of tabloid enthusiasm. England had for 15 years been copying the methods of the teams who beat them – turning to West Indian-born pacemen during the 1980s, for example – so there was no inconsistency in their choosing a pair of perky, loud-mouthed boys with Australian accents. Both claimed to be all-rounders. Adam Hollioake, in the words of one Englishman, was 'one of those players who, when you saw him bowl, you figured he must be a batsman, and when you saw him bat, you figured he must be a bowler'. He had an interesting line in banter, however, claiming before the Test that he enjoyed cricket more the tougher it was. A hard man, indeed.

Australia's batting came together at last on the first day at Trent Bridge. They sold themselves a little short, no individual making a century, but 427 in the first innings gave them dominance in the match. The best England could do was 303, thanks largely to a counterattacking 87 from 107 balls by Stewart, who had returned to his favoured position at the top of the order. Yet this masterful batsman still remained without a century in eight years of Ashes Tests, and there was little backup as McGrath and Warne kept the wickets flowing. Australia's second innings, a competent 336, left England an insurmountable 450 runs behind with a little more than four sessions remaining.

Nobody could have expected the rapidity of their collapse. Even the Australians evinced surprise at England's lack of fight. After losing Atherton (to McGrath) just before tea, England lost their nine other wickets in the last session. It was a bewilderingly careless display, each batsman trying to emulate Stewart's shotmaking from the first innings. Heaven knows what the debutant Hollioakes thought of this approach. Gillespie stormed in, went for eight runs an over, took three wickets and injured his back so badly he was to miss much of the next two years. That loss was obscured by Australia's stampede to victory. Graham Thorpe scored 82 not out from 92 balls, but even his cavalier batting set no example for his teammates.

At 7pm, Mark Waugh pouched an edge from Devon Malcolm at slip, off McGrath's bowling, to give Australia the Ashes for an unprecedented fifth time running. Steve Waugh was the only current player, from either side, to have played in an Ashes series (1986-87) won by England. The Australians lived in expectation of victory, the Englishmen in expectation of defeat. Australia's celebrations were boisterous, Warne dancing with a stump and spraying champagne from the Trent Bridge players' balcony. Retaining the Ashes was, of course, a great achievement, but each time it lost a little of its lustre. England were hardly worth the celebrations; the celebration was rather for the completion of a spectacular nine-month sequence, Taylor's men beating the West Indies, South Africa and England under the most stressful and gruelling of pressures.

The final Test, at The Oval, was a strange affair. After retaining the Ashes, the Australians had travelled to Canterbury, where they had beaten Kent. More pressingly, they had signed a deal with sports entrepreneur James Erskine (see later chapter) to represent them in their negotiations with the ACB on improved conditions, both for themselves and for Sheffield Shield cricketers. There were suspicions that other things were on their minds when they returned to London.

They played a typical 'dead rubber', a match characterised by poor cricket (on both sides) and unpredictable collapses. Batting on a powdery, loose-crusted wicket, England scored 180 and 163. Winning a Test match with such scores owed more to Australia's efforts than their own, although the recalled Phil Tufnell deserved credit for exploiting the awful wicket. The ball broke through the surface of the pitch and popped unplayably from all lengths. McGrath took seven wickets in the England first innings, Michael Kasprowicz seven in the second, Tufnell eleven for the match. Ben Hollioake was dropped, but Adam should have been. The elder brother was humbled on day one, leaving a Warne ball which did exactly as it promised to do, pitching on leg, spinning mildly to the off and hitting middle stump.

Injuries forced change on Australia, Reiffel and Gillespie joining the long queue at the infirmary. The tour selectors had to call on reinforcements from county and league cricket, and on match eve were faced with the barely palatable choice of giving Tasmania's Shaun Young or NSW's Shane Lee a Test debut. Neither was considered quite up to the mark, but Young, who was playing for Somerset, was preferred.

On day one, England started well but collapsed. On day two, Australia did much the same, gaining a lead of just 40. England lost Butcher, Atherton and Stewart before erasing the difference, and Hussain just after. Four wickets down, they were 12 runs ahead. Thorpe and the recalled Mark Ramprakash showed some enterprise, charging down the wicket at a tired Warne, whose efforts to lift himself through the pain barrier for the vital middle Tests were now exacting their cost. After Taylor caught Thorpe for 62, however, England lost 6/32 and left Australia 124 to win. The task was never going to be straightforward given the state of the pitch and Australia's historic hesitancy when chasing such paltry totals. A weary Elliott, who was fast losing his freshness for cricket after such a mighty leap from State to international level, was out early. Taylor and Blewett reduced the target to 88, with nine wickets in hand, before Taylor was trapped by Caddick. The Australian captain had made 317 runs for the series at 31.70. Although moderate, it was more than he might have expected in May. But 260 of his runs had come in three innings, at Edgbaston and Trent Bridge, each of them immaterial to the results of those games. He had totalled 57 runs in his other seven innings. Nonetheless, his last-gasp revival at Edgbaston had lifted a curse off the Australian team, and thereafter they were able to function as a cohesive unit. In the overall scheme of things, Taylor's Edgbaston century did more than just save his career.

In their last innings of the endless tour, the Australian middle order crumbled like the pitch. Warne slogged, batting with a runner to spare his injured groin, but the visitors fell 19 runs short amid the predictable English delirium. A 3–2 result flattered the hosts into believing they had made up ground since the previous series – a hope that was proved illusory, yet again, in 1998–99. For Australia, the match was both anti-climax and bitter repetition of their strange diffidence when chasing small targets. The Oval was, from an Australian point of view, the Test they had played after their minds had started the journey home. Once they got there, there was no ticker-tape parade from a public who had grown accustomed to, even bored with, beating England.

But point of view is everything. For England, delusions or not, this match meant something. Matthew Engel, greeting patriotic glee as a rare and powerful visitor, referred to it in *Wisden* as 'a contest fit to rank with the great games of Ashes history'. Taylor took possession of the replica Ashes urn after play – sparking calls, not for the first time, for the original to be sent to Australia – but, Engel wrote, 'this was greeted with only casual applause. It was a moment for England, and not just for the team. For the administrators, desperate to keep the game alive in the hearts of the public in difficult times, it was a priceless victory.'

Two years earlier, when England had won another dead rubber, Gideon Haigh viewed it this way:

Adelaide probably explained more about England's mercurial streak than it exposed any Australian fragility. England rolled Australia at The Oval in 1993 and the West Indies at Bridgetown last year after three tramplings because, given elbow room, it can come out swinging, but toe-to-toe it lacks the assertiveness born of regular success. Until that's remedied, Mike Atherton's team will only play for parity and never supremacy.

England in Australia, 1998–99

All cricket teams are, one way or another, prone to misfortune. Australia's 1995 tourists to the West Indies could have felt they had embarked under a bad sign when their strikeforce of Damien Fleming and Craig McDermott were ruled out with injuries before the first Test. In England in 1993, the Australian party suffered worrying early days when McDermott was sent home with a twisted bowel and his possible replacement, Wayne Holdsworth, lost all semblance of the form which had won him selection. And four years later, the Ashes tourists were blighted by injuries to Andrew Bichel and Brendon Julian, the heavy spring rains, Taylor's effort to break his slump and the consequent inability of Michael Slater or Ricky Ponting to enjoy any worthwhile time in the middle.

Yet all those tours ended with resounding success. There was something resistant about the Australian team in these years. Strokes of ill luck literally brought out the best in Taylor's players. It was not simply that they coped with setbacks; it was that players such as McGrath, Warne, the Waughs, Taylor and even backups like Julian (in the West Indies), Merv Hughes (in 1993) and Reiffel (1997) actively lifted their games when luck appeared to have turned its back on them.

Conversely, there was something brittle about the English teams of this period, something that made them particularly vulnerable to misfortune. From the beginning of the 1998–99 tour, there was a feeling that the English squad were cursed. In the opening week in Perth, it was clear that several of their players had arrived with injuries. Seven of the 17 squad members had undergone surgery since their last Test match, against Sri Lanka two months earlier. In that first week, their two key men, Alec Stewart and Michael Atherton, succumbed to chronic back injuries. For their long-term rock, Atherton, it was to be an injury from which he did not recover for the entire tour, and which became a worsening misery the longer it wore on. Stewart, who had assumed the triple burdens of captaincy, wicketkeeping and opening the batting, could ill afford to suffer injury as well. His confidence was undermined early, and the string of ducks he made before the first Test match were a sad omen for the rest of the tour.

In their first first-class match, moreover, opener Mark Butcher was put into hospital, second ball, when he ducked into a bouncer from West Australian tearaway Matthew Nicholson. Butcher was to go into the first Test with a total of nine runs under his belt. He recovered with a fine century in Brisbane, but his form tailed away badly after that.

Bowlers Dean Headley and Ben Hollioake also injured themselves in Perth. Headley did not recover fully until Christmas, and Hollioake, whose abilities at this level were questionable anyway, had one of those nightmare tours when his few on-field opportunities met with humiliation.

During the third first-class match, against Queensland in Cairns, middle-order batsman John Crawley was beaten up while walking back to the team hotel one night. The English team smuggled Crawley to Brisbane before the press were aware of the bashing. Officially, the story was that he had been bashed by an unknown assailant, who made no identification of him as an English cricketer, while walking alone near the Cairns harbour. Yet nobody was caught, or came forward. There was no apparent provocation for such a strange 'bashing'. It was not long before rumours circulated that Crawley had, in fact, been in a fight with one of his teammates. His demeanour, sullen and evasive, only strengthened the rumours.

From its earliest days, then, the England tour relied heavily on a tiny core. Nasser Hussain and Mark Ramprakash were the English batting, insofar as resistance was concerned. They top-scored in the first match, in Perth, and continued as mainstays of the top and middle order for the entire Test series. When Graham Thorpe was sent home with a back injury, England's back woes were complete - they had a full set. Likewise, Darren Gough and the improved Alan Mullally carried the English bowling, notwithstanding cameos from Alex Tudor and Headley. Their spinners, Robert Croft and Peter Such, were as ineffective as their past records would suggest, and Angus Fraser had come to the end of his tether. The management of Fraser was odd indeed. Having observed that he needed 'miles in his legs' during the opening match, the England selectors failed to select him in the two other lead-up games. Similarly, Tudor was fast-tracked into the team for the second Test in Perth, starred with four wickets in the first innings, and did not play another Test until the unsuitable fifth rubber in Sydney, where he was to bowl only one more over than the part-time spinner Ramprakash.

So why were England so vulnerable to the bad luck that accompanies most tours? Why did the English have such trouble recovering? One answer could be that the Australians did not let them fight back. The Sheffield Shield teams played uncompromising cricket against them, Nicholson blasting out seven wickets and Ryan Campbell a century during the first game, after which captain Justin Langer slammed the English for playing for a draw. Australia's Test team also affirmed their old psychological edge from the earliest encounter and, despite the absence of Warne, kept their foot on the English throat the way they had since 1989.

Yet the Australians were distracted mid-series by the revelations that Mark Waugh and Warne had been fined for their bookmaking links in 1995, and that Australia had concealed this from the Pakistani match-fixing inquiry in 1998. Australian cricket was in uproar for the third Test in Adelaide, yet it was they, not the English, who summoned the dominant effort for that match.

England did bring much of it on themselves. Their selection oddities reflected a broken chain of authority between tour selectors Stewart, David Lloyd (coach) and Graham Gooch (manager), and the other selectors, David Graveney and Mike Gatting back in England. There was no consensus on how to benefit from Stewart's versatility as a batting keeper. One day, they would opt for five specialist bowlers and six batsmen; the next, without any reason connected to the conditions or the opposition, they would choose seven batsmen and four bowlers. Partly, the problem was that Hollioake was way out of his depth in international cricket and so the all-rounder option was lost. But partly, also, Stewart was not allowed the freedom a captain should be given to run a tour his way. The affable

Lloyd held strong ideas, and was happy to bow to the judgment of Stewart, but Gooch was a malign influence as both manager and selector. His presence intimidated the younger players and irritated the older ones. To younger tourists, he was the brooding 'spy' from the selection panel, and to the older men, he was a constant reproach. When an English batsman returned after another failure, he had to walk past the gloomy figure of the prodigious opening batsman, who then went out and spoke to the press, to the effect that he could have done better himself and why didn't these lads show some of the commitment that had given him nearly 10,000 Test runs.

While Gooch was surrounded by incompetence, the English management created a bit of their own. They focused, with an unhealthy obsession, on Warne, recruiting Australian spin coach Peter Philpott to demystify the art for them. Philpott taught their batsmen how to bowl leg-spin, reasoning that if you know how to bowl it, you'll know how to bat against it. As things transpired, Warne played no real part in the series, and a completely different kind of leg-spinner, Stuart MacGill, tore through them in three Test matches. Five and a half years after first facing Warne, the English still had no idea how to play leg-spin. As early as 1993, Pakistan's Mushtaq Ahmed had said: 'I found out last summer that English players don't play leg-spin very well because they don't see much of it. I found that by pinning them down early, they got to the stage where they were tentative to play a stroke and, when they did open up, it was often to the wrong ball.' His words were no less apt in 1998 than they had been in 1993.

Also, England earned derision for not agreeing to play under lights if the cloud cover became too heavy. Their argument was that Australia had done so before, which gave the hosts an advantage. Any player could have told them that the adjustment was not difficult, yet the stubborn refusal seemed to exemplify England's divided attitudes, which manifested themselves in muddled or inconsistent output.

The Ashes series, which Australia won 3–1, could as easily have been 5–0 or, given Australia's bouts of carelessness, 2–2. It was a topsy-turvy summer in which Australia lost only two or three sessions and were clearly the better team, yet could have thrown away the series in the last two Tests.

In Brisbane, Taylor's 100th Test, England were saved from MacGill's last-day burst by a Noachian storm. Centuries from Healy (134) and Steve Waugh (112) had pulled Australia back from 4/106 to 485 in the first innings, England contributing with some key dropped chances. Butcher made a century and Hussain, Thorpe and Ramprakash fifties in their reply, which fell 110 runs behind when McGrath came through with a six-wicket rampage on the fourth morning. Michael Slater blazed an old-fashioned second-innings hundred as Australia put the match out of England's reach, and it was left to the spinners to mop up in the second innings. This was going perfectly to plan on the fifth day, MacGill's vicious wrong'un bowling Hussain and Mark Waugh bluffing out Stewart and Thorpe, until the rains washed it all away when Australia needed four wickets in about 40 overs to win. Already, England were praying for rain. It wasn't a good start.

Australia had the luxury of dropping MacGill for the second Test. Nicholson's spell in the Perth first-class match had shown that the WACA was back to its slippery, bouncy best, and Australia's selectors banked on Jason Gillespie's pace with Colin Miller's seam-and-spin to provide variation. Surprisingly, perhaps, it was Fleming's hooping swing, into the Fremantle Doctor, that went through England in 39 overs on the first morning. England's seven-batsmen trick was worth little in the first innings, No 7 Graeme Hick only worrying Gillespie for two balls. Stewart, inept against spin in Brisbane, top-scored with a belligerent 38 in 29 balls at No 4. For Australia, Taylor's 61 on the first afternoon was worth a century. The second morning saw the pitch quicken noticeably, Mark Waugh grinding 36 runs off 128 balls as Tudor and Gough roared in. England did well to restrict the hosts to 240, a lead of 128; but a two-day Test loomed suddenly, as Fleming got rid of England's top four in his first spell. At 5/67 after tea, the second two-day Test in history was a strong possibility. Yet this hyper-aggressive match took another turn when Hick started blasting Gillespie for sixes over mid-wicket. At stumps, England were on terms, with five wickets in hand. If they could add another 150, they had a real chance. Was this to be the day, finally, when Hick won a Test match? Some Australian journalists, who had written that England were mentally shattered in their previous day's editions, chewed their fingernails as Hick continued hitting on the third morning. With the obdurate Ramprakash, he got the lead out to 48 before Gillespie charged in with the Doctor and knocked over the last five wickets for 33. The 64 Australia was set looked momentarily challenging, as the openers and Langer were out for 36, but the Waughs steadied and ensured a 1-0 lead.

Against the scandalous backdrop in Adelaide, Australia relied on Langer's unbeaten 179 to bat England out of the series. Only Hussain (89) and Ramprakash (61) could resist the superb Australian bowling on the second day, MacGill returning for Gillespie to take four wickets and McGrath, Miller and Fleming chipping in with two each. Slater repeated his Brisbane second innings to set up a declaration, and the pacemen made England look feeble for a second time. A 205-run win, somewhat hollow given the turmoil off-field, secured the Ashes for a sixth straight series. Two Test matches were still to be played. By all objective criteria, England had gone backwards since 1997. Wilfred Rhodes had written nearly a century earlier that 'To win in Australia, you need to be 25 per cent better than they are.' England teams of the 1990s would flatter themselves to say they were 25 per cent worse.

Their tour hit its nadir the next week. Bob Willis had opined publicly that Australia's Second XI could beat England's Firsts, and the solid summer form of several Australian fringe candidates had enlivened speculation, much of it mischievous, that Australia A should play a Test match to make things interesting. This English squad had been spared games against the Cricket Academy, after all, because it was feared that the tourists might record the same 0-2 scoresheet as in 1994-95. So England came to their match against an Australian XI in Hobart in a state of apprehension. They had just scrambled home in a one-dayer against the Prime Minister's XI, thanks to an over of leg-spin by Taylor to Angus Fraser, which cost 16 runs – the same margin by which England won the match. A relieved Stewart said he had been preparing to bowl the last over in a gesture of goodwill, but observers at the ground could have sworn they saw him tell Ben Hollioake to warm up.

The match in Hobart was ruined as a true contest on the first day, when the pitch was revealed to be slow, low and murderous on bowlers. Australia's Gavin Robertson pulled out of active duty with a back complaint, and as it was too late to call for a replacement, he stayed in the line-up. It became a nine-man team when Reiffel broke down in his second over, and then eight when Kasprowicz seized up in his 19th. Brendon Julian remained as the only frontline bowler. He shared the load with the bits-and-pieces men: Stuart Law, Michael Bevan and Greg Blewett. The conditions were ideal for stand-in captain Atherton to restore confidence with an unbeaten double century, and Hick reinforced his name as a flat-track bully with an entertaining 125.

Blewett was enjoying a Bradman-like season in Sheffield Shield. He and Matthew Elliott, whose appetite for cricket and runs had returned after a period in the wilderness, put on 206 for the first wicket. When the Australians declared at 4/293, nearly 180 runs behind, Blewett's season tally was 962 runs at 120.25, Elliott's 793 at 88.11. Blewett was undefeated on 169.

Butcher and Crawley slogged the part-timers second time around, and Atherton was able to make a match of it by declaring at 3/199. It left the Australian team four hours, or 78 overs, to make 380. By anyone's reckoning, it should have been a good contest – anyone's, that is, except the Englishmen's. Manager Gooch disagreed with Atherton's declaration, arguing that he should have killed the match and used the afternoon for batting practice. The bowlers appeared to agree with Gooch. They staged the equivalent of a go-slow, bowling half-heartedly, disgracefully for a national team. Blewett (213 not out) and Corey Richards (138 not out) seized on their opponents' disunity and belted the runs in quick time – seven an over – achieving the win with 22 overs to spare. It was an amazing afternoon, partly for the quality of the batting, but more for the absence of any pride or spirit in the bowling. Atherton was hung out to dry, Gooch criticising his decision to a stunned press. Only the English, it seemed, could turn on their captain for trying to turn a snooze into a real cricket game with a competitive finish. It was almost a mutiny. Atherton had never been given clearer cause to celebrate the fact that he was no longer their leader full-time.

Overconfidence, in the circumstances, was always going to be Australia's enemy in the Boxing Day Test. They called up the former under-19 player of the year Matthew Nicholson when Gillespie revealed a foot injury he had been trying to hide. Nicholson, possibly the fastest bowler in the country, also had a history of injury and illness, notably a bout of chronic fatigue syndrome brought on, his doctors told him, by a cocktail of Ross River fever, salmonella and malaria he had picked up on a youth tour to India.

Boxing Day itself was washed out, but once the game started, McGrath was into his work, firing out Atherton and Butcher in his first two overs. Nicholson removed Hussain in his first spell, and only a typically flashy 107 from Stewart gave England any respectability. The captain had finally recognised the inevitable and handed over the gloves to Warren Hegg. Promoting himself to his favoured position at the top of the order, he was well warmed-up by the time MacGill entered the attack. Australia were skittish rather than focused in the field, and their batting looked vulnerable. Taylor and Slater failed, Langer and Mark Waugh made starts but could not sustain concentration, and Lehmann, replacing the out-of-form Ponting, played a magnificent upper-cut almost over the point boundary before giving his wicket away. Steve Waugh, meanwhile, played one of his best Test innings. He added 58 with Healy and 26 with Fleming before the fall of Nicholson, yorked by the irrepressible Gough, left him 77 not out with only MacGill and McGrath to come. As was his wont, Waugh gave MacGill unrestricted access to the bowling. MacGill revelled in the responsibility and scored 43. Waugh improvised some exciting cuts over gully and tennis-like slogs over mid-off, and was uncharacteristically jubilant when he reached his century. He made 122 in all, hitching Australia's lead up to 70 runs before MacGill and McGrath were out in three balls.

England's second innings was only four runs better than their first, Stewart and Hussain making fifties and Hick top-scoring with a fiery 60 off 82 balls at No 7. Mullally, an even greater bunny than McGrath,

Bring Back Warney ... The English had prepared for Shane Warne, but found Stuart MacGill a bigger handful. Here the leg-spinner bowls Alec Stewart after the England captain's first century against Australia, Melbourne 1998. Joe Armao/Age

annoyed his rival by hitting three boundaries, an act so galling that McGrath abused him verbally and received a suspended fine. Still, the Australian juggernaut rolled on, and a 175-run winning target seemed a formality, particularly at 2/103 when Langer and Mark Waugh were travelling along comfortably.

Then Ramprakash took the catch of the summer at square leg to remove Langer. But still he looked somehow ridiculous as he ran around, his eyes spinning, trying to rev up his teammates. The Waughs carried the score to 3/130, only 45 from the win, before Mark Waugh drove lazily at Headley and edged to Hick in slips. Headley was bowling with gusto, the full voice of the Barmy Army behind him. It was one of those surreal summer afternoons when there seemed a weird electricity in the air. The Australians were in a hurry to win the match, and both sides were stretching their capacities on a day of record length. To make up time for the lost Boxing Day, the teams were effectively playing four days in three. The last session on day four lasted four hours – too long for the Australians, as it turned out. Lehmann received a bad decision, his bat clipping the ground but given out off the edge, and Healy and Fleming went for ducks. Headley, bowling the spell of his life, got them all. Steve Waugh was still there, but Australia had lost 3/0, their situation deteriorating from 35 runs with six wickets to 35 with three. Nicholson, whose bowling debut had confirmed his wicket-taking ability, stuck around with Waugh, who decided not to take stumps but rather force the exhausted English bowlers to keep going. The score edged up to 161, another 14 to go, before Nicholson was caught behind off – who else? – Headley, who had transformed himself into Malcolm Marshall in an hour. As in the first innings, Waugh chose to expose MacGill and McGrath to the strike, but this time he was condemned as selfish because they weren't up to the task. Amid the expected English pandemonium, the tourists won by 12. It was an astounding afternoon, showing that a team can lose every session but one and still win a Test match. A livid Taylor blasted his side's 'lazy' cricket. Their last-day display was one of their least professional in five years.

For Sydney, Warne selected himself. Unsettled by MacGill's fast progress, Warne was desperate to come back and remind the world of his existence. He also wanted badly to go to the West Indies at the end of the season and needed to win back his spot. His Sheffield Shield form had been unconvincing: he had bowled accurately but unthreateningly. Publicly, he said he was coming back because the Waughs and Slater had complimented his bowling after a pre-Christmas Shield match in Sydney. Privately, Warne had the privilege of selecting himself. He told the panel of Trevor Hohns, Allan Border and Andrew Hilditch that he was ready to play, and they, for their sins, picked him. As the world was to discover in the next two months, he had come back too early.

The New Malcolm Marshall? ... Dean Headley traps Damien Fleming, on his way to a match-winning six wickets and an unbelievable win, Melbourne 1998. Patrick Eager

Steve and Mark Waugh dominated the first day on their home ground, adding 190. Steve managed to set a world record for innings interrupted in the nineties when, on 96, he was bowled by Peter Such. Mark, his reputation so badly scarred by the bookmaker revelation, went some way to redeeming himself with a century before his family and friends. Gough gave a late, late show, taking England's only Ashes hat-trick of the 20th century in the 88th over. Bowling from the Paddington end, he beat Healy for pace and got a catch behind the wicket; speared an inswinging full-pitcher through MacGill; and bowled the ball of the series, an outswinging yorker to Miller, to round out the great moment. The funny thing was, a hat-trick looked inevitable from the moment he got Healy.

'I'm not one of those bowlers who says he knows what he's bowling every ball,' was Gough's non-explanation later. 'I just bowl it down the other end, and if it swings, whichever way, if I don't know which way it's going to swing, I don't think the batsman will. I bowled it at the stumps and it shaped out, which helped, obviously. It ended up being probably the best ball I've bowled all series.'

Warne took Butcher's wicket leg-before in his first over, but took no more as England battled to 220, a deficit of 102. MacGill took five. Australia's batting had another attack of the lazies in the second innings, Taylor completing a miserable second half of the series and only the belligerent Slater scoring more than 24. It was his third century of the series, all in the second innings, but had he not scored it, Australia may well have lost the match and drawn the series. When he was out, he had scored 123 of 180 runs. England needed 287, and challenged briefly before MacGill started turning it square on the fifth day. The familiar story unfolded, English batsmen utterly flummoxed by leg-spin, only this time Warne was effectively a spectator as MacGill did the job. Taylor said there was little real difference between Warne's two wickets and MacGill's 12 in the match, but that was akin to saying there was little real difference between Warne's 300 and MacGill's 30 in their careers. As Warne had shown, the trick is not to bowl well, but to take wickets and win matches.

Taylor caught Ramprakash on the last day, off McGrath's bowling, to pass Border's world record of 156 catches. He wore his cap at the presentation on the last day, a signal to many that despite his statement of availability for the West Indies tour, he had decided to retire. At the end of his speech, he said to the crowd: 'See you next year.' In the press conference later, he admitted that he didn't know whether that would be as a player or commentator.

Without announcement, then, with no more than hint, question and hedged denial, the Taylor years were over. Australia had won a Test match through the batting of their NSW core and the bowling of a leg-spinner. They had won a series against England for the sixth straight time, in a canter, with only a few late wobbles once the win was achieved. England's players went to Yabba's Hill to reciprocate the Barmy Army's applause, and ended the series with some hope, possibly false, that they were getting closer to the Ashes. The series had been entertaining and very well supported – historic sell-outs on the first days of the Sydney Test, a dead rubber, attested to England's ongoing popularity – but, in its way, it was merely a depressing re-run of those that had gone before. The more things change, the more they stay the same. Taylor knew that the West Indies were waiting, and while there had been much change and revolution over there, the essential challenge remained the same: outstanding, aggressive fast bowlers would make life a nightmare for opening batsmen. He had to decide whether he was up to it one more time. But playing even more on his mind was the ongoing sadness of being a Test-only player. In his heart, the Taylor years had been winding down since 1996.

Sri Lanka: Under the Skin

SRI LANKA WAS the surprise pebble in Australia's shoe during the 1990s. They provided stout resistance in the Test arena in 1999, when they stole a home series from Steve Waugh's team on the strength of some keen swing bowling and the mesmerising spin of Muttiah Muralitharan. But it was in one-day cricket that Sri Lanka earned their standing as genuine rivals. They attacked Australia on their own aggressive and abrasive terms during 1995–96, and then belted the Australians, twice, on their own soil. They saw themselves as standing up to a bully and testing the notion, successfully, that bullies like to dish it out but not to receive it. From 1996 the Sri Lankans were world one-day champions at Australia's expense. It took the Australians some time to swallow their pride, but eventually they were forced to adopt some of the Sri Lankans' progressive one-day tactics. This had unforeseen repercussions, notably the omission of Mark Taylor and Ian Healy from Australia's one-day plans in the 'two-teams' structure. Eventually, however, the Sri Lankans did Australia a great favour. By facing up to their shortcomings, Australia was able to revamp its one-day approach and succeed Sri Lanka as world one-day champions in 1999.

Sri Lanka in Australia, 1995–96
Australia in the 1995–96 season hosted twin tours, by the world-class Pakistanis and the cheeky Sri Lankan team led by Arjuna Ranatunga. Unexpectedly, the Pakistan series was a bloodless affair compared with

I'll Raise You 100 Rupees . . . Gambling man Shane Warne staying out of the casinos, Sri Lanka 1999. Mark Ray

the other tour. If Sri Lanka arrived with a chip on their collective shoulder, it was deepened by their poor treatment at the hands of cricket authorities. The ACB felt it had done the island nation a good enough turn by offering it a three-Test series, and indeed it had, particularly compared with England, for example, who could not find room in their program to play a single Test series, at home or away, in Sri Lanka's first 18 years as a Test nation. Having offered them such a fine opportunity, however, the ACB then gave them a rough schedule and substandard facilities in their build-up.

In three weeks of preparation, Sri Lanka lost to Queensland twice on poor wickets at Cairns and Mackay, and scrambled a one-day win and a four-day draw against Tasmania in Devonport and Launceston. The slow, uneven wickets there were no preparation at all for the WACA blitzkrieg of McGrath and McDermott in the first Test, and Sri Lanka did well to score 251 and 330 in their two innings. It was hard to imagine even teams like Pakistan or India scoring so well with such limited forewarning. Sri Lanka did unearth their ability to at least frustrate the Australians, with Hashan Tillekeratne scoring 119 in the second innings and Romesh Kaluwitharana, Asanka Gurusinha, Roshan Mahanama and Ranatunga all making sound contributions.

Their bowling, on the other hand, posed few questions to an Australian team which piled up 5/617 in its only innings. Slater belted 219 off 321 balls, a welcome return to form, Mark Waugh scored his tenth Test century, and Taylor made 96. Ricky Ponting, who with Stuart Law (56 not out) was making a Test debut in place of Steve Waugh (injured) and Greg Blewett (dropped), was on 96 when a Chaminda Vaas ball hit him in front of the stumps. It would have passed a good 20 centimetres over the bails, but Pakistani umpire Khizar Hayat gave him out.

Hayat, who had been at the centre of the Mike Gatting furore on England's 1988 tour of Pakistan, and had umpired in Australia's infamous Karachi Test of 1994, had an interesting match in Perth. He made several poor decisions that went both for and against the Australians, but his most significant contribution was to summon Ranatunga to explain the condition of the ball in the 17th over of Australia's innings. Hayat told Ranatunga that he believed the ball had been tampered with illegally. Ranatunga protested his team's innocence against what was, after all, a serious accusation. Yet it was not so serious that Hayat would impound the ball. Instead, he and fellow umpire Peter Parker warned the Sri Lankans and allowed them to continue using that ball, a bizarre decision which effectively destroyed the evidence. The match referee, New Zealand's Graham Dowling, made a statement that night, based on Hayat's submission, that 'the condition of the ball was clearly altered ... by a member of the Sri Lankan team', yet, without the ball to examine, he could do nothing other than issue a warning. There was some subsequent speculation on Hayat's role in the affair, with unsubstantiated allegations made of his supposed connections with Indian and Pakistani bookmakers. The matter of the un-impounded ball, however, seemed a case of clear and simple incompetence.

In that match at Perth, Warne took his 200th wicket in his 42nd Test appearance. Only four bowlers had reached the mark in faster time. Two years later, a fifth bowler was to get there faster than Warne. That was

Sri Lanka's off-spinner Muralitharan, who passed 200 when he took 16 wickets to destroy England at The Oval in a one-off Test in 1998.

Muralitharan was lucky to progress so far, given the humiliation inflicted on him in the Melbourne Test of 1995-96. It is well documented that Australian umpire Darrell Hair, believing Murali's action 'diabolical', called him seven times for throwing - twice in his fourth over, three times in his fifth and twice more in his sixth - before Ranatunga removed Murali and left the field to consult with Dowling. Returning to the field, Ranatunga switched Murali to the opposite end, where New Zealand umpire Steve Dunne did not call him, despite Hair encouraging him to stand back from the stumps so as to examine the bowler's action. Hair did not call Murali from square leg either, although he wrote in his book *Decision Maker* that he could have called Murali as many times as he wanted. He restrained himself, feeling his point had been made. It all happened before an MCG crowd of 55,239, the best for Test cricket in Australia for 10 years. Many were Sri Lankan Melburnians, their bewilderment and anger an embarrassment to the ACB.

Hair gives his own explanation of events:

When it became clear that Steve (Dunne) was not going to call him I should have continued to make the calls from square leg. This would have left Arjuna with no option but to remove Muralitharan from the attack. However, as the tea break was nearing, I thought, perhaps naively, that I may have one last chance of resolving the matter off the field ... During the break I again spoke to ICC Referee Graham Dowling and basically pleaded with him to request that the Sri Lankan management instruct Arjuna not to bowl him again. The reason for this request was that it was obvious to me that Arjuna was not the man in charge even though he was the appointed captain on the field. It seemed clear that Arjuna took instructions from his administrators, which to me indicates a lack of on-field control. Unfortunately, the referee did not agree with my ideas about how the matter was to be resolved and he reiterated that matters such as this should be settled on the field.

That the situation was untenable should need no stating, except that it was repeated later in the tour, when Murali was called for throwing during a one-day international in Brisbane, and yet again in 1998-99, when Ross Emerson called him in a one-dayer against England in Adelaide. That three years were not enough to deal with this matter reflected poorly on most of those concerned.

The relevant law of cricket states that the umpire must be 'satisfied' that the bowler is bowling fairly. Thus, the burden of proof is on the bowler. This is the first flaw in the situation, because it should not be up to a bowler to prove to an umpire that he is bowling fairly; rather, the umpire should have to prove that he is correct in endangering a bowler's career. If this were the case, umpires such as Hair and Emerson might have taken steps to examine Murali's action more closely. To the naked eye, certainly, his action appeared strange. His right arm is bent throughout, and it twists around the vertical axis as he delivers the ball, giving it the appearance of straightening. To the naked eye, then, most of his deliveries appear illegal. This had been noted by several umpires and match referees before Hair made the decision to call Murali on the MCG. It was also the belief of many Test cricketers who had played against Murali, including the entire Australian team, that he threw.

From Hair's point of view, he was doing what an umpire should be doing - upholding the laws of cricket. Likewise Emerson. The umpire's authority is inviolate, contrary to the official solution that concerns about a bowler should be referred to the ICC. That is all very well, and Murali was referred to the ICC, which appointed a panel to assess his action. That panel did not 'clear' Murali, as was claimed by the Sri Lankans, but rather passed on a recommendation to the Sri Lankan board that Murali work on his action. The ICC had no power to compel a national board to take any action, such as omitting a bowler from its team until he straightened his action out. Moreover, it made no such recommendation to Sri Lanka, who continued to choose him.

Hair criticises the Sri Lankans for this, recalling that video footage of Murali's action had been sent to their board: 'This procedure would, of course, only be successful if the relevant home cricket board acted swiftly to ensure the player altered or modified his action to some extent. Sri Lankan authorities, however, chose to ignore the very clear alarm bells which had been rung discreetly in their direction.'

Taylor believed that it became 'almost irrelevant' whether or not Murali was bowling fairly. Indeed, this is how it began to seem to the participants. Steve Waugh wrote in his *World Cup Diary*, 'Forget whether that bowling action was legal or otherwise.' The Murali problem became one of process – how to spare the umpires and the bowler from controversy? – rather than of proof – is Murali's action legal or not? By bogging down in process, however, the issue took away the umpires' power to make decisions on the field. It is all very well to say an umpire should refer his concerns quietly to the ICC, but what if a bowler wins a Test match with a clearly illegal action? Is an umpire to stand and watch? Absolutely not. Given their beliefs, Hair and Emerson were correct and courageous in doing what they did, and deserved more support than they received from their board. Instead, Hair claimed that he was put under pressure by the 1995-96 ACB not to stir the nest any more, and in 1998-99 he was let know, through indirect channels, that it would be advisable for him to stand aside from games involving Sri Lanka. In that latter season, journalists were chastised by ACB chief executive Malcolm Speed for writing that Hair had been pressured to stand aside. Yet it was merely a matter of semantics. No, the ACB did not place any direct pressure on Hair. But yes, it was spread around through other umpires, who duly passed on the information to Hair, that his career might be endangered if he caused another furore by calling Murali. When Emerson did so, he received minimal support from the ACB, which did not select him as an international umpire the next season. Emerson sued Denis Rogers and others for defamation over comments Rogers made at the time.

The two umpires had every reason to feel they had been abandoned by their board and their colleagues. When Emerson called Murali in 1998-99, an English player approached Emerson's partner, Tony McQuillan,

I'm Taking My Bat And Ball And Going Home . . . Arjuna Ranatunga calls the boys out after Murali was no-balled. Adelaide, 1998–99. Hamish Blair/Allsport

and quipped: 'If I was in the trenches, I wouldn't want you there with me, mate.' Hair and Emerson had made what they believed to be a principled stand, yet they were isolated for doing so.

Hair felt particularly let down after a match in Perth 1995–96, during which he had queried Sri Lanka's acting captain Aravinda de Silva about the constant substitution of fieldsmen during drinks breaks. Later, Hair gave de Silva a poor-looking leg-before wicket decision, and de Silva responded by vandalising the dressing room. Hair said:

> Steve Randell and myself were in Melbourne the following Tuesday and we were summoned from the breakfast table at our hotel for an urgent meeting with Graham Halbish, the CEO of the Australian Cricket Board. On our arrival in his office, Graham Dowling joined us and our report from Perth was discussed. It was obvious Halbish and Dowling did not want us to take any action. Halbish said that while it was up to the umpires to apply the laws of the game and the ACB would always support umpires who did so, we could find ourselves "between a rock and a hard place". I then realised we may well be left out to dry with no prospect of support and that hurt me immensely.

What was never properly examined was the primary and obvious question. Perhaps it was too obvious, and slipped under everyone's guard. But really, in fact, was Murali a chucker? Even some of Murali's supporters in the Australian media believed he threw the ball, but objected to the manner of his treatment.

Was he really a chucker? Several universities, in Australia and overseas, conducted tests on Murali which showed that the double rotation of his bent arm created an optical illusion that his elbow straightened – went from partially bent to less partially bent – as he delivered the ball. These were the nearest anyone had to a sober, scientific assessment of the bowler's action.

'I'm In Charge Here' ... Arjuna Ranatunga showcases the art of gunboat diplomacy.
Clive Mason/Allsport

Yet, in cricket, these kinds of studies are invariably pooh-poohed. The common objection is that Murali might improve his action for the biomechanicists' cameras, but it will go 'bad' again under the pressure of a Test match. Hair wrote that 'it is easy to bowl legally when you know you are being filmed, but you may do something completely different when the trial is over. Sort of like driving under the speed limit when a police car is following you.' There is only one way to test this theory, which is to bring the umpires into the laboratory (actually, a cricket net) and have them call Murali for throwing. Indeed, as Hair and Emerson have said, they could have called Murali on innumerable occasions, not just the odd big-turning ball under pressure. The situation could be solved thus: Hair goes to a net practice with Murali, watches him bowl, and says, 'Yes, I would no-ball those balls.' Hair can then view the many-angled, slow-motion replays of Murali's action, which show that he has been tricked by an optical illusion. Case closed.

Alternatively, the ICC umpiring panel can view videotape of the balls on which Murali has been no-balled, and only those balls, thus making an assessment of whether the umpire has called them correctly. If the balls are illegal, the Sri Lankan selectors must then decide if they will risk a bowler who occasionally bowls no-balls. They may do so. Australia, after all, selected Paul Reiffel for nearly a decade when he never solved his problem of overstepping the popping crease! On the other hand, if the umpire has no-balled Murali unfairly on those balls, then that umpire is clearly incompetent to officiate in matches in which that bowler is playing. It does not mean the umpire is biased; simply that he is mistaken.

But cricket does not work that way. If every Australian player says Murali throws the ball, telling journalists, officials and umpires, whose naked-eye judgment concurs, then they are not going to believe any fancy university laboratory evidence to the contrary. When Richie Benaud says, as he did in commentary on a one-day game in Hobart, 'The doctor says (Murali) can't straighten his arm but at the moment of delivery it looks pretty straight to me', thousands of Australian minds are instantly made up on grounds of belief in Benaud and national arrogance (just as many Sri Lankans' minds are made up on the equally arrogant ground of supporting 'their' man). As we have seen with the bribery scandal, cricket has a dearth of men who will place the interests of the game above the interests of their nation. Administrators are home-team boosters – and the only administrators who have a non-partisan position, the ICC, are the ones who hold no real power. And then, when a controversy blows up, everyone points the finger at the ICC, saying they should act. Yet none will give the international body sufficient power to do so. It is a recurrent dead end, doomed to repeat for as long as the game is played and run by men with big egos, grand passions and more cunning than statesmanship.

Australia won the Melbourne Test convincingly, Boon making a swansong century and Steve Waugh and Gurusinha also shining with the bat. Relations between the teams were so strained by the ball-tampering and Murali affairs, however, that the one-day series interposed between the second and third Tests was a quarrel on a slow-burning fuse.

If the Sri Lankans were really going to get under the Australians' skins, it would be when they could translate their feisty self-confidence into success on the field. The arrival of an underperforming West Indian team as the third participant in the one-day series gave them that chance. Sri Lanka had been placing great emphasis on their one-day cricket, in preparation for the World Cup which they were part-hosting, and had crept up with some good results in those Asian tournaments that go largely unnoticed by the rest of the world. They were ready when they came to Australia, cruising by the West Indians in Adelaide in the first match of the pre-New Year block (Australia won the other three, plus the famous New Year's Day win over the West Indies in Sydney when Michael Bevan hit Roger Harper for four to win on the last ball). The West Indians beat Sri Lanka twice after the break, but the masterstroke came in the ninth match of the series, when the Sri Lankan selectors promoted wicket-keeper Kaluwitharana from No 7 to the top of the order for a match against Australia in Melbourne.

Kalu could boast series scores of 8, 0, 8 and 0 to that point. Chasing 213, the little right-hander ignited a 60,000 MCG crowd by launching into McDermott and Reiffel with a series of audacious off-drives played on the up. He hit 77 off 79 balls and was third out at 127 in the 24th over. Sri Lanka were able to pace their run home, winning in the 48th over. Thus was their World Cup destiny marked out on a warm Melbourne evening. The old one-day orthodoxy, of preserving early wickets and building an

Shower, Anyone? ... Shane Warne prepares to demonstrate some Aussie culcha, Old Trafford 1997. AP/AAP

Out of the shadows ... Here saluting the SCG crowd after taking 12 wickets against England, Stuart McGill eclipsed the injured Shane Warne in 1998-99. But not for long. Warne seems to know that when it comes to making decisions, he'll always have the inside running. TRENT PARKE

Diabolical Bowler, or Diabolical Umpire? ... Darrell Hair watches Murali, Melbourne 1995.
JACK ATLEY/AGE

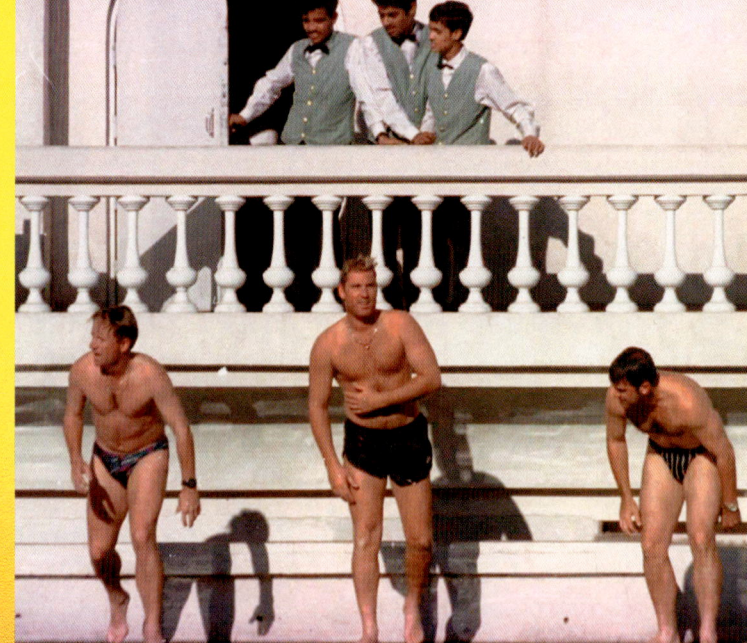

On Your Marks ... Ian Healy, Shane Warne and Mark Taylor training at the hotel pool prior to their World Cup encounter with Kenya.
VISAKHAPATNAM/REUTERS 1996.

A Kiwi Fighter ... Young Craig McMillan has always tackled Australia head on. Here he drives strongly on the up against England, Old Trafford 1999. *Patrick Eagar*

Taxi! ... Sachin Tendulkar's Man of the Series award gets a test drive from his team-mates, Sharjah 1998. India had just beaten Australia by six wickets in the final. *AP/AAP*

Free Spirit ... Relieved of the captaincy, Tendulkar was ready to tear the Australians apart in 1998. Here, in Calcutta, he clubs a six as Ian Healy looks on.
KAMAL KISHORE/REUTERS

Indian bowler Anil Kumble and wicketkeeper Nayan Mongia go up unsuccessfully against Steve Waugh in New Dehli, 1996.
Kamal Kishore/Reuters

The Run Machine ... A revealing picture of the Steve Waugh style, WACA nets 1997.
CRAIG GOLDING/SYDNEY MORNING HERALD

Pigeon Racing ... Mark Waugh, head of the department of silly sunglasses, prepares to field the ball AND place a bet on the fastest homing pigeon, Melbourne 1997.
TRENT PARKE

No, You First ... Taylor had to share the captaincy with Steve Waugh from 1997. When he came back to the Test team, Mark Taylor felt as if he had lost his ownership of the side.
TRENT PARKE

Creature from the Deep ... Photographer Trent Parke proved that Mark Taylor could talk underwater. TRENT PARKE

Last Laugh ...
Despite being caged by untold pressures, Mark Taylor tried to keep his sense of humour.
TRENT PARKE

The Establishment ... Denis Rogers leads the way for the new and 40th Australian cricket captain, Steve Waugh. Malcolm Speed brings up the rear. IAN WALDIE/REUTERS

innings, was displaced by the idea of hitting over the top in the first 15 overs, when only two fielders are allowed outside the restrictive circle. If early wickets are lost, it does not matter; the later batsmen, carrying less pressure to build the run rate, can push the ball into the gaps and keep the rate at around five an over.

Next match, coincidentally, Australia replaced an out-of-form Slater at the top of the order with Mark Waugh. Whether they knew it or not, they were beginning to mirror the new Sri Lankan style. Waugh made 130 in that game, but Sri Lanka bounced back two days later to achieve a rare win over the West Indies on the WACA. Kaluwitharana made 50 off 55 balls, his partner Sanath Jayasuriya 28 off 44. Sri Lanka had to win the final qualifier, against Australia in Melbourne, to make the finals. Despite Steve Waugh's maiden one-day century, in his 187th international, Sri Lanka hunted down Australia's 242 after Kaluwitharana again gave them a blazing start, this time hammering 74 off 69 balls. Sri Lanka had knocked the West Indies out of the finals series.

Sri Lanka could not maintain their momentum in the first final, notwithstanding a fine bowling effort to limit Australia to 201. Bevan, who this season started carving out his place as the world's best limited-overs batsman in the middle order, took his series tally to 357 runs at 178.5 with a good 59. Kaluwitharana started out in a scorch once more, but McGrath, after taking some stick, trapped him in front and the Australians ground the match home in their trademark suffocating style.

Taylor (73) and Mark Waugh (82) set up a 273 score in the second final in Sydney, but a thunderstorm during the interval delayed the resumption until 8.50pm and changed the complexion of the game. Sri Lanka's revised target was 168 runs in 25 overs – a high run rate, but a chase well suited to their slash-and-burn style. Kaluwitharana was out, again leg-before to McGrath, first ball, and Aravinda de Silva fell cheaply, but Jayasuriya and Gurusinha threw the bat so effectively that Sri Lanka were always in the hunt. Under a humid night sky, on a wet field, tempers frayed. McGrath shouldered Jayasuriya mid-pitch, provoking an ugly confrontation. The Australians fielded badly, spilling the ball under pressure, and the Sri Lankans suffered some terrible umpiring decisions, including some clearly wide balls not being called and Ruwan Kalpage being out to a McDermott full toss which was almost chest-high. On 30, and building a possibly matchwinning partnership with Tillekeratne, Ranatunga called for a runner. Healy approached him and said, 'You can't call for a runner just because you're unfit, Porky.' It was a tactic often used by Ranatunga, a clear breach of the rules, and the umpires waved off the runner, Jayasuriya. Shortly afterwards, Ranatunga convinced the umpires that he did indeed have cramps, and, against the Australians' protests, Jayasuriya was allowed on. A win hovered before Sri Lanka until Taylor reintroduced Warne, who removed Ranatunga and Kumara Dharmasena. Mark Waugh wrapped up the final with a brilliant run-out of Tillekeratne, cutting down the Sri Lankans eight runs short.

Who, Me? ... Ian Healy and Arjuna Ranatunga are equally innocent, Sydney World Series final, 1996. Steve Christo/Sydney Morning Herald

It was a dramatic and bilious match; in Steve Waugh's words, it was 'the one [he] enjoyed the least' of all his international appearances. After the game, the Sri Lankans declined Taylor's offer to shake hands and would not acknowledge Australia's receipt of the trophy. 'Our win meant nothing to me,' Waugh wrote. 'All I could think of was how little I had

Arjuna Says Hands On Heads ... Mark Taylor's offer to shake hands and be friends at the end of the 1995–96 World Series fell on deaf Sri Lankan ears.
Trent Parke

enjoyed being involved, and how sad it is when affairs reach the point where opponents can't shake hands after the contest has been won.'

The final conflagration was the sum of what had gone before. After the ball-tampering accusations in Perth, the throwing calls against Muralitharan in Melbourne and Brisbane, and a long line of umpiring decisions so poor, and so heavily weighted towards the Australians, that the Sri Lankans could only see it as persecution, the visitors had had enough. Apart from the howlers in the second final, a leg-before decision that went Steve Waugh's way and a caught-behind in Reiffel's favour in Melbourne were the most egregious of the umpiring errors. It may well be argued that these were merely temporary instances of incompetence, and the Sri Lankans should not have been complaining of bias; yet, when the same happens in the subcontinent, Australian players are equally quick to fall into a persecution mentality.

Between the acrimonious final and the third Test, to be played in Adelaide, there were attempts to smooth out the differences between the teams. Australia were due to travel to Colombo to play their first World

Cup match six weeks later, and already McDermott, Warne and coach Simpson had received death threats from the island. Reiffel recalled 'standing in a bar in Sydney that night when two Sri Lankan girls came up to me and said, "You're going to die when you get to Sri Lanka. You're going to get blown to bits." I laughed, but I have to admit that they put the wind up me. I wasn't alone.' McDermott received a letter saying his home would be bombed, and alerted the Federal Police. Darrell Hair also received death threats, and the ICC chose never to send him to umpire in Sri Lanka after 1995–96.

Three days before the Adelaide Test, the Australian team met with Denis Rogers, Graham Halbish and ACB director Des Rundle to canvass their World Cup options. A full boycott was ruled out, and when the option of boycotting just the Sri Lankan leg was raised, Halbish said: 'I'm hearing what you're saying, but if you do decide to pull out of that first game, it will take 10 years at least to rectify the situation.' Halbish said such a boycott would only inflame further the supposedly dangerous elements in Sri Lanka and entrench their dislike of the Australians.

Guarantees were sought and given. The Australians would have Head-of-State status in Sri Lanka, travelling with armed guards and protected by 24-hour security. A worldwide security firm, Group 4, was contracted to look after the Australians' safety. The players were given the following assurances:

- Separate exit and passport control at airports.
- Cars cleared from both sides of roads while team travelling on them.
- Armed guards on team bus.
- One bus for players and another for luggage.
- 24-hour security guards.
- Team to have own hotel floor, with that and floors above and below secured by guards.
- All incoming phone calls screened.
- Practice sessions supervised by security guards.

The Australian players felt better after these assurances were made, and decided to meet again towards the end of the Test match.

Taylor also ventured to build bridges. He wrote later that it was his greatest regret of that season that he didn't invite the Sri Lankans to the Australian dressing rooms during the one-day series. That, he felt, may have alleviated the tensions. There was some socialising during the Adelaide Test match, but it also became clear that Ranatunga was going to use the hostilities to his own advantage. He did not play in Adelaide, citing injury, and instead made stupid and inflammatory statements, such as: 'We are looking forward to playing Australia in our own country, before our own crowds and with neutral umpires.' The Sri Lankans may well have borne a grudge over what had happened during that Australian summer – they would have had some right to do so – but for a national captain to project these sentiments to an already overheated public was irresponsible in the extreme.

Meanwhile, ACB director Malcolm Gray went to Calcutta, for meetings at the Taj Bengal Hotel with the World Cup organising committee. He was verbally abused over Australia's moves towards a World Cup boycott, and for apparently influencing the West Indies to follow suit. The Sri Lankan board chairman, Coca-Cola executive Asa Punchihewa, tried to conciliate the Australians, but Punchihewa had little control over his own team in Australia, who issued a terse written statement rather than attend the press conference after the Adelaide Test.

The Test match was another one-sided one, Sri Lanka dropping seven catches in Australia's first innings of 9/502. Steve Waugh scored 170, and Boon, playing his last Test, was given a let-off first ball when he appeared to be caught behind. He made 43. Sri Lanka batted sturdily in both innings, Jayasuriya hitting his maiden Test hundred in the second and late replacement Sanjeewa Ranatunga, the captain's brother, eked out a 60 and a 65. McDermott was also playing what turned out to be his last Test match, and succumbed to an injury in the Sri Lankans' second innings. His first-innings dismissal of Ranatunga, caught by Steve Waugh, was the 291st and last of a grand Test cricket career.

A fractious summer had ended with something of a whimper. The big bang, however, was only days away.

World Cup, 1996

'After taking centre, I glanced around the field, checking out exactly where the Indians were, and couldn't help but notice how close the spectators seemed to be. It was as if they were all cardboard cut-outs, joined together with faces everywhere and eyes all looking straight through you. The playing arena seemed almost too small and claustrophobic, and the air had a distinct smell about it, a kind of musty incense-like aroma. The atmosphere was as thick as pea soup. This, I thought, is what it is all about.'

Steve Waugh had plenty of time to develop his writing skills during Australia's 39-day World Cup campaign. Playing cricket occupied just six of those days. Countless hours of practice, travelling and sitting in airport lounges beneath indicators displaying that most common of Indian destinations — 'Delayed' — occupied the others.

It was day 15 of the tour, 23 February, before the Australians played their first match, against Kenya in Visakhapatnam. This delay was caused in part by the threats Australian players had received from Sri Lanka during the tumultuous summer series, and partly by the suicide truck bombs that exploded in Colombo at the end of January. The Australians had, in their discussions on the penultimate night of the Adelaide Test match, voted to go ahead with the first leg of their World Cup tour, in Colombo, where they were grouped with Sri Lanka — and where Arjuna Ranatunga had talked so boastfully about looking forward to playing the Australians. But at around 11am on 31 January, a truck drove into Colombo's business district, and stopped outside the nine-storey Central Bank, disgorging a number of gunmen from the Liberation Tamil Tigers of Elam (LTTE). The gunmen started firing indiscriminately into the lunchtime crowd. The commotion brought hundreds of panicky office workers out onto the street. Minutes later, the truck, loaded with explosives, drove into the front of the bank and exploded. Eighty were killed, more than a thousand injured. The Central Bank was gutted, and buildings across and down the street, as far as 50 or 60 metres away, were ripped by shrapnel.

The hotel and business centre of Colombo is quite compact. The city's three main hotels – the Colombo Hilton, the Taj Samudra and the Lanka Oberoi – are all within a kilometre of the Central Bank. The Australian players were due, a week later, to settle into the Taj Samudra. While there, they would expect to visit the business district regularly for shopping and sightseeing. News Limited's Ron Reed, who was in Colombo when the bomb went off, put it succinctly in his report: 'If the directors of the Australian Cricket Board had been in Colombo yesterday morning to accompany me on a grim walk through the horrific aftermath of Wednesday's suicide bomb atrocity, I have no doubt they would quickly arrive at a unanimous decision. Australia must either forfeit the opening World Cup match against Sri Lanka or insist that it be moved to India or Pakistan.'

While there was no evidence that the LTTE wanted to target Australian cricketers – their spokesmen promised the contrary – and while the death threats against particular players were almost certainly a brand of bellicose, cowardly intimidation, the players' apprehension was quite understandable. Shane Warne put into words the fears of many when he said that anyone who was shopping in Colombo on the wrong day may lose his life. Warne was lambasted by the Sri Lankan sports minister, and the World Cup organising committee, PILCOM (Pakistan India Lanka Committee), withheld Australia's Cup bonus of $US200,000 for most of the next year in reprisal. World-record holder Kapil Dev angered the Australians by writing in the *Indian Express* that Australia and the West Indies 'should not only have been thrown out of the competition, they should also have been barred from playing the game for at least one year'. Yet the decision not to tour, after consultation with Australia's foreign affairs department, was a quick and easy one. The West Indies decided similarly, and Sri Lanka were awarded the points for those two games. Colombo hosted one game in the Cup, between Sri Lanka and Zimbabwe on 21 February.

With some relief, the Australians set up camp in Mumbai, where they undertook a strenuous campaign to keep themselves fit and occupied. Meanwhile, the World Cup opened with a tight match in Ahmedabad between New Zealand and England, the underdogs prevailing over an English team which was already betraying itself with a combination of inept fielding and lethargic attitude. That was a Group A match, the side of the draw through which South Africa powered undefeated, finishing ahead of Pakistan, New Zealand and England, in that order. The key match was between South Africa and Pakistan in Karachi, when Aamir Sohail's blazing 111 set up a sound target of 242 for the Proteas to chase. They did it with remarkable ease, good scores from Daryll Cullinan (65), Gary Kirsten (44), Andrew Hudson (33 off 26 balls) and Hansie Cronje (45 not out) making light of Pakistan's vaunted attack. That result meant Pakistan would play the third-placed team in Group B in the quarter-finals. With Sri Lanka certain to lead Group B, given their forfeit wins, third place and the toughest quarter-final would be decided between Australia, India and the West Indies.

Kenya were keen to throw a spanner into the normally predictable workings of World Cup group matches. Against Australia, they put up a spirited chase after Mark Waugh's 130 had given them 305 to get. In 24 overs, Kenya were 2/132, Kennedy Otieno and Maurice Odumbe crashing the bowlers around. The Kenyans had taped Australia's recent one-day games from the ESPN coverage there, and devised plans to counter each Australian. Certainly they were better prepared than their rivals, who nevertheless won by 97 runs after Bevan's Chinamen stemmed the flow. This was the unlucky McDermott's last international match. After three overs, he broke down with a torn calf muscle. As on the 1993 England tour and the 1995 West Indies tour, he was sent home to recover. This time, however, there would be no comeback.

The Kenyans took enough from the game to approach their next, against Zimbabwe in Patna, with some optimism. But rain shortened the match and Zimbabwe's dominance shortened it still further – they cruised to a five-wicket win. There was no hint of what was to happen in Pune two days later, especially when Kenya could score only 166 against Curtly Ambrose, Courtney Walsh, Ian Bishop and company. On losing the toss, Kenyan captain Maurice Odumbe even said on television: 'I think we've already lost – the game is over.'

The underlying disunity in the West Indies camp, bubbling along since Richardson's absence through 1994, suddenly exploded on the field. Only Shivnarine Chanderpaul (19) and Roger Harper (17) made double figures in a lamentable effort lasting just 35.2 overs. The winners of the first two World Cups were knocked over for 93, giving the Kenyans a memorable win over their idols. Richardson announced that he would retire after the Cup. Coach Andy Roberts and manager Wes Hall were to follow, exasperated by their inability to foster any common purpose among the players. Roland Holder told Steve Waugh at a hotel function: 'We can't go home!' Brian Lara caused a storm after the game when he visited the Kenyan dressing room and spoke words to the effect that if the West Indies had to lose to anyone, they would prefer it was to the Kenyans than to a white team like South Africa. An Indian journalist heard and reported Lara's remarks. The hypothesis, in any case, was soon to be put to the test. The result shunted the West Indians down to fourth in Group B, pitting them against the fearsome South Africans in the quarter-finals.

Pakistan's knockout rival was decided, when Australia beat India at the Wankhede Stadium in Mumbai. Mark Waugh's second straight century (a first in World Cup cricket), 126 off 135 balls, and Taylor's 59 set the platform for a solid 259, before the Indians started their reply under lights in Mumbai for the first time. This was the game Steve Waugh referred to in his diary as 'claustrophobic' – it encapsulated the very best of cricket on the subcontinent, and was a perfect antidote to the controversy and inactivity of the previous fortnight. Despite losing Ajay Jadeja, Vinod Kambli and Mohammed Azharuddin early, the Indians' innings would always revolve around the great Tendulkar, who hit 90 runs off his first 89 balls. Foreshadowing what would happen in the same city two years later, Tendulkar flat-batted his first ball from Shane Warne back over the bowler's head for a spanking boundary. At 3/143, India had the target in their sights. Tendulkar's 90th ball was a wide, curving off-spinner from Mark Waugh. Tendulkar advanced and missed. Healy stumped him as umpire Steve Dunne signalled a meaningless wide. The Australians won by 17 runs, a great relief and boost after their troubled lead-in. Steve Waugh, who, now that McDermott was gone, was the only survivor from the 1987 World Cup victory, said he sensed in this win an echo of Australia's one-run defeat of India in Mumbai in that tournament. 'Our time together tonight, coming on top of our success,' he wrote, 'has been enough to convince me that we now know we will be the World Cup winners in three weeks' time.'

The Australians could feel that they had South Africa, India and the West Indies covered, yet they feared Pakistan and certainly did not discount the Sri Lankans, who seemed to have picked up an extra gear since their Australian tour. The Kaluwitharana–Jayasuriya partnership, nascent in Australia, surged on home pitches. Aided by low bounce and small boundaries, the exhilarating openers started making a habit of scoring eight, 10, even 15 runs an over in the early stages. Against Kenya, they propelled their team to 102 runs in the first 10 overs before Aravinda de Silva's 145 firmed up a record score of 398. Against the hapless English in a quarter-final at Faisalabad, their score was 1/52 after three overs. Jayasuriya was out for 82, in an astonishing 44 balls, in the 13th over. The score was then 113 and the Sri Lankans were home. Steve Waugh, watching from Chennai, had his doubts, however: 'I still get the feeling the Sri Lankans' "slash and burn" tactics in the early overs will backfire on them sooner or later. I just hope we have the opportunity to try and achieve this in the final.'

In Bangalore, meanwhile, India was continuing its successful record against an apparently stronger northern neighbour. This was the first international between India and Pakistan on the subcontinent for seven years. Before the game there were the requisite high security and panicky forecasts of violence; after the game there were the requisite suicides and effigy-burnings in the losing country. The game leant India's way from the start, when Tendulkar played an observer's role as Navjot Singh Sidhu went on one of his rampages, scoring 93 off 115 balls. Tendulkar was first out, having contributed just 31 to an opening stand of 90. India looked set for a score around 250 or 260 until Ajay Jadeja smashed 45 off 26 balls from a tiring Pakistan attack. Waqar Younis's 10 overs conceded 67 runs, while captain Wasim Akram watched from the sidelines, apparently injured. After a swift opening stand of 84 in 10 overs, Pakistan never threatened India's 287, prompting attacks on Akram's home and accusations that he had feigned the injury because bookmakers had bribed him not to play. Evidence was given in the 1999 Pakistani judicial inquiry that Wasim had stopped the team doctor examining him. Wasim countered that he did not know the doctor in question. The doctor stated that he had given Wasim treatment over a number of years. Pakistan's run chase ground to a halt as 39-year-old Javed Miandad, playing his sixth World Cup, scored 38 off 68 balls. It was a sad end for the great batsman, who had been recalled for political rather than cricket reasons, as became painfully evident as Pakistan's hopes withered.

The action-packed quarter-finals continued in Karachi, where the resurgent West Indians made good Lara's threat and applied the chokehold to South Africa. Lara's 111 off 94 balls was one of the innings of the tournament, helping his team to 264. Still, South Africa looked certain winners at 3/186 in the 38th over. Then they collapsed to the spin bowling – or rather, slow bowling – of Jimmy Adams and Roger Harper. It would not be the first or last time Hansie Cronje's team would implode under real pressure.

On to Chennai, where Australia were playing the fourth quarter-final against New Zealand. At a pre-game meeting, when the Australians were discussing their likely dangers, they came to all-rounder Chris Harris and dismissed him. According to Paul Reiffel, they said: 'He's never made a run against us. He won't do anything. Forget him.' Harris, of course, blazed a remarkable 130 from 125 balls. Wicketkeeper-captain Lee Germon, another nondescript non-danger, made 89 from 97. The supposed threats – Nathan Astle, Chris Cairns, Steve Fleming – all failed. Steve Waugh later likened Harris to Fine Cotton, the horse at the centre of the ring-in scandal in Australian racing in the 1980s. 'If only,' he wrote, 'we could have worked out who this "Chris Harris" really was.' Fortunately for the Australians, Harris tired in the heat and humidity and New Zealand only managed 74 in their last 15 overs, for a still-challenging total of 9/286.

Mark Waugh answered Australia's crisis with his third century of the tournament. With able help all down the line, an effective pinch-hitting appearance by Warne – on the suggestion of Steve Waugh and Ian Healy – and a fine cameo from Stuart Law late in the innings, Australia made the runs with 2.1 overs to spare. 'I think the calm and clinical way we went about our task this evening even surprised most of us,' Waugh wrote, 'but it was a pleasant discovery, almost as if we ... added another dimension to our game.'

None of the four semi-finalists from the previous World Cup – Pakistan, England, South Africa, New Zealand – had qualified for the last four of this one. 'This,' Steve Waugh wrote, 'just goes to show the evenness of most of the Test-playing countries in world cricket, and also underlines the fact that no international side has been able to hold centre stage in the abbreviated game for any length of time. All teams today seem to know not only their own games well, but also how their opponents go about things. Mind you, this isn't surprising when you consider how much one-day cricket is being played. It will be interesting to see whether or not the World Cup is won by a side using conventional tactics or by improvising and unorthodox methods. Only time will tell!'

As well, the remaining teams were all from the controversy-hit Group B. Sri Lanka's dashing openers had propelled them to this stage, but were to play little part in the final two matches. In their semi-final against India at Eden Gardens, in Calcutta, Jayasuriya and Kaluwitharana were both back in the pavilion after four balls, caught identically – slashing to third man off Javagal Srinath. Azharuddin was later blamed for inviting Sri Lanka to bat first, but the Sri Lankans had thrived on chasing and certainly Azharuddin's decision looked warranted when the openers, plus Asanka Gurusinha, were gone early. Aravinda de Silva, however, was enjoying one of those periodic surges of self-belief that characterised his career, and made a wonderful counterattacking 66 off 47 balls to steady the innings. The old heads paced Sri Lanka to a competitive 251, and their innocuous-looking bowlers tightened the screws on India. Once Tendulkar was gone, stumped off Jayasuriya for 65, India succumbed limply. The riot that ended the game prematurely was only a formality, as India were well out of the running from around the 25th over.

Playing Their Final A Few Days Early ... Damien Fleming leads the Australian celebrations over the escape from the West Indies in Chandigarh, World Cup Semi-Final, 1996. Shaun Botterill/Allsport

Australia played what was, in effect, their final in Chandigarh against the West Indies. They seemed defeated twice. The first time was when they were 4/15 after nine overs of Ambrose and Bishop. Twenty runs later, Law was caught off Bishop and the game was as good as lost. But Bishop had bowled a no-ball, and Law survived to engineer a steady fightback with Bevan and Healy. Australia's 207 never looked like enough, and at 2/165, with eight overs to go, the West Indians were cruising to a regulation victory – hardly regulation, however, given their loss to Kenya just 15 days earlier. Shiv Chanderpaul played a bad shot on 80, and suddenly Harper was in at No 5. McGrath and Warne captured him and Ottis Gibson, and a mild stutter was in an inkling a major panic. Jimmy Adams and Keith Arthurton could not stay with Richie Richardson, who watched aghast as his career came to an end. The West Indies needed 10 off the last over, bowled by Fleming, and Richardson hit the first ball for four. The second hit his toe, and Ambrose called a single which he did not make. This took Richardson off strike. Taylor told Fleming to bowl a yorker at Courtney Walsh, and Fleming bowled a good length ball which hit the top of the off stump. Steve Waugh wrote that the delirious Australians were 'almost unable to comprehend what had just happened ... Flem couldn't recall his last two overs, I couldn't remember the crowd's reaction at the end'. Waugh, Reiffel and Taylor were to write that it was the greatest one-day win of their careers. It also provided the greatest obstacle to winning the final. Twice the Australians had appeared to have been knocked out of the tournament, but in Chennai and Chandigarh they had impossible escapes. By the time they arrived in Lahore for the final – after more protracted and mishandled travel – they were emotionally spent.

Sri Lanka's appearance in the final was, according to Waugh, 'a popular one with the Australian team, because we are all very keen to have a crack at them. As I think I've made clear, we haven't been impressed with the "cry baby" antics that were employed during their summer tour of Australia, where they were given cricketing lessons in all three Tests but, according to their "butter-wouldn't-melt-in-his-mouth" captain, weren't served at all well by the umpires.'

When he arrived in Lahore, Ranatunga was again the provocateur, saying Warne and the Waughs had been overrated by the press. His mastery of mind games was complete. This time, the Australians were fired up for everything except anti-climax. And that was what they got, in a final strangely devoid of atmosphere. The Australians were flattened by not being able to train the night before the final, or two days before, due to organisational hitches, and thus never discovered how heavy the dewfall was in Lahore at that time of year. It rained heavily on match morning, and Taylor told the team, mistakenly, that the match was unlikely to start on time, if at all. He and Simpson travelled to the ground at midday, to discover that the Gaddafi Stadium had drained well. They made a panicked call to the team, who were scattered around their hotel and arrived late at the ground. Preparation, on which Australian cricketers so prided themselves, let them down. They were unsettled before the match, and surprised by the subdued ground. Only about 30,000 were present for the national anthems, and the crowd was kept more than 30 metres away from the boundaries. The Australians walked off after the national anthems – or what they took to be the anthems – only to discover that the wrong one had been played for Sri Lanka. Their walk-off was taken, inevitably, as a snub.

Even with all these excuses, the balance had shifted so much since the Australian summer that the Sri Lankans would probably have beaten them in any circumstances. Taylor and Ponting batted well at the start, but Jayasuriya, Muralitharan and de Silva extracted good turn from the pitch to apply the sleeper-hold to Australia's middle order. Australia stumbled to 241 – more than they had made in Chandigarh, but the momentum was all different this time: they had not lifted themselves out of an impossible position but squandered a good one.

Still, they fired themselves up during the dinner break, only to be stalled again as the lights failed. After a brief delay, they removed the Sri Lankan openers, thus reviving their own hopes. But, as in the semi-final, Sri Lanka showed a steely middle. Gurusinha, de Silva and Ranatunga were not to be denied. Law, Fleming and Warne dropped vital catches, Healy missed a stumping, and Warne was unable to grip the dewy ball. Indeed, Warne had performed great deeds during this Cup in spite of a worsening finger injury that had kept him from practising throughout the tour. Finally, at the last hurdle, he was worn out. McGrath, Fleming and Reiffel could not step in with the heroics, and Sri Lanka won the match in third gear.

After an oddly subdued final, the crowd broke into mayhem at the conclusion. The presentation ceremony had already teetered on the shambolic, with presenter Ian Chappell shunted to one side of the podium by Prime Minister Bhutto's retinue and other dignitaries, and Taylor committing the (unwitting) faux pas of trying to shake her hand.

Slipping Away . . . Unable to grip the dewy ball, Warne bowled badly in the 1996 World Cup final, and here he drops a hot caught-and-bowled chance from Arjuna Ranatunga. Aravinda de Silva runs. Rayner/Age

Then, when Ranatunga took the Cup, the crush of fans overwhelmed the rickety podium, and it collapsed. The last pictures of the World Cup, then, were of Ranatunga on the ground, beneath a pile of fans and players – and still, a beatific smile on his face. The oversized winners' cheque was stolen, but Sri Lanka were able to return home as heroes: they had proven themselves the best one-day team in the world and had avenged their humiliation in Australia.

For Taylor's team, the final was to prove not a hiccup – which was how they read it at the time – but a prophetic turning point. Warne returned home for the finger operation that threatened his career. This would be followed by a shoulder operation two years later, and ultimately changed him from a constant to an occasional matchwinner. Australia's one-day tactics had failed, really, before the final. They relied on heart and team spirit to overcome New Zealand and the West Indies, but their Simpson-era strategy of quiet accumulation and defensive bowling was growing predictable. Sri Lanka's improvisational style had triumphed. While Australia would persist with their old ways for another year or so, still believing the World Cup final loss had been an aberration, they would eventually have to accept that their methods were outmoded. That they were able to revolutionise their approach to one-day cricket between 1997 and 1999, and emerge as winners of the next World Cup, was testimony to their adaptability, common purpose and the sheer quality of their champion players. But they would do so without Taylor, without Healy, and without Simpson, the man who had masterminded their rise from the bottom to the top of the pile in a long decade at the helm. In the 1996 winter break, the ACB rejected Simpson's re-application, replacing him with one of his own protégés, former Test opener Geoff Marsh.

The Worm Turns ... Sri Lanka gained revenge in dewy Lahore, March 1996. Trent Parke

Australia in Sri Lanka, 1996

Another bomb exploded in Colombo during the winter, killing 70 people at a railway station in July. If the Australian players had been reluctant to tour Sri Lanka during the World Cup, many were downright scared now. The ACB's first reaction was to ask the Sri Lankan board to modify the tour program from a five-week, two-Test tour into a 24-day schedule made up solely of one-day matches in Colombo.

Fearing a reprise of the World Cup boycott, the Sri Lankans obliged. A palace revolution had overturned their board of control after the World Cup, with a new group of 'young Turks', headed by plastics manufacturer Upali Dharmadasa, seizing control. The board also appointed Arjuna Ranatunga's brother, former Test batsman Dhammika, as its first full-time chief executive.

Into August, the ACB still delayed its final decision on whether to tour at all. It was soon apparent that some of the leading Australians would not go to Sri Lanka. When the Australian team went into camp in Brisbane on 15 August, Taylor was hobbling, bent almost double, with a recurrence of his back injury. It required immediate surgery. He had ruptured a disc lifting weights, ironically with the purpose of strengthening his back. Warne's spirits were high, and he ran around geeing up his teammates during a practice match at the Gabba, but he failed a test on his spinning finger, which was still healing from his off-season operation. McDermott was available to tour, but given his injuries and his past reluctance to go to Sri Lanka, after the death threats he had received a few months earlier, he was overlooked by the selectors anyway.

It was not until 16 August – four days before the leaving date – that the ACB announced the tour would go ahead, under Healy as captain. The first time an Australian captain had missed a tour since Greg Chappell in the early 1980s, this was to be a great test of Healy's leadership skills. The team in his charge was to include one surprise face. Western Australia's Bradley Hogg, a competent middle-order batsman who had turned his hand to left-arm over-the-wrist bowling during the previous summer, was taken as Warne's replacement. A fitness-conscious but painfully shy country boy, under the wing of new coach Geoff Marsh, Hogg found it hard to believe he was part of the Australian team. In the Lanka Oberoi Hotel, where the team stayed under armed guard throughout the short tour, Hogg was often left to his own devices, spending solitary hours in the restaurant and the gymnasium. Asked why he was eating alone, he said: 'I'm rooming with "Bevo", and he didn't want me hanging around.'

There were ripples of unease in the Australian team over the demanding schedule ahead. The ACB was serving them a smorgasbord of 24 Test matches and up to 57 one-day internationals on nine separate tours in the next 20 months. Michael Slater said: 'I don't know how we're going to get through it.' Slater did not, as it turned out. Perhaps thinking too far ahead of himself, he lost form during the first leg of the marathon and would be dropped within two months.

The Sri Lankans, meanwhile, were in their element. Richly rewarded for their World Cup win, Ranatunga's men were basking in the glory of now being able to parade their wares on home soil. Beating Australia again, Ranatunga said, would give his team particular pleasure. In the Lanka Oberoi, the Sri Lankan players buzzed around with mobile telephones pressed to their ears. Poolside, Ranatunga would promenade up and down the deck, eating ice creams with his wife and children while his teammates did their physical exercises in the pool. The hubris and indiscipline that would haunt the team by the time of its demise in the 1999 World Cup, and which would drag Ranatunga into disrepute, were already evident.

But in 1996 the team was playing very good cricket. In fact, the problem with the four-nation Singer World Series was that Sri Lanka were such a clear grade above their opposition that only one match, out of the seven in the tournament, was a real contest. Australia thrashed Zimbabwe by 125 runs first up, Sri Lanka beat India by nine wickets and Australia by four wickets, and both India and Sri Lanka feasted on the substandard Zimbabweans in games four and five. It was not until Australia played India at the Sinhalese Sports Club, the winner progressing to the final against Sri Lanka, that the fans witnessed a close match. Heavy rain had pushed the match back a day, to 6 September, and further delayed the start, reducing the rubber to 45 overs a side. The Australians seemed to have got out of the wrong side of bed, fielding poorly when India batted first and dropping three catches. Steve Waugh held three, however, two of them brilliant ones (of Sachin Tendulkar at point and Ajay Jadeja caught-and-bowled), as the Indians faltered to 6/89 on a seaming track. Saurav Ganguly and Sunil Joshi fought back for India, adding 100 for the seventh wicket, and the Australians lost their cool. McGrath kicked the crease and the ball in his frustration at repeated no-ball calls, and Steve Waugh argued with umpire B.C. Cooray at an unjust (in Waugh's opinion) call of a wide ball he had bowled to Ganguly. Waugh was to be reported, and given a suspended fine of 30 per cent of his match fee, for dissent and bringing the game into disrepute. It was the first disciplinary fine levied on an Australian since Taylor's first series as captain – and it happened while Taylor was at home nursing a back injury, away from the helm.

The Indians scrounged 201, but crucially failed to bat for more than 41 of their allotted 45 overs. Slater and Mark Waugh put on 50 for Australia's first wicket, but those two and Ponting were dismissed in a blur, and it was left to Steve Waugh and Stuart Law to add 113, in the stabilising fourth-wicket partnership that set up Australia's chase. Waugh was dropped early at mid-wicket by Vinod Kambli, showing that the Australians were not alone in having an off day in the field. In truth, it was a low-quality match all around. In the steamy heat, even the umpires lost their composure. Australia faltered late, losing Law and Waugh within three runs, and then nine runs later Healy was given not out on a run-out appeal, when Mohammed Azharuddin threw down the stumps from backward point. Sections of a vehemently anti-Australian crowd, seeing the replay on their television screens, started booing and hissing the decision. India's captain, Tendulkar, hearing the reaction, approached the umpires to ask them to consult the video umpire – an illegal move, but one the crowd applauded when K.T. Francis made the square sign. Healy said to his partner, Michael Bevan: 'I knew he was going to change his mind.'

Healy was ruled out, on the strength of the replay, but Bevan hoisted the Australians over the line with three balls and three wickets to spare. The Australian manager, Cam Battersby, protested the Healy run-out decision after the match.

If the Australians were not enjoying the tour, it was at least in part their own fault. Many of the players were bored and claustrophobic from being guarded in the one hotel for nearly a month. They had enjoyed

Sri Lanka on previous tours, and said they wanted to get out and see some of the country. But the high-security cordon was of their own making – they had asked for it. And when an opportunity to get out of Colombo for a day was organised, at great difficulty to the locals, only two Australian players – Steve Waugh and Glenn McGrath – obliged by taking the trip down the south coast. It was embarrassing to Australian cricket, and Australia in general, that when local delegations put on the red-carpet treatment in their beachside towns, wanting to welcome the Australians, only Waugh, McGrath and two of the support staff were there. The other players stayed by the hotel pool.

There were other security concerns. Healy was reported in the local press as having been caught trying to smuggle a Sri Lankan ex-beauty queen to his room. Healy replied that he had known the girl on previous tours and had had dinner with her and her parents that evening. If she was trying to get onto the Australian team's floor of the Lanka Oberoi, Healy said, that was none of his doing.

Healy was not having the best of tours as captain. His derogatory comments about Ranatunga, in his book *Playing for Keeps*, were widely reported in the Sri Lankan press. Many Sri Lankans saw this tour as their chance to exact revenge for the perceived unjust treatment of their boys in Australia the previous summer. Healy was jeered every time he made an appearance, and even umpire Darrell Hair was booed in absentia. Nothing was forgotten from the recent tour, and nothing was forgiven. Healy made the right diplomatic noises in public, but he did not smooth his path in private. Battersby was frustrated by Healy's lack of punctuality for official functions. At one, Healy did not even appear. Battersby's end-of-tour report on Healy was not glowing, and when, six months later, Healy was stripped of the vice-captaincy, he would point back to this Sri Lankan tour as the time when the ACB had 'marked his card'.

Yet Sri Lanka, puffed-up with World Cup victory, was at times a hostile location for Australian tourists. The sons of a local official showered water on the Australian players inside their viewing area during the game at the SSC. I had some experience of this myself. I wrote a colour story about the Premadasa Stadium in Colombo, pointing out the rustic sights of goats and dogs snuffling for scraps under the grandstand and the problems with mites during matches – twice, play was held up while men with large insecticide guns came out to spray the bugs away from the cricketers. My article was 'bounced back', or faxed from Melbourne to Dhammika Ranatunga, who did two things with it. Firstly, he protested to ACB chairman Denis Rogers, who was visiting, with chief executive Graham Halbish, for a week in the middle of the tour. Rogers called me down from my room, along with the three other touring Australian journalists, and carpeted us for obstructing his task in smoothing down diplomatic relations between the countries.

'But I will support you,' Rogers said, 'because we're all Australians here together.'

The senior journalist on the tour, *The Australian*'s Trent Bouts, said drily: 'We'd prefer that you support us because we have a free press in our country.'

The second thing Dhammika Ranatunga did with the article was give it to a local newspaper, *The Sunday Leader*. It reprinted parts of my article accompanied by its own editorial, commenting: 'Perhaps it was Jayasuriya's knock which annoyed some Australian journalists. A couple of knocks like this will keep some KNOX quieter.' What was disturbing was not the local press's attempt at humour, but the number of threatening telephone calls I received that Sunday morning. Before I asked the hotel switchboard to block incoming calls, I received about 10 of them, all anonymous, from men promising to 'get' me while I was in Colombo. Two of them remarked on my 'convict origin' – a precursor to Arjuna Ranatunga's racist comments on Australians during the 1999 World Cup. It was hard not to take the threats seriously, though some of the Australian players assured me that they were so used to death threats from Sri Lankan callers that they no longer paid them any heed. 'It's just the way they do things here,' one player said.

The tournament final was another match to be hampered by rain, but nothing could stop the Sri Lankan juggernaut. Jayasuriya and Kaluwitharana were irresistible, slaughtering the Australian new-ball attack. McGrath, Reiffel and Fleming all went for 10 runs or more an over during their first spells. Jayasuriya scored 27 off 20, Kaluwitharana 58 off 45, and de Silva an unbeaten 75 off 64 as the hosts charged to 3/234 off their 35 overs. On form, Australia would have struggled to match this score in 50 overs, and they were never a chance after Slater, Mark Waugh and Ponting all failed. To a mounting cacophony of drums, horns and high-pitched whooping, the Sri Lankan bowlers tightened their grip. Only Steve Waugh, playing his 200th one-day international, passed 50 in the Australian reply of 184. It was a one-sided finale to a one-sided tournament, concluded fittingly when Roshan Mahanama took a miraculous one-handed running, diving catch to dismiss McGrath. Aravinda de Silva had finished the tournament with 334 runs in five innings, at better than a run a ball, without once being dismissed. The Sri Lankans were World Champions in fact as much as in name. Bouts wrote, in *Wisden*, that Sri Lanka showed 'they had the depth to hold sway in one-day cricket for some time'.

New Zealand: A Minor Theme

The Pay Dispute

Tracing the history of the Australian cricketers' near-strike in late 1997 is akin to chronicling any war. It was not a single dispute. What happened in the acrimonious second half of that year was a coming together of many ongoing disputes; as such, it had no single point of origin.

In one sense, the origin went back as far as 1911–12, the only other time Australian Test cricketers had gone on strike against their board. One of the key points of conflict in that strike was the appointment of the team manager. The cricketers wanted a professional manager rather than a board member taking advantage of the opportunity for an overseas holiday. Amazingly – or perhaps not so amazingly, given the speed of board-player reforms – that same issue was one of the Australian Cricketers' Association's (ACA's) log of claims in 1997. It was not until February 1998, when former selector Steve Bernard signed a three-year contract as professional manager, that the players' request was met.

In another way, the players' dispute was about the business of cricket; in particular, the cricketers' claim on the game's burgeoning income from television rights and merchandise sales. The origins of that dispute were more recent. The exclusive Australian telecast rights, held by Kerry Packer's Nine Network, were to expire in 1998. Entrepreneur James Erskine, who was to become the cricketers' chief negotiator and, in the view of the ACB, chief antagonist, saw the opportunity to break Packer's stranglehold over cricket rights and force an auction between Nine and rival networks. The entry of the confrontational Erskine into the arena, in mid-1997, can also be seen as the dispute's starting point.

The Hatchet Man ... James Erskine saw a way to get his foot in the door of the cricket business, but was accused of being an 'imposter'. Kylie Melinda Smith/Sun Herald

On yet another level, the players' dispute evolved when a core of senior, long-term members of the Australian cricket team formed around Mark Taylor. In Allan Border's decade-long tenure, there were too few regular members of the team to build any kind of power base – they were too busy protecting their positions as cricketers – and Border was neither militant by nature nor stimulated by financial need, at least not sufficiently to start a pay revolt against the ACB. Players' associations had come and gone since Ian Chappell's time as Australian captain, but under Border they entered a long dormancy. It was only when Taylor and his key teammates – the Waugh brothers, Ian Healy and Shane Warne – each of whom had a strong awareness of their earning potential, won the Frank Worrell Trophy together in 1995 that the Australian Cricketers' Association was re-formed. Taylor telephoned Test off-spinner and chartered accountant Tim May after that tour, and May agreed to act as the players' union leader. Discontent brewed through 1995 and 1996, Steve Waugh remarking drily during the 1996 World Cup:

> The biggest winners, regardless of who triumphs out on the field, look like being PILCOM. What they will eventually profit by is anyone's guess (though some educated estimates put the figure as high as between $US50 million and $US80 million), but whatever it is, I'm pretty certain it will make the first prize cheque of $US30,000 look obscenely small, and annoying, from the players' perspective. Without us, their profit would be zero.

The ACB granted the ACA $25,000 a year to assist with secretarial costs. May, who had retired from the game in 1995–96, continued running his nightclubs in Adelaide and Melbourne, and had no pressing desire to provoke conflict with the board. Certain players whinged now and then about their money and conditions, but negotiated changes through their personal managers. The ACA might have continued in a quiet advisory role if not for the rise of important influences outside cricket.

The Union Rep ... Tim May went from spinner to spin-doctor in the players' dispute.
Dominic O'Brien/Sunday Age

Rupert Murdoch's News Limited's raid on rugby league in 1995, when it paid clubs to break away from the 87-year-old Australian Rugby League and form a separate competition, had a profound effect on the cricketers. Money was Murdoch's only leverage with league players, and the News Limited raids blew a hyperinflationary bubble into football salaries. By 1997, more than 200 league players were earning more than $100,000 a year from their sport. Rugby union turned fully professional, powered by News Limited's long-term broadcast agreement with SANZAR, the amalgamated body of the South African, New Zealand and Australian rugby unions. Competition from rugby league clubs also pushed up union players' salaries.

The cricketers saw the matter quite simply. As Taylor said, 'We're playing in a bigger national and international sport than these guys, yet we're seeing them paid a lot more than we are.' While this was not literally true about Taylor himself, who earned as much as the top league players, he was correct with regards to the overall pool of money available to cricketers. Only six or seven Australian cricketers earned more than $100,000 annually from cricket. The percentage available to cricketers from the Australian game's total revenue was also considerably lower than in other professional sports. Of course the ACB believed that the inflation of rugby league and union salaries was bound to injure, if not destroy, those sports. Nobody in football, except for the new golf-playing, property-buying class of player, argued that the wages boom was causing anything but great harm.

All these issues might have been negotiated calmly and sensibly. None was insurmountable. Certainly Taylor, May and the other ACA executive members, Steve Waugh and Shane Warne, were reasonable men whose primary consideration was cricket. They wanted a dispute no more than did the ACB.

Why then did a routine difference of opinion between employer and employee erupt into a brawl which threatened to destroy a season? How could money rupture lifelong friendships in the game? What went wrong with the management of the dispute?

A key moment at the start was in January 1997 when, without prior warning or subsequent explanation, the ACB dismissed its long-serving chief executive, Graham Halbish. An old-style sporting bureaucrat, Halbish had risen through the ranks of cricket administration, succeeding David Richards as ACB CEO when Richards left to take over the ICC's secretariat in London. A tall, bespectacled former district bowler who wore a moustache and spoke with a stentorian voice that magnified an instinctively authoritarian temperament, Halbish had for several years been perceived as a capable chief executive. He was for the most part popular with players, who saw him as a 'can-do' man who could expedite matters through a cautious and ponderous board. Certainly Halbish saw himself that way. Soon enough, the board began to grow concerned with Halbish's increasing autonomy. When Tasmania's Denis Rogers ascended to the ACB chair in 1995-96, he was soon alarmed by how much business Halbish was taking upon himself without reference to the board. Halbish saw this as the only efficient way to proceed, and past ACB chairmen had been either happy or uninterested enough to let him go on. Rogers, however, demanded ever-greater accountability from Halbish, and the two were barely on speaking terms for some weeks before the board terminated Halbish's contract and locked him out of the ACB offices in Jolimont, Melbourne. The two sides agreed on a pact of secrecy over the circumstances of the dismissal.

Four months later, Halbish resurfaced on the payroll of the ACA. May and the players reasoned that there was no greater store of information on the board's financial affairs than Graham Halbish. May lacked confidence in his own negotiating skills, and sought Halbish's advice on how to play tough with the board. Halbish was happy to be employed. Rogers, meanwhile, was enraged. In South Africa at the time, Rogers asked Taylor what was happening. Taylor told Rogers, in a conciliatory tone, that the ACA was only trying to act in its members' best interests. Rogers gathered the travelling Australian journalists in Durban's Crowne Plaza Hotel and told them that the ACB was taking legal action to prevent Halbish acting for the ACA. That action failed to eventuate, but the threat of it created a poisonous relationship between the two parties. Rogers would not deal with Halbish. For the duration of the dispute, the ACB chairman could not rise above this personal enmity. As arrogant and domineering as Halbish had been, Rogers failed to see that Australian cricket could not afford to be bogged down in a war of personalities between two officials. It was not his last failure of leadership on the issue.

Even so, the two key actors in the eventual dispute had still to enter the scene. In May 1997, Malcolm Speed and James Erskine could never have guessed that they would see out the year as the hatchet men of the ACB and ACA respectively. Speed, the chief executive of Australia's National Basketball League, had been introduced to Rogers – by Halbish, ironically – at a cricket match a year earlier. A barrister with sound academic and sporting qualifications, Speed impressed the ACB with his firm manner and experience. He became Halbish's replacement, on a handshake deal, in May 1997. Speed was left in no doubt, from the very start of his tenure, that countering the ACA's push for improved money and conditions was one of his prime tasks.

May, meanwhile, was introduced by a mutual friend to Erskine in Melbourne. Erskine had for 18 years headed the International Management Group's operations in Australia. A former medical student from Lancashire, Erskine came with a reputation for winning deals at the cost of popularity. He was a brash, oleaginous customer who promised May that he could secure unheard-of increases in the cricketers' salaries. In July 1997 Erskine formed his own company, Sports and Entertainment Limited (SEL). Soon after, he and Halbish formed SEL (Cricket) Pty Ltd, taking Halbish out of his direct employment by the ACA and protecting May's organisation from any ACB threats to withdraw its funding unless Halbish went.

In August, Erskine travelled to England to meet the touring Australian cricketers. He addressed them in a secret meeting in Canterbury, Kent. While many of the players took an instinctive dislike to Erskine's smoother-than-silk manner, he projected such confidence that they nevertheless trusted him to fight their case. His grasp of the wider entertainment–media issues, such as television and sponsorship revenues and the importance of free agency, was certainly more secure than May's or Halbish's. Under the supervision of John 'Strop' Cornell, one of the architects of Packer's World Series Cricket revolution in 1977, the ACA signed an agreement with SEL (Cricket), whereby Erskine and Halbish would collect 15 per cent of any rise they could negotiate on the players' current total income. In turn, SEL (Cricket) would bankroll the ACA for around $150,000 a year.

Rogers and Speed assumed a war footing from the moment of

Erskine's entry. Erskine raised the temperature of the debate in September by telling the *Sydney Morning Herald* that cricket had been 'undersold' and could be raising more revenue than the ACB had done. It was at this time that he first raised the prospect of competition for free-to-air television rights. Erskine had dealt with Packer in the past, as IMG head, but now he was reconciled to taking sides against the mogul. In response, the ACB argued that if cricket had been undersold, hadn't Halbish been the man doing the selling? After all, as chief executive, Halbish had negotiated the prevailing rights deal with the Nine Network that Erskine now said had been too cheap. This counterattack was another example of the ACB's preoccupation with personalities instead of issues.

As the phony war escalated, May refused to rule out strike action and the ACA began spreading details of the players' ACB contracts to the media. I was told that players such as Taylor, Steve Waugh and Warne were earning around $200,000 from the ACB, while lesser lights such as Michael Bevan were earning just $50,000. When I called the ACB to confirm these figures, the board decided to ambush the ACA by releasing, in full, details of exactly how much senior players received from the board for playing cricket. According to the ACB's release, which was front-page news around the nation, five players – Taylor, Steve Waugh, McGrath, Warne and Healy – earned around $440,000 each. A second tier of five players earned around $250,000. A third tier earned around $100,000. Rogers later claimed that this release was 'our masterstroke'. Public opinion turned hard against the cricketers. It was a blow from which they never really recovered in the course of the dispute. When the strike seemed imminent in November, television commentator and former Test captain Bill Lawry said: 'I can't understand how blokes on $400,000 can strike.' A masterstroke indeed.

The image of the cricketers as petulant millionaires persisted when Warne was photographed arriving at Victorian training in a Ferrari with Paul Reiffel. Both players threatened the News Limited photographer, Reiffel snarling, 'If Warney doesn't get you, mate, I will.'

If any doubts remained about the ACB's strategy, Rogers erased them with an incendiary speech in Melbourne. The occasion was the official season launch at the MCG. Patrick Keane, the ACB's media officer, had written Rogers a nice speech welcoming and flattering the gathered media and wishing everyone well for the coming season. Keane stood to one side as Rogers went through it. Towards the end, Keane's eyes popped out. Rogers was suddenly departing from the script, uttering veiled warnings about 'the imposter who has only self-interest at heart', and warning the Australian cricket community to shun this unnamed figure.

As ad libs go, Rogers's effort was calculated. It was a keynote digression, because it proclaimed the ACB's hardline policy for its coming negotiations with the ACA. Rogers did not believe that Halbish, or Erskine, had any legitimacy to act on the players' behalf. Rogers would maintain that stance until the end of the dispute. Persistently, he tried to drive a wedge between the players and their appointed agents. He was happy to deal with May, and with the individual players' managers, but he simply would not recognise Erskine or Halbish as anything other than opportunists whose only incentive was to provoke unrest in the game and line their own pockets.

The ACB's hardball approach was typified in the first formal meeting between the two parties, in Melbourne two and a half weeks later. When the players who were offered ACB contracts refused them, directing the ACB to the ACA, the ACB was forced to meet with May and Erskine on 21 October. As Erskine, Halbish, May, Speed, ACB director Bob Merriman and two legal advisors sat down, May handed over a 20-page document, which the ACB delegates left the room to peruse.

It was an extraordinary log of claims. Financially, the ACA wanted a pool of at least $12.5 million, rising to $17.5 million by 2000, to be split between a minimum of 24 ACB-contracted players and 120 State players. This would, however, rise if the board's 'Total Cricket Revenue' exceeded $40 million a year. If the board's gross revenues, including all cash and contract deals, were in excess of $60 million by 2000, the players' cut would be 45 per cent, or $26 million. This did not include overseas tour fees and prizemoney, which would be an added sweetener for the international players.

Other claims were:
* The ACA president (currently May) and two non-playing ACA appointees to sit on a committee, with three ACB nominees, to determine player payments and a raft of matters involving the players; if the committee was deadlocked, an independent arbitrator would be appointed by consent or, failing that, a member of the Australian Industrial Relations Commission;
* The attendance of two ACA members at every ACB meeting, and one ACA member at every State Association meeting;
* A requirement for the ACA's 'input [into] and consent' to tours and tour itineraries;
* Top-level medical cover paid for by the ACA and States;
* Free tickets for players' families and 10 members' area premium reserved tickets at every match in Australia for the ACA;
* A fee of at least $1.26 million to be paid to the ACA, increasing to as much as $10 million by 2000, calculated as 20 per cent of the increase they won for the players on present arrangements.

The ACB team returned with a hastily drafted reply, objecting to 'the right of veto to changes to the ACB's or States' business ... tours and programs', and 'the handing of fundamental decisions about the conduct and future of the game to an unknown third party outside cricket'.

Then they walked out. The meeting had lasted 28 seconds.

Outside, Speed told the media the document was 'an attack on the fundamental principles of cricket administration. What most disturbed us were several catch-all sections demanding a right of veto on areas of the board's business ... This went way beyond the proper role of a players' association. It is a massive attack on the way this sport or any other sport that I know of is administered.'

May said: 'We're extremely disappointed. [A strike] is an option. It's something no one particularly wanted to think about prior to this meeting.' He said the claim was 'a very responsible document'.

Speed said: 'We went into these meetings expecting a discussion of player welfare. Instead we received a document that goes well beyond player welfare into areas that are not the business of a players' association.'

Asked if it amounted to an attempt by the players to take over the running of the game, Speed paused before saying: 'It is an attempt by the ACA to play a role in the management of Australian cricket which is completely inappropriate.'

He chose deliberately to distinguish between 'the players' and 'the ACA'.

It was a distinction put to the test over the next few days. Concerned that the media had taken sides with the board, and that players in far-flung regions would receive a distorted impression of what had happened in Melbourne, the ACA delegates flew around the country to hold meetings with the players. NSW and Victoria were engaged in a Sheffield Shield match at North Sydney Oval, and May met with Warne, Steve Waugh, Greg Matthews, Taylor and Tony Dodemaide in Sydney. There were comical scenes as the group, led by the harlequin-trousered Matthews, ran the gauntlet of cameras and microphones in Darling Harbour, where they ate at a sports bar co-owned by Ian Healy.

Halbish and Erskine flew to Cairns, meanwhile, to meet the Queensland players, who were playing the touring New Zealanders. In a long meeting at the Tropical Gardens Motor Inn, Erskine outlined the ACA's plans and answered the players' questions. The players left after three hours, and Erskine invited the waiting media – four print journalists – to join him and Halbish, and the Queensland ACA delegate, veteran left-arm spinner Paul Jackson, in finishing off the esky of beer he had brought for the Queensland players. A long and frank discussion ensued. Halbish, who was well known to the journalists, took a quieter role as Erskine continued to sell the players' case. For all his faults, Halbish left us in no doubt of his love for cricket. In one exchange, Erskine was saying cricketers should earn comparable amounts to other artists, such as singers and rock stars. I interjected that a lot of artists – singers, rock bands, painters, writers – earned a pittance. An Australian writer

'*Rogers Won't Cop Graham*' ... *Former ACB CEO Graham Halbish leaves Sydney Airport with Tim May, October 1997. Days later, Halbish stood aside from his role as ACA negotiator.* Craig Golding/Sydney Morning Herald

the Nobel Prize, I said, yet be earning less than $20,000 a year. Halbish boomed: 'What's the Nobel Prize? Our guys are *playing cricket for Australia!*'

After a long and wearying discussion of the issues, Erskine asked the journalists to predict what would happen. My contribution was to say that nothing would move very far while Halbish remained involved as a negotiator.

'Why's that?' Erskine said.

'Because Rogers won't cop Graham.'

'That's Denis's problem.'

'Maybe, but he just won't deal with you.' Halbish nodded acknowledgment. The next day, he announced that he was standing aside as an ACA negotiator.

The ACB fulfilled its promise to make public its financial position, after an independent audit by accountants Coopers and Lybrand. Income was $54 million, almost half of it from television rights and sponsorship. Expenses came to $56.5 million, of which player payments formed $9.5 million. About 60 per cent of that went to international players, 40 per cent to State players. The cricketers' share of the revenue pool was 18 per cent. The ACA questioned some of the figures and asked why the ACB was holding $13.2 million in cash reserves, while the States held $8.3 million in the bank. Rogers replied that the administrators, as guardians of the entire sport in Australia, needed to make provisions against wet seasons and to guarantee ongoing work on cricket grounds around the country.

Stirring The Pot ... Greg Matthews lost some friends in the media during the dispute, but didn't mind having a go at interviewing Mark Taylor himself. Steve Waugh, Tony Dodemaide, and Shane Warne look on. Steve Christo/Sydney Morning Herald

The heat rose in succeeding weeks. Taylor, dropped from the Australian one-day team playing an Academy XI for its 10th anniversary match in Adelaide, travelled to Coffs Harbour to play for NSW against the New Zealanders. The Australian captain had stood aside from the rough-and-tumble, but in Coffs Harbour and then Newcastle he asserted the players' solidarity with the ACA and promised that if a strike were the only option, the players would take it. 'You might think Erskine's a bastard,' he said, 'but he's our bastard and we're behind him.' Friendships were strained and enmities deepened. At the four-day match between NSW and New Zealand in Newcastle, Greg Matthews and News Limited journalist Robert Craddock had a shouting match on the concourse of the Newcastle No 1 Sports Ground. Matthews felt Craddock had misrepresented the players' side. His outburst reflected a real worry among the ACA members – that they were losing the public relations battle. Craddock returned to his word processor and wrote a stinging item in his Sunday column, saying there were too many old spin bowlers in State cricket blocking the way for youngsters to come through, and as a result Australia had no spin bowling depth beneath Warne. Craddock's piece was directed at Matthews, but in an unintended consequence, Queensland's Jackson, a friend of Craddock, took offence and told him so. Meanwhile, Erskine tried to regain the PR initiative by going on ABC Radio in a long interview with Tim Lane. Lane gave him a torrid time, questioning his sometimes glib responses. Erskine looked rather foolish when, after criticising the ACB for not knowing how many children Steve Waugh had, or taking any interest in its players' personal welfare, he referred to Michael Bevan as 'Tony Bevan'. It was an unfortunate slip: Tony Bevan was a former Wollongong mayor who had been in the news as an accused pedophile.

Behind the scenes, the first signs of agreement between the ACB and the ACA were emerging. Journalists were becoming active players in the drama, and the war was becoming too publicly spiteful for either side's comfort. On 2 November, the ACA and the ACB agreed to refrain from commenting to the public at all. A Test match, the first of the season, was five days away and both sides felt it was in their interest to let the brawling subside and allow the players to concentrate on their cricket.

Australia won the first Test in Brisbane on the fifth day, a decisive but hard-fought victory over a New Zealand team which had lifted from its terrible tour form. The caravan moved on to Perth, where the second Test was to be played back-to-back with the first.

The dispute, however, was bubbling along. Former Test batsman Dean Jones, who had fallen out with Warne in the faction-riven

Victorian team, stated that if the top players were to go on strike, he would lead a strike-breaking team. Allan Border joked that he would play in a strike-breaking team, but there were many who took him seriously. Tasmanian David Boon said he did not like the idea of a strike, and may not obey any such call. West Australian veteran Tom Moody said his teammates would not blindly follow any eastern-States dictate; it took an emergency mission from Justin Langer, a close friend of ACA secretary Steve Waugh, to bring the West Australians into line.

Cricketers are, politically, a conservative group. With some exceptions, they tend to admire authoritarian politicians in the mould of former Victorian premier Jeff Kennett. Yet they can also, in groups, gripe and moan about their employers, the State and national associations. It's a common pastime. While Rogers and the board believed this was no more than the usual whinge – which would come to nothing – they misjudged the fraternal spirit being forged among the players. Most cricketers are happier to follow the herd, and Rogers calculated that the herd would pull back from militant action. Yet at some stage in October – probably when the ACB walked out of the first round of talks – a critical mass was reached whereby the players' mood, as a whole, came to a militant consensus. They were proud of their new association, and for the most part they believed the ACA's leaders were acting in the interests of the lowliest State players, who were having to dedicate their lives to cricket full-time while receiving pay of only $20,000 to $40,000 annually. The weak and the wavering moved into line with the hardliners. Only the crusty veterans with nothing to lose – the Joneses and the Boons – bucked the trend. (Boon had always been a pro-board soldier, even in 1988 in Pakistan when the actions of Col Egar and Bob Simpson had almost seen the Australians walk out of their tour. Boon wrote: 'I thought "C. Egar" was magnificent. Basically, he put the politics to one side and backed the players. We needed that, to have someone in authority recognise we had a case.' That, at least, was one player's point of view. Others recognised that no matter how poor the umpiring or how arrogant the local officials, the very fabric of international cricket would be torn if a white team abandoned a tour of the subcontinent.)

When a petition was passed around the country in early November, asking the players to give authority to the ACA to call a strike, nearly all 120 ACA members signed. The 'strike' matches would be Australia's one-day internationals against South Africa and New Zealand on December 4, 7 and 9, and the December 14 match with Australia A. These were all high-revenue matches in Sydney and Melbourne, the cancellation of which would hurt the board and the Nine Network profoundly.

As the signed petitions were making their way to Perth, where the Test team was gathered, one fell into the hands of the ACB. Some Victorian players accused Jones of leaking it. Speed said it had not come from Jones. Whatever its provenance, the ACB used the petition to launch a bold counterattack. Breaking the unwritten truce about not letting the dispute intrude into a Test match, Speed chose the first morning of the Perth Test to release the petition to the public.

Reiffel recalls: 'I'd been at the crease batting for about a quarter of an hour during the Second Test against New Zealand in Perth when I suddenly realised that I wasn't at all tuned into the game ... [The dispute] absorbed all the off-field hours during that match, and just about all our concentration, on and off the field. We had meetings that went all night, and when rain held up play for three hours one day, we spent that time in meetings, too. It made it extremely difficult to concentrate on the cricket. I guess I can't speak for all the guys, but I suspect that none of us had our minds fully on the game. It was quite alarming to discover myself in the middle in a Test match, but not really there at all.'

After an uproarious day, where talkback radio was flooded with public opinion, for the most part opposing a strike – and where Australia took the initiative in the Test match – Steve Waugh and Shane Warne gave a press conference. They said they would sign the strike petition, and expected all of their Test teammates to do so. Momentum for the strike seemed irresistible.

Another interesting angle emerged from that conference. Asked about the free agency provision in the ACA's log of claims, Waugh and Warne shrugged and said they did not know what free agency meant. But, as Reiffel was to reveal later, 'This was what worried the ACB from the beginning: that by demanding a form of free agency, we were giving ourselves the option of signing up with, say a Rupert Murdoch or a Kerry Packer in the event that a Super League-style competition was launched. In fact, they thought that our refusal to sign our new contracts meant that we had already been offered better money by a third party. They were convinced we had a hidden agenda. But it just wasn't true.'

At the time, the players did not quite understand why their demand for free agency panicked the board. Their ignorance of the issue confirmed the ACB in its view that Erskine, not the players, was driving the debate.

That day, 20 November 1997, was to be the pivotal moment of the dispute. By the end of the day's play, the cricketers appeared locked into action for the strike.

All along, though, a kind of Loch Ness monster had been sleeping beneath the turbulent waters of the dispute. The participants were fooling themselves if they believed Kerry Packer would stand by and allow the lynchpin of the Nine Network's summer programming to be disrupted by a strike. A few weeks earlier, Taylor had said privately that when it came to the crunch, he believed in his heart that Packer or his son James would step in and somehow keep the cricketers on the field.

The Packers' leverage on the ACB side was obvious – Nine paid the board $15 million a year for television rights – and it was equally well calculated on the players' side. When he had raided cricket in 1977, Packer had found it easy to buy players who were earning a few hundred dollars for Test matches generating hundreds of thousands. Sportsmen's loyalties, he reasoned, were always for sale when they were being underpaid. So in the mid-1990s, Nine signed the top Australian players to six-figure media contracts which required them to do very little. Sometimes they read the television news previews written for them by staff journalists, and sometimes they appeared on television specials, but often, as in Taylor's case, the cricketer picked up a huge salary for no active duties at all. Taylor, Healy, Warne, Michael Slater and, since October 1997, Steve Waugh were beneficiaries of Packer's apparent generosity.

So when the strike action became public, Packer's lieutenant in Perth, Nine's director of sports Gary Burns, invited Taylor, Waugh, Healy and Warne out for dinner. Of all the pressing matters and people surrounding them that night, these four top players had dinner with Kerry Packer's man. Hours before, Waugh and Warne had predicted the strike. Hours later, when I bumped into Burns, he said:

'I think you'll find the players will back off.'

'What did you tell them?'

'I just said how Nine would like to see the cricket go ahead as planned.'

'Was there any message from Kerry Packer?'

'Would I tell you,' Burns smiled, 'if there was?'

The next morning, 21 November, Taylor slipped out of the Australian rooms during a rain delay and met Denis Rogers. Taylor admitted he was feeling uncomfortable about the whole affair. Yes, he had been an instigator of the ACA's formation, and yes, he believed strongly that the Shield players deserved better conditions, but as Australian captain he felt a greater responsibility to the game's welfare. Rogers wanted to negotiate personally with Taylor – to raise the matter above the ugly mess into which the hatchet men had dragged it. Rogers, who never lacked a sense of the importance of his office, envisioned himself and Taylor as grand statesmen who could settle the issue man-to-man and present a peace deal.

Taylor and Rogers had a number of discussions through the day. Essentially, what Rogers was offering was a continuation of the prevailing contract schemes – a repudiation of collective bargaining and the ACA's right to act as the players' negotiating agent – but a more consultative approach to spreading resources among State players.

Taylor took the proposal to a team meeting. It was rejected. Erskine was flying to Perth to meet the players that night, and the group wanted to hear what he had to say. Taylor returned to Rogers with the news. Rogers told the public, with regret, that the deal had fallen through. At a cocktail party, Rogers gathered a group around him and said, with deep regret: 'The captain's gone. He's been rolled.'

But Rogers had miscalculated on two fronts. His first error was to think that Taylor would be able to sell the deal to his men. The second was to think Taylor's survival was tied to this peace deal. Taylor was smarter than that. While he would have liked to end the dispute, he knew he was only one of 120 or, within the team, one of 12. He had no mandate to come over the top of Waugh, Warne and Healy and the other members. So when they rejected his proposal, he shrugged his shoulders and moved on.

It was Gary Burns, not Denis Rogers or Mark Taylor, who was able to pull the strings. The 'Packer Four' changed their minds about the strike after dinner with Burns, but they wanted to follow at least a semblance of democratic process. They heard out Erskine, when he met them at the Perth Sheraton on 21 November, but at the end of a painful meeting they told him they would not strike. The ACA had no written constitution, so the votes of 100 State players did not necessarily outweigh those of the 12 Test men. The strike was called off. Essentially, not through its own crash-through-or-crash battleship diplomacy, but through Packer's intervention, the ACB had won. Now that it knew the players were not prepared to strike, the board could conduct negotiations, holding the upper hand.

Talks continued privately through December and January. At times, May and Erskine were sufficiently exasperated to utter threatening comment – and there was some talk of the players boycotting the tour of India – but the ACB softened in February, and proposals were exchanged with relative civility. While in Calcutta for their disastrous second Test match, the Australian team received their new contracts and sent them back, signed, to Melbourne.

It was 15 September before the ACB and ACA finally signed off on their new agreement. The State squads received $300,000 more from the overall pool of payments, achieving the ACA's primary aim of raising the standard wage for a first-class professional cricketer. Players in the top tier received pay cuts. Most severely affected were Taylor and Healy, whose lack of involvement in one-day international cricket deprived them of the 'double-whammy' contracts enjoyed by the Waughs, McGrath and Warne. Taylor's contract was subsequently topped up, though not to its former level, in a special grant from the ACB after he scored his 334 not out in Pakistan. The senior men also had to pay up to $80,000 each in fees to the ACA, but only Mark Waugh, effectively a non-contributor to progress during the pivotal periods of the dispute, complained publicly.

The board tried to score one last propaganda point in August by condemning the $1.5 million SEL would take over two years as its commission. Rogers and Speed had long been spinning the line that this was 'money lost from the cricket community', a reprise of the old 'impostor' insinuation. Their accusations were scarcely credible, given that they were happy to see commissions paid to the players' individual agents, not to mention the board's own payments to external service providers. Erskine and Halbish broke their partnership, Halbish forming his own promotions company, Left Field Solutions, with Dean Jones. Erskine withdrew from ACA business, and the board agreed to subsidise the ACA with a grant of $250,000.

It was true that Erskine profited financially from the dispute, but that was a matter between himself and the players, negotiated through John Cornell in England in 1997. It was none of the ACB's business. The board's last stab at Erskine typified the futile personal politics endemic to the entire dispute. From the earliest phase, participants tired of Rogers calling on them to describe Erskine as 'a failed medical student', and of Erskine saying Rogers was 'a Tasmanian public servant who never got over being able to ride in Kerry Packer's helicopter'. The protagonists' hairy-chested egomania did nothing for the players or the cricket public. The negotiators were driven by an irrational obsession with 'winning'. The dispute edified no one. Speed, in particular, was

> left in the invidious role of having to do the ACB's hard talking, being their tough guy, as his first significant job as chief executive. As a result of this introduction, most players felt alienated from the man whose day-to-day job was to run cricket. It was unfair to both sides.
>
> And unnecessary. The enduring emotion after the settlement was that much energy and money had been wasted to achieve some overdue commonsense reforms. The end result – a fairer payment scheme, more appropriate benefits to all players, a clear voice for the players' association, a more transparent board – was eminently sensible. The route there was anything but.

New Zealand in Australia 1997–98

The New Zealand tour was a disappointing minor theme of Taylor's fourth summer as captain. Since the retirement of Richard Hadlee and Martin Crowe, New Zealand had still to produce the one or two star players who could lift their overall standing in cricket. While they had beaten Pakistan in Pakistan, taking advantage of one of the Pakistanis' periodic mental seizures, and stretched Australia in the World Cup quarter-final at Chennai, New Zealand were still an acknowledged member of Test cricket's 'second division', exchanging close-fought series with Sri Lanka, Zimbabwe and England.

Steve Rixon, the former Australian wicketkeeper and NSW coach, was the dominant figure in a youthful touring party. Rixon had raised New Zealand's professionalism and fielding standards, using the excellent new cricket headquarters in Christchurch to at least lift those areas which relied less on natural talent than on application. As a result, the team, led by left-handed batsman Stephen Fleming, arrived with the air of a hardworking if limited group with the modest aim of perhaps winning a Test and making the World Series finals. There were no stars of the Hadlee or Crowe class, but the careless, headstrong tendencies that had characterised their decline in the early 1990s were now erased. Chris Cairns was playing closer to his potential, and another willful individual, keeper Adam Parore, had been brought into the fold.

'Just Win The Toss And Hope For The Best' ... Steve Rixon gives Stephen Fleming the inside info on how to beat the Australians, indoor training before the first Test in Brisbane, 1997. Greg White/Sydney Morning Herald

Their hopes were dented badly in the first fortnight of the tour. Even while Australia's cricket community squabbled, the New Zealanders failed to capitalise on it. Fleming described their innings loss to Queensland in Cairns as 'pathetic', and when they followed up with a similarly heavy defeat to NSW in Newcastle, Rixon was apoplectic, telling his team 'We can't do any worse than that.' New Zealand needed their senior players to perform at their best, but Nathan Astle was dreadfully out of form, Bryan Young not much better, and their inadequacies against spin bowling did not need Stuart MacGill's hat-trick in Newcastle for advertisement. Their only encouragements during that fortnight were the form of youngsters Daniel Vettori and Craig McMillan, and the hope that Australia would self-destruct.

Had it not been for a poor umpiring decision on the first morning in Brisbane, New Zealand may well have ambushed their hosts. Heavy rain had kept the pitch covered during the lead-up week, and Fleming's correct call of the coin unleashed his bowlers on the Australians on a typically humid, seam-friendly Gabba. Simon Doull and Geoff Allott sprayed the new ball but Cairns roared in with a wonderful four-wicket spell. Cairns's hostility earned the Australians' respect – a considerable achievement, as they had long regarded the all-rounder as a 'pussycat'. On New Zealand's 1993–94 tour of Australia, Cairns had been sledged mercilessly; so much so that he was accused quite improperly of withdrawing from the second Test match with a faked heel injury. This time, he returned the Australians' fire. Later in the season, he was to announce his arrival in the 'club' when he defended the Australian players publicly against an article which alleged that they had taunted him tastelessly about aspects of his personal life in 1993.

As Cairns announced his return as a bowling force, Australia slipped to 4/52. They could have been 5/56 had umpire V.K. Ramaswamy given Ponting out when the Tasmanian tickled a Doull delivery down the leg side. Ponting survived to add 56 with Taylor, and the New Zealand momentum was lost when Healy (68) and Reiffel (77) built on the captain's century to give Australia a first innings of 373.

Taylor refused to acknowledge that his 112 was a payment on the debt he owed his teammates. The ability to compartmentalise his thoughts, which had saved his sanity during the previous 12 months, was evident in his assessment that he was simply doing his normal job. But if some of his teammates were sick of having carried the captain in early 1997, they were grateful for his salvage effort in this innings. He batted for 313 minutes and saved Australia from a humiliating collapse. He added 117 for the sixth wicket with Healy. It was the first time that the pair had batted together in two years, and it was a partnership laden with meaning, as it had been Taylor's batting slump which, indirectly, robbed Healy of his vice-captaincy.

The out-of-form Young and Astle went quickly, but Blair Pocock (57) and Fleming (91) steered New Zealand to a competitive reply before the 21-year-old debutant McMillan (54) and Cairns (64) hit hard in the middle order. New Zealand trailed by just 24 runs when Allot was last man out. Unfortunately, the visiting bowlers had spent their powder in the first innings, and on what was a dry track by day three, the Australians were giving no second chances. Mark Waugh (17) failed again, continuing his wretched run from the Ashes series. The New Zealanders exploited his nervousness, Adam Parore murmuring: 'See the hard hands? Hard hands!' when Waugh pushed defensively at Vettori. Waugh, launching an ill-timed autobiographical book called *A Year To Remember*, quipped that he still had several months of failures to go before the selectors could drop him. The reference to Taylor's slump was only half in jest. Taylor's survival had set a new benchmark, in the minds of senior players, for tolerance of failure. This benchmark was not to be truly tested until the 1999 tour of the West Indies, when Warne appealed to the Taylor precedent to keep his place in the team after he had taken four wickets in four Test matches. Steve Waugh, the new captain, cursed the Taylor precedent but dropped Warne anyway.

New Zealand, in any case, were a spent force after their failure to penalise Australia on the first day. Australia's second innings was 6/294, Blewett hitting 12 fours in his 91. Ponting, with 73 off 85 balls, was disappointed when, feeling he was half an hour from his century, he was called in by Taylor. Five New Zealanders failed to score in their second innings 132, McGrath ignoring his worsening abdominal strain to take 5/32, including one spell of 4/4.

The tourists' performance in their next match, against Sheffield Shield laggards Victoria at Princes Park in Melbourne, was so bad that Rixon put them out in the rain on fielding drills. They lost their 20 wickets for 255 runs, Astle again a worrying double failure. Victoria were little better, but did enough to win the match by five wickets in two-and-a-half days.

Australia's internecine wars offered New Zealand their best chance of a surprise, the ACB breaking the unwritten 'Test match truce' over the strike issue by releasing a document outlining plans to strike on the first day of the second Test. McGrath withdrew, replaced by a Taylor pick, NSW right-armer Simon Cook, who had flourished since his move from Victoria. Taylor argued that while Cook may not be the next-best fast bowler going around, he had a similar style of high-arm, impact bowling to McGrath. Taylor hoped Cook would be able to exploit the cracks that had opened so alarmingly in the WACA pitch during the previous season's Test match against the West Indies. WACA curator David Crane resigned nine days before the match, leaving Adelaide's Les Burdett to oversee preparations.

With the advantage of all these factors and another won toss, New Zealand gave another pallid batting effort on the first day. Only McMillan and Cairns passed fifty, and they were all out for 217 an hour before stumps. Mark Waugh caught Cairns with a startling horizontal leap at mid-wicket, captured by a hobby photographer whose method was to follow one player for a block of overs at a time. Her good fortune was to be following Waugh, and the photograph appeared in newspapers around the world. Waugh admitted later that the catch threw a switch in his mind, and suddenly his confidence in his ability returned. The following day, he scored 86 and featured in a 153-run stand with his brother. Mark Waugh advanced to Vettori and hit one of the biggest sixes seen, a steepling on-drive that bounced on the roof of the Lillee–Marsh Stand. Local estimates put the distance of the shot at 138 metres. Healy contributed 85 and Steve Waugh 96 – his seventh Test innings to finish in the 90s – as Australia piled on a 244-run lead. The late-night meetings and brinkmanship over the pay dispute seemed only to concentrate the Australians' minds more closely on their cricket. They wrapped up the match in businesslike manner on the fourth day, Cook aiming at the cracks and taking 5/39 as Australia won by an innings and 70 runs.

Most importantly, perhaps, this otherwise forgettable match was the first Test in which floodlights were used to keep play moving during periods of bad light. The ICC had approved the measure during the year, and Fleming and Taylor agreed to play under lights if need be. Lights had been used for 21 years in limited-overs cricket, and one wonders at cricket's slowness to adopt such commonsense for Test matches. A year later, a clue to that retardation emerged when, in the same circumstances, England refused to play any part of a Test match under lights.

The Test series well lost, New Zealand showed some enterprise and form, finally, in the third match, in Hobart. Rain and a slow pitch appeared to condemn the match to stalemate, Australia scoring 400 runs in 554 minutes in their first innings, which ended on the third day. Elliott (114), Blewett (99) and Mark Waugh (81) worked hard for their runs. None played anywhere near as well as New Zealand's Matthew Horne, who gave not a chance in his 133, his maiden Test hundred. Daringly, Fleming declared 149 runs behind. For once, Taylor was made to appear negative as a captain when he batted slowly and declined to play up to New Zealand's challenge. He argued that he was not going to be suckered into giving away a contrived Test match. He was also in a sour mood over his and Healy's omission from the one-day team, announced during the Test. When he declared at 2/138 at lunch on day five, New Zealand needed 288 to win in 61 overs.

Horne and Astle blasted 72 runs in 39 minutes to reduce the one-day-style target to 216 in a very manageable 54 overs. But Reiffel staunched the flow, dismissing both openers, and Warne moved in for a familiar-looking kill. He took five wickets, including the dangerous Fleming and Cairns with clever Healy stumpings. Yet the New Zealanders, showing new resolve, held out for the final overs, Doull and O'Connor surviving a tense assault from Warne. McGrath's absence was noted, not least in the field, where Cook spilt possibly the decisive chance of the day, dropping Parore off Warne at backward square leg. Despite his five-wicket performance in Perth, Cook would be dropped after this match, almost certainly never to play Test cricket again. He suffered a broken foot the following summer when a steamroller ran over him at work, and was seen only sporadically in State cricket. The ruthlessness of international cricket was never more apparent.

New Zealand were combative during the one-day series, playing the best compressed match of the summer against South Africa in Brisbane, only losing on the last ball when Lance Klusener took an excellent running catch on the boundary. Despite their athleticism and competitive vigour, however, this New Zealand team lacked sorely in class. McMillan and Vettori showed promise for youngsters, but there was little leadership from Fleming's generation, at least in terms of solid figures. Fleming seemed a mature and capable captain, but was let down by Astle, Young and Doull. When the New Zealanders left Australia in January, Rixon was expounding the same views as when they had arrived: that they needed more hard competition, perhaps by joining the Sheffield Shield, if they were to avoid slipping permanently to the international game's second division.

India: The Last Frontier

THE FINAL FRONTIER remained unconquered while Mark Taylor was Australian captain. India was the only opponent his teams failed to beat in Test cricket. This was due to both poor preparation and political relations between the two countries, which kept India from touring Australia between 1991-92 and 1999-2000. Given India's record in Australia, it would be hard to argue against Taylor's chances of winning the Border-Gavaskar Trophy on home soil.

But as it was, Taylor took two teams to India, in 1996 and 1998, and both were beaten soundly. On the first instance, a shambolic tour left the Australians in no state to combat the Indians on a crumbler at Delhi. On the second, Australia's first full tour to India since 1986, they met a home team which, in Ian Healy's words, was the most confident and mentally strong opposition he had faced since the West Indians in their heyday. They were far better prepared than the Australian team, which was hobbled by injury and wearied by 20 months on the road, and they handed Taylor's men the worst Test match defeat an Australian team had suffered since 1938.

Yet that tour was a great learning experience for Australia, and they could attribute their historic win in Pakistan later in 1998 to the lessons they had learned in India.

While Taylor, with his 334, was a central cog in that revenge over Pakistan, he was to retire before Australia savoured a Test win over India, at home in 1999-2000. Just as he had held the World Cup, Steve

Waugh took, in the Border–Gavaskar, another trophy denied his predecessor. In so doing he reinforced the view that Mark Taylor's retirement was a speed hump, rather than a road block, in Australia's path.

Australia in India, 1996

Only three weeks separated the Australians' return from Sri Lanka and their departure for a six-week tour of India. Australia's and India's boards had endured a long period of enmity, which had resulted in no Australian Test tours there since 1986 and no Indian tours to Australia since 1991–92. The frost was seen to have thawed when, at the beginning of September 1996, the Border–Gavaskar Trophy was unveiled as the prize for Test supremacy between the two nations.

Although Taylor's back had healed enough for him to make the tour, and thus continue his unbroken Test-playing record during his captaincy, the tour was hastily prepared and poorly scheduled. A three-day match in Mumbai, against an Indian Cricket Board XI, planned to start on 3 October, was cancelled when the Indian board failed to produce a team. With only a week remaining until the Test match, the Australians flew to Delhi and caught a slow train for the 200km journey to Patiala. When they arrived at their hotel, Ricky Ponting and Steve Waugh were assigned a double room – with a double bed – and caused offence when they refused to sleep together. As if that weren't enough, it rained hard enough overnight to wash the covers away, and on 5 October, the first day, only two hours of play were possible. Several of the Australians made the most of their batting practice, Bevan scoring a century and Slater, Taylor, Ponting and Healy all making scores of more than 40. Of concern was the bowling attack, however. McGrath, Fleming and Reiffel took two wickets between them, while Mark Waugh was left to claim a career-best 6/68 with his off-spinners. The match was drawn, inevitably, and an underdone, disgruntled Australian party caught the snail-like train back to Delhi on the evening of 7 October. The slowness of this train trip was to cause Australia's infamous 'no plane, no game' threat on their 1998 tour of India. So unwilling were they to undergo what they saw as the horrors of another train journey, they would rather forfeit a match than travel that way again.

Worse news awaited them in Delhi. The Feroz Shah Kotla ground had not hosted a Test match since March 1993, and it was immediately apparent to the Australians why. The weed-strewn terraces of the small ground (capacity 25,000) were literally disintegrating before their eyes. Surveying the grey, pocked, jigsaw-cracked wicket, umpire Peter Willey said it was the worst first-day pitch he had seen and that he would take a piece of it home to England as proof of such atrocities. One Australian wondered aloud why the Indians had chosen only four spinners in their team. They ended up taking three into the match: left-arm finger-spinner Sunil Joshi, off-spinner Aashish Kapoor, and the master leg-spinner, Anil Kumble.

Struggling with all these things, the Australians also had to put up with a poorly policed dressing room. After Taylor had won the toss and decided to bat, the waiting batsmen were besieged by unauthorised visitors, both Indians and Australians, including the High Commissioner in New Delhi, Darren Gribble.

While each of the top four battled for at least 50 minutes, none was able to make the big score Australia needed. Slater was the best, with 44, but Taylor (27), Ponting (14) and Mark Waugh (26) could not build on their starts. Ultimately, their concentration failed them. Steve Waugh, who later blamed himself for watching too much of the first two sessions on a television monitor and overestimating the amount of spin in the pitch, lasted five balls before edging Kapoor. Bevan (26) and Healy (17) tried to mount a fightback, but after 73 overs Australia were out for 182, eight wickets falling to Kumble (4), Kapoor (2) and Joshi (2).

Steve Waugh was particularly agitated by his failure. He felt that Border was owed better for a trophy which bore his name. Border told him that night that if he were batting on such a pitch, he would 'play straight, occupy the crease and try to sweep'. The same night, McGrath had a drink with Ian Chappell, who said he thought McGrath had looked more batsmanlike in the first innings than Waugh had. When

McGrath saw Waugh at breakfast next morning, he gleefully relayed Chappell's opinion. Waugh was not amused.

'I said, "Fucking hell, I'll show him",' Waugh later told Greg Baum. 'For some reason, it really pissed me off that a guy could say that after I'd faced five balls. That niggled away at me for a bit. I thought, "Gee, he's taking the piss out of me after I'd faced five balls. The No 11 looked better than me! I'll bloody show him in the second innings."'

When India replied, the man to set the example was their wicket-keeper–opener Nayan Mongia. The right-handed Mongia had an unusual block-or-slog technique. He was happy to kick or bunt the ball away, with complete lack of interest, if it was outside his scoring zones. Yet when it was inside, he took a massive swipe. Mongia put his front foot outside the line of leg stump and cleared room to hit Australia's two wrist-spinners, Peter McIntyre and Brad Hogg, over mid-wicket. With Saurav Ganguly (66), Mongia saw the Indian total almost up to Australia's before the second wicket had fallen. Solid down the order, the Indians massed around Mongia's 152 (in 497 minutes) and compiled a formidable 361, a lead of 179. Brad Hogg picked up his first Test wicket, but was again left thinking he was only in the team on sufferance, while Warne's finger healed. It had been Hogg's dear desire to hear Healy give him the same sort of encouragement he gave Warne. But instead of hearing 'Bowling, Hoggy' or some such from behind the stumps, Hogg was left with a lonely silence. He bowled a reasonable 17 overs, taking Ganguly's wicket, but was dropped later, probably never to bowl in Test cricket again.

Australia's second innings started disastrously. After Taylor had scored four off Venkatesh Prasad's first over, Slater faced up to the young fast bowler David Johnson. Johnson had a wild, sprinter's run-up and a great mop of hair. Playing as the replacement for an injured Javagal Srinath, Johnson was not, in all honesty, a Test-standard opening bowler, even by India's thin standards. His first ball was a wide, outswinging half-volley. Slater cracked it straight to cover. The next ball was similar, only wider. Slater went for a repeat of the shot, edged it, and Mohammed Azharuddin pulled down a wonderful right-hander at slip. Slater, who had top-scored in the first innings, was not to play another Test match until Australia's return to India, 16 months later.

Ponting (13), Mark Waugh (23) and Taylor (37) did much as they had done in the first innings, and soon after Steve Waugh's arrival Australia were 4/78 and facing an embarrassing innings defeat. Waugh, who had watched Mongia's innings hawkishly, decided to bat, as Mongia had, with the aim of 'boring' the bowlers into putting the ball where he wanted it. Waugh decided boldly that he wanted to face as much of Kumble as possible.

'He's probably the best spinner in the world on that type of wicket, yet it was almost as if I wanted to get down his end and face him,' Waugh said. 'I didn't mind not scoring off him. I knew if I wore him down, I'd get a few loose balls eventually. I let a lot of balls go in that innings that just missed the stumps.'

Waugh had read an article by South Africa's Hansie Cronje saying that the Proteas had dealt with Kumble by treating him as a slow inswing bowler rather than a leg-spinner.

'You can see which ones he's trying to turn because he gives them a bit more air,' Waugh said. 'You play them as a leg-break or a toppie or whatever. Generally you play him as a slow-medium inswing bowler, but he's obviously better than that.'

Waugh had decided not to play the cut shot. The uneven bounce militated against it, and he was confirmed in his view when his brother was out cutting at Kumble. Steve Waugh had fretted after the first innings about the absence of his lucky red rag, which he wore in his hip pocket for every innings. It was symbolic of Australia's rushed preparation for this tour that Waugh had overlooked packing his lucky rag when he left home.

'When I got a duck in the first innings, I did think: "Well, I know the reason: I didn't bring the rag." Then I thought: "No, you're being stupid here. If you come to rely on superstitions, you're going to be in a bit of trouble, aren't you?" It's a bit of a comfort thing. If I've got that rag, I say to myself: "It's nice to have it here." But it's not going to play your shots for you.'

Basing his game around an impenetrable defence, as Mongia had, Waugh set to work frustrating the Indian bowlers. He was not content to think about saving the game. Australia were 100 runs behind, and Waugh felt that if they could make up that deficit and score another 150, they could have India under pressure in the fourth innings. He was certain he could do it, but needed a partner. It was a trademark of Australia's cricket in the Taylor years that the batsmen tried to bat in partnerships. In 1994–95, Gideon Haigh wrote: 'Greg Chappell has made the point that the Australians always aim for joint ventures: they bat in complementary styles, delegate responsibility for particular bowlers, back up and run hard.'

After Taylor was out, Michael Bevan joined Waugh. It was Australia's last realistic chance for the one big partnership. While Bevan batted in silence, Waugh offered him constant encouragement from the other end.

'Nearly every ball,' Waugh said, 'I was saying something. "Well watched." "Well played." "Remember, soft hands, cut your backlift down, just keep going." I think it's important to talk to batsmen. The fielding side encourages bowlers all the time. I don't see any reason why you can't do that when you're batting, especially with tailenders.

'A lot of the time I talk to myself in the middle. I say "Now", or "Come on", or "Concentrate". The players in close can hear it. Probably they think I'm crazy. But doing that lets them know that there's no way I'm going to give in easily. I'm going to keep fighting all the way.'

India's spinners bowled 30 of the 33 overs between tea and stumps, trying to lure Waugh into an impatient shot. He scored from 21 of 100 balls. Kumble dismissed Bevan after an hour and a half, and then had Healy stumped. Even at 6/159, with Brad Hogg coming in, Waugh was thinking about possible victory.

Hogg kicked the spinners away, and Waugh said to him between overs: 'Hope you've played a bit of soccer.'

'It's the way I play spinners,' the nervous Hogg replied. He lasted until stumps.

The next morning, Waugh packed himself a separate shirt and pair of socks for each session. He expected to bat out the day and put Australia in a winning position. Under the eerie yellow-grey light of a hazy Delhi morning – Delhi has more cars than in the rest of India combined, and commensurate air pollution – Waugh had Stuart Law imitate Kumble's style for his pre-play throwdowns, and practised the flicks to leg he would need to survive the day.

Hogg and Reiffel fell early, however, and Australia were only 12 runs ahead when McIntyre joined Waugh. Still, Waugh urged McIntyre to concentrate, saying that a lead of 100 runs may be good enough. They set targets of 10 runs at a time. As usual, Waugh let McIntyre take as much of the strike as he wanted. Waugh would be criticised at times for not protecting tailenders from the strike, but he felt that positive reinforcement gave them confidence, and conversely, that the cat-and-mouse game of farming the strike only added a complication which both batsmen could do without.

Waugh urged McIntyre to play fully forward, and they lasted together until lunch. The lead was 50. Waugh was thinking that only another 50 could put Australia in a winning position. Also, he was feeling as if he had blunted the Indian bowlers psychologically, and that there was no way they could get him out unless he threw his wicket away.

His dreams of an incredible matchwinning innings evaporated, however, 11 balls after the break. McIntyre, after batting for an energy-sapping 20 overs in 73 minutes, was trapped on his crease by B.K. Venkatesh Prasad. McGrath nicked Prasad a few minutes later, and Australia were dead, only 56 runs in the black. Waugh had played an innings which he rated one of the five best of his career – 67 not out in 273 minutes off 221 balls – but ultimately, it meant nothing. Australia did take three cheap wickets in India's second innings, including Mongia for a duck, but the match was over in an hour.

Afterwards, Geoff Marsh slammed his players' 'millionaire' approach to practice. Taylor ticked him off for his public outburst. It was the first conflict between the captain and the new coach, and also the last time for some years that Marsh was to speak so unguardedly. The team rules were quite clear now. Unlike in the Simpson era, where the coach shared authority with the captain, nowadays the captain was running the show and the coach was his assistant. Marsh learned his lesson well – sometimes too well, to the agitation of journalists who became so tired of his anodyne responses that they ceased asking him questions altogether. This was to rebound on Taylor a few months later when, during his form slump, he was unable to call on Marsh to take the fire of the constant questioning. But Taylor wanted it this way; that was his decision, and he never shirked its consequences.

Even though the Australian team knuckled down at practice, their batsmen concentrating on simulating match performance rather than entertaining the hordes of spectators with their big hitting, the Indian tour did not improve after the bad seven-wicket loss in the Test match. Australia's only point in the triangular Titan Cup series was from a rained-out match against India in Cuttack. Despite this, they were only six runs away from qualifying for the final. South Africa were so dominant in their lead-up games that Australia needed only to beat India in Mohali in the last preliminary game to nose ahead of the hosts for a match-up against the Proteas. Aided by a run-a-ball 62 from Sachin Tendulkar and 94 from Mohammed Azharuddin, India scored 289. Australia looked like winning when Bevan (40) and Slater (52) put on 86 in 71 balls for the fifth wicket, and even when it came down to the last over, Australia had a fair chance, needing six runs off six balls. Tendulkar bowled the first to Brad Hogg, and appealed unsuccessfully for lbw. Hogg, deranged by the noise and the pressure, left his crease and was run out by wicketkeeper Mongia.

India won the final when South Africa choked in a high-pressure match once again. Yet it would have been an even greater poetic injustice had Australia qualified. Their one-day tactics were looking antiquated. Taylor was batting well as sheet-anchor, but Australia were still failing to match their opponents' fast starts. Their fast bowling was a liability on the flat Indian wickets, McGrath conceding 4.62 runs an over and taking only four wickets at 53, Reiffel bowling only slightly better, and Jason Gillespie going for 5.44 runs an over and taking two wickets at 79 apiece. Healy's wicketkeeping suffered when he strained his hamstring, and Adam Gilchrist was flown out to make his international debut in Healy's place for the matches in Faridabad and Gauhati. Recognising the challenge to his cherished Australian position, Healy remained with the team and came back to play in the final match at Mohali. Yet his form had slipped enough, and his stocks as an alternative captain had fallen sufficiently on the short Sri Lankan tour, for the selectors to start questioning his place.

Only Taylor, who topped the averages and aggregates, improved his reputation on the one-day leg of the tour. His captaincy was also courageous in trying conditions, notably in the match against India in Bangalore. The crowd of around 55,000 rained bottles and other objects onto the field when Azharuddin, given out lbw to Gillespie, gave an irresponsible show of incredulity. *The Hindu* wrote: 'The Aussies played their own heroic role in this high drama. They stayed on the field when very few international teams would have risked limb and psyche by being prepared to play on in such a riotous atmosphere.' After sulking for 10 minutes, Azharuddin was persuaded to come out and walk the boundary, calming the crowd, and the match resumed. Bravely, Taylor went to the rope and fielded at deep mid-wicket, in front of the most riotous section. 'I didn't want the game called off or anything stupid like that,' he said. 'I wanted to play. But I didn't want my players hit by glass bottles either.'

Even though there was every reason for Taylor to walk off – he'd scored a century, his first in 98 limited-over internationals, and Australia were moving into a commanding position (which they surrendered when Kumble and Srinath added an unlikely 52 runs for the ninth wicket and won the game) – Taylor was again giving a conspicuous display of calm authority when it was most needed. The crowd's behaviour was dangerous, and many of Taylor's men were genuinely frightened. Unfortunately, the captain's bravery was to make no difference to crowd behaviour in the long run; all this incident did was foreshadow outbreaks of similar volatility to come, in India, Australia and the West Indies.

Australia in India, 1998

Many international cricketers love watching cricket almost as much as they love playing it. For those player-fans in the Australian touring party to India, there was no shortage of cricket to watch on satellite television in their hotels. They would return from the rigours of a day playing India or an Indian provincial team, cocoon themselves in their hotel rooms, and tune into the Test matches in South Africa, where Pakistan's team was undertaking an eventful three-Test tour. After play in the Pakistan–South Africa matches finished, Rupert Murdoch's Star TV would switch to the Caribbean to take up the start of play on each day of the series underway between England and the West Indies. Being part of a wall-to-wall international cricket feast, involving the world's six leading Test countries, and comparing their own performances with those of their rivals across the globe, preoccupied some of the Australian players. Touring life in India is seen by many as a hazardous course, and seclusion with one's television set is seen as the only alternative to being mobbed by autograph-hunters and other fans ready to put their foot into the slightest crack in the door.

By the end of their eight weeks in India, the more perceptive members of the Australian squad were able to look upon that television experience

Captain & Son ... 'How could anyone dislike me with a kid like this?' Mark Taylor with son William before leaving for India, February 1998. Mark Ray

as one which held the most instructive reasons for Australia's loss in the Test series. There was, of course, the obvious cultural alienation which more frequent tours to the subcontinent might have helped overcome. While some of the Australian players, especially Steve Waugh, engaged with Indian culture and exhorted their teammates to follow suit, many others withdrew into the lonely, bored, restless cell of their heavily fortified hotels. When frustrated with matters on the field, many of the Australians lacked the bedrock of cultural awareness that would have warned them to retain their composure.

The more profound lesson in the television story lay in what technology had done for the hosts. As Geoff Marsh observed, 'They see so much cricket here, they knew our games inside out before we even got here. They had a plan for our batsmen and our bowlers.'

Indian crowds everywhere seemed familiar with the Australians' games, from Warne and Taylor down to such lesser lights as Darren Lehmann and Paul Reiffel. They had seen every recent Australian game on television – indeed, Australia's home series of 1994–95 against England was being repeated even during this tour – and knew the tourists' strengths and weaknesses. Satellite television penetrated into every apartment block in every Indian city. Due to the satellites' inability to split the signal between receivers in high-density areas, resourceful Indians were able to rig up 30 or 40 families' television sets to a single dish, reducing the cost per family to no more than two or three dollars a month.

Their Test cricketers, who lived in a manner where such improvisations were unnecessary, made full use of their advantage. Before the Australians arrived, Indian coach Anshuman Gaekwad, captain Mohammed Azharuddin and former captain Sachin Tendulkar laid out meticulous profiles on each Australian player. Foremost in their minds, of course, was Warne, due to play his first Test series on Indian soil. The Indian brains trust observed that, without Glenn McGrath, the Australian attack would depend heavily on Warne. Their plan was to assault him from the first ball, to shake his confidence with unremitting attack. They also knew that Warne, who had missed the short tour to New Zealand, might be troubled by his sore shoulder. If this tactic of all-out aggression did not work at first, they could then reassess. But from the start, they resolved to smash Warne into submission.

Tendulkar assumed responsibility. Before the Australians arrived, he went from his home city of Mumbai to the Madras Rubber Factory cricket academy in Chennai, and went on an exclusive diet of leg-spin. Among those bowling to him was the former prodigy Laxman Sivaramakrishnan, making a comeback to first-class cricket after mysteriously losing form during his short Test career in the mid-1980s. Sivaramakrishnan had lost none of his guile, and was one of the best leg-spinners in India. Tendulkar had him bowl around the wicket, as he knew Warne would do. Then, mindful of Warne's powers on last-day pitches, Tendulkar used his own spikes to rough up the area outside leg stump. Sivaramakrishnan bowled into the rough, and Tendulkar set about destroying him.

The Australians, ensconced in the majestic Taj Mahal Hotel at the Gateway to India in Mumbai, were likewise occupied with questions of spin. They had brought three slow bowlers on tour: Warne, Stuart MacGill and journeyman NSW off-spinner Gavin Robertson. Aged 32, Robertson had been recalled after playing one Sheffield Shield match in the previous three seasons, though he had also bobbed up in one-day international cricket now and then. The theory behind Robertson's inclusion, strongly promoted by Warne, was that an attack containing two leg-spinners would lessen Warne's danger. Warne argued that the Indian batsmen were so used to spin bowling that MacGill would only accustom the right-handers to the ball turning away from the bat. As evidence, he pointed to the final Test match against South Africa in Adelaide, which South Africa had dominated, and where MacGill had taken five wickets to Warne's three. Instead, Warne argued, he needed to bowl in tandem with a tight off-spinner whose accuracy could tie batsmen down and whose variation would protect the leg-spinner's element of surprise. He wanted another Tim May. Taylor and Steve Waugh pitched strongly for Robertson, who found himself not only a surprise selection on the tour but an automatic Test pick, as he, not MacGill, was chosen for the two lead-up games to the first Test match.

MacGill may have played in the second lead-up, and applied some

Shaving, Warney ... The new vice-captain gives the reporter a good stare before deciding on the short answer or the long answer. Kandy, 1999. Mark Ray

pressure for selection, if not for what happened to Warne in the first. Playing against the Ranji Trophy champions, Mumbai, at the genteel Brabourne Stadium, with its wicker chairs and white P & O style pavilion, the Australians declared late on the first day at eight for 305. Michael Slater, back in the Test squad for the first time since October 1996, top-scored with 98. The real action, however, happened on the second day. Tendulkar, against common practice, decided not to hide from the touring bowlers and came out to assert himself. He came to the wicket at No 4, when Warne was bowling. His first ball from Warne he let run off the face of his bat to third man for a single. Former Test batsman Sanjay Manjrekar, playing his final first-class game, was his partner. Manjrekar blocked Warne away until the next over, when Tendulkar was on strike again.

What followed was a shot which rang through the Australian team's psyche for the next eight weeks. Warne pitched on Tendulkar's legs, the ball turned to off, and Tendulkar clouted the ball into a small but enthusiastic group of fans over the mid-wicket boundary.

With that shot, Tendulkar started an astonishing assault on all the Australian bowlers, but most of all on Warne, whose figures in Mumbai's 6 (declared) for 410 were 0/111 in 16 overs, his worst in first-class cricket. While taking some apparent risks, and scoring faster than a run a ball, Tendulkar still retained his wicket, declaring Mumbai's innings after he had gouged 204 runs from 192 balls. It was his first double-century at that level, a feat of concentration ominous in both intent and effect.

The Australian batting, not for the last time on this tour, appeared shell-shocked by Tendulkar's foray. They collapsed meekly for 135, five wickets falling to the left-arm spin of Nilesh Kulkarni, losing the match by 10 wickets early on the third day. It was the second recorded win by an Indian State team over a touring squad, following Karnataka's defeat of the West Indies in 1978–79. Not only that, but four of Mumbai's first XI were absent, touring Pakistan with India A.

Taylor responded calmly, assuring reporters that his men were enjoying the Indian experience and looking forward to the next match, against a Board President's XI in the eastern industrial port of Visakhapatnam. Some Australians had experience of that ground – a placid pitch and fast outfield – from their World Cup encounter with Kenya there in 1996. What they didn't expect was that having endured a 'dry' (alcohol-free) week in Mumbai, owing to voting in federal elections, they were bound for another in Visakhapatnam. The voting rotated through the States, and the dry week rotated with it, from Maharashtra to Andra Pradesh. While the Australian players appreciated the emergency supplies, officially approved if not quite legal, provided by tour sponsor Foster's, who were setting up breweries in India, their frustrations at being denied the usual comforts were mounting already.

Against this background, a psychologically shaken team needed everything to go their way. In Visakhapatnam this was not to be. The selection of local batsmen played with painful studiousness, trying cynically to bore the Australians into the red Vizag dust. Sadagopan Ramesh, V.V.S. Laxman and Hrishikesh Kanitkar, all of whom were to sparkle at international level in the next 12 months, led a numbing first innings of 4 (declared) for 329 in 517 minutes. Umpiring decisions went against the bowlers, heightening the Australians' exasperation and entrenching, in the minds of some, the feeling that the gods were against them. Moreover, Steve Waugh and Mark Taylor were down with stomach and chest complaints and Warne was still unable to make headway against the local batting. Australia's response was wildly aggressive, Slater belting 207 from 236 balls and Ricky Ponting 155 from 237. The Australians batted 13 minutes longer than the Board President's XI, and scored 238 more runs. The match fizzled out as a contest. If the Indian players were working to a strategy of sapping the Australians' enthusiasm, they were successful here.

Taylor's men came to the heaving Chidambaram Stadium in Chennai, scene of the tied Test of 1986 and the great Mark Waugh-led escape in the World Cup quarter-final against New Zealand in 1996, with little to rely on but their confidence that they would lift, as usual, for the big occasion. Their preparation, in contrast to India's meticulous work, had been uncharacteristically scratchy. Steve Waugh hadn't batted on tour, Warne had taken two wickets in two matches, and Taylor had scored six runs in his two innings in Mumbai. The backup bowling lacked spark, while MacGill languished, unwanted. In spite of Taylor's and Steve Waugh's best efforts to engage the team with local cultures, some players sat in the dressing room during the match at Visakhapatnam speculating on how many millions they would insist on as payment to play full-time in India. Only Gavin Robertson, who was still holding down his job as a manager with grocery firm Davids in Sydney, expressed any willingness to play in India for less than a million dollars a year. A lot of his teammates just didn't want to be there.

The cultural divide found focus in some players' rejection of Indian food. A group of players, among them Warne, complained to team management that they would prefer eating tinned baked beans or spaghetti to chapatis, dhal and rogan josh. One of the Australian journalists following the tour found out about the request and passed it on to his newspaper as a light-hearted story along the lines of 'Shane Warne is fading away – send beans please!' The Heinz company saw the opportunity for promotion and flew several hundred tins of baked beans and spaghetti to the team. Warne became known as 'Mister Bean' and was teased relentlessly by Indian crowds for the rest of the tour. Indicative of some Australian players' mistrust of India was not simply the fact that they preferred tinned plain food to Indian food, but that they would not even let the hotel kitchens heat their tins for them. Warne regularly dispatched his Victorian teammate Reiffel to the room of the team liaison officer to collect some tins, which they would heat up over the stove in their team common room.

Australia did lift on the first day of the Test, played on a hard-baked pitch that seemed to invite a three-spinner attack, such as India selected, rather than Australia's – Warne, Robertson, Reiffel and Kasprowicz. After Nayan Mongia and Navjot Singh Sidhu put on 122 for the first wicket, Australia reeled the hosts in, Warne dismissing Tendulkar, caught edging a big drive to slip, for four. The Australians' suspicion that Tendulkar would struggle to bat freely under Test match pressure seemed, so far, to be warranted. Warne and Robertson took four wickets each as India made 257.

Taylor and Slater saw off the Indian opening bowlers, but the magnitude of their task was put into perspective when Anil Kumble came into the attack on the half-hour. The Australians had seen little of the Bangalore leg-spinner – but had seen enough when he destroyed them in Delhi in 1996. Their tactic was to play him as if he were a medium-pace leg-cut and inswing bowler. Easier said than done, as was clear from his first ball to Slater, one that exploded off the pitch and struck the batsman on the arm. In a spell of greater consequence in the mind than on the scoreboard, Kumble bowled Slater for 11 and Steve Waugh – not offering a shot –

for 12 with an inswinging wrong'un. Only Mark Waugh (66) showed any aptitude against Kumble and his spin posse, Venkatapathy Raju and Rajesh Chauhan, as Australia slumped to 8/201.

A seeming deficit was turned around by the effervescent Healy and Robertson, who added 96 for the ninth wicket on a steamy third morning. Resisting for 257 minutes, Healy played one of the innings of his career. Robertson's 198-minute 57 was certainly the innings of his life. He was the first Australian since Gary Gilmour in 1973–74 to take four wickets and score a half-century in the first innings of his debut; but the heat, humidity and effort so drained him that hours later he was still supine and red-faced on his bed.

The late revival had given Australia a 71-run lead. They had a session to bowl at India after tea on the third day, and this was, if not recognisable at the time, the moment Taylor and Waugh would later name as the turning point in the series.

Blewett trapped Mongia for 18, prompting an outburst that left the Indian wicketkeeper-opener with a fine from ICC match referee Peter van der Merwe. Australia saw their chance, but without McGrath, Gillespie or an in-form Warne, they were unable to take it. Instead, it was India's Sidhu and Rahul Dravid who seized the day. Sidhu launched a withering assault on Warne, literally running down the wicket at the bowler and clouting him over straight-hit. The Australians tried to unsettle the Sikh with verbal tactics, but they had picked on the wrong man. Sidhu, a veteran of 15 years in and out of Test cricket, and several heated exchanges with Azharuddin, had walked out of India's tour of England in 1996, after Azharuddin humiliated him, telling him he had been dropped even as Sidhu was padding up to open the batting in a Test match. Sidhu was no weakling. He erased the deficit and created the platform on which the great Tendulkar batted the next day. To the constant din of the Tamil crowd, Tendulkar replaced Sidhu at 2/115, 44 runs ahead, and carved 155 runs off 191 balls. He hit 14 fours and four sixes in a replay of his Mumbai innings. Reiffel broke down with injury, and no bowler was spared from either the heat, the noise or the belting as India amassed 4/418 before declaring. Australia were set 348 to win, the same as India had needed in the fourth innings of the tied Test here 12 years earlier, but the target was rendered moot when Slater, Blewett and Taylor all fell in the minutes before stumps. English umpire George Sharp, standing in his first match in four months, made a series of poor decisions on the fifth morning, notably giving Ponting out lbw to Raju when the ball had not hit his leg at all, but his bat, as Australia folded to lose by 179. Still, Taylor refused to blame the umpiring: 'When you're on top, and crowding the bat, and appealing all the time, the run of the decisions always seems to go your way. It's worked for us in the past. Our problem here was that we couldn't get ourselves into that position in the first place.'

Taylor was having to balance a phlegmatic acceptance of defeat with the urgency of the situation. He might have wished to criticise his team's play, even behind closed doors, and spark them into resistance. Yet the fractious players were in no mood to be told what to do. When told that there was no flight chartered to transport the 20-strong party from Calcutta to Jamshedpur, in Bihar, for the tour match after the first Test, the Australians said: 'No plane, no game.' A special train was commissioned for a five-hour trip (against one hour in the plane), but still the Australians held firm. In the end, a 15-seat plane was found and Paul Wilson, Adam Dale and Michael Kasprowicz accompanied officials on the train. Secret arrangements between railway staff and local villagers saw to it that the train stopped through the night throughout Bihar, where hundreds of local people had come out to chant their support and catch sight of the Australian cricketers. Dale, who wanted to open his door and show his appreciation, was warned to keep it shut, or the carriage would be invaded.

Warne's shoulder, meanwhile, was showing serious signs of wear. He and physiotherapist Errol Alcott could not see eye-to-eye on its treatment. There was concern in the team at the damage Warne was doing to his shoulder, and pressure would be placed on him not to play the full complement of one-day matches in India and Sharjah after the Test series. As a marker of his sensitivity on the issue, Warne reacted irritably to these suggestions. Later, when he had had the serious surgery that followed the tour, he complained that Alcott had urged him to play when he didn't want to. Alcott disagreed, saying that Warne would not stop playing, even when cautioned about the damage he was doing himself.

Warne did rest – his only missed match of the tour – for the three-dayer against India A in Jamshedpur, home of the giant Tata steel corporation. A somnolent affair, it ended in a draw when India A reached 2/241 in their second innings. The only real highlight was the performance of MacGill, who took six wickets. It seemed surprising that when Australia were in such need of penetration with the ball, they could not find a place for MacGill in the Test team. Taylor and Waugh, while supporting Warne's theory that a second leg-spinner would dilute his threat, simply felt that MacGill was still too raw to cope with the kind of attack Tendulkar, Sidhu and Azharuddin would mete out. They felt that his confidence might not recover. Perhaps they were right. MacGill, who disagreed, cut an increasingly isolated, frustrated figure in the touring party. He tended to socialise separately from the team, and joked that he was happy to stay out of the Tests, because his six wickets in Jamshedpur left him with the best average on tour.

Thoughts of playing MacGill at Eden Gardens in Calcutta were quelled by the grassy, bouncy strip that awaited. Taylor opted for Wilson to make his debut as Kasprowicz's partner. Reiffel had a shoulder injury and Dale joined the sick list, leaving only MacGill and Wilson. What unsettled the team further was the announcement on match eve that seven of the party would be going home for the one-day series. Taylor knew already that he and Healy would be returning to Australia, but he was furious that the touring party's momentum, already so difficult to generate in India, would be upset further by such wholesale changes.

Already shaken, the Australians were fully stirred in the first over of the match. In front of 80,000 Bengalis, Javagal Srinath had Slater caught at short leg and bowled Blewett in that over. It was the first time two wickets had fallen in the first over of a Test since S.J. Snooke did it for South Africa in 1911–12. Mark Waugh and Taylor went soon after, and Steve Waugh strained his groin while battling for 80 runs. He was out when Blewett, his runner, became mixed up in a call with Robertson.

Australia's 233, feeble-looking already, was blown away on the second day when India piled on the runs. Tendulkar's 79 was almost a failure, as Sidhu (97), Laxman (95), Dravid (86) and Azharuddin (163 not out) decimated Australia's bowling. Warne resorted to bowling wide outside the off stump and hoping for a mistake as his figures blew out to 0/147 in 42 overs. India's 5/633 was more than enough. At times, Australia were at the point of calling on coach Marsh to field. When Wilson fell over in his 12th over, tearing an abdominal muscle, the injured Reiffel took his place as substitute: MacGill and Dale were ill, and only Marsh and the manager Bernard remained. The day was almost surreal as the Indians plundered the bowling at four, five, six runs an over, hour after hour. Robertson, fielding on the fence to Warne, gave a shrug and a philosophical smile. Then, remembering himself, he quipped: 'Nothing to smile about today.'

Capitulating for 181 in their second innings, Australia suffered their worst loss since Len Hutton's Test at The Oval in 1938. It ended Taylor's nine-series run without a defeat, going back to his first series against Pakistan in 1994. Significantly, this was also in the subcontinent. As *The Australian*'s Mike Coward said, 'Australia are world champions in Test cricket except in one regard – they cannot win on the subcontinent – and if they cannot win here, what sort of world champions are they really?'

Again, though, Taylor's response was calm. He felt his team was tired, and sapped by injuries. McGrath was missed and the top order was making insufficient runs to place pressure on India. One might have expected the captain to react more stridently, but such was the despondency over their cricket that Taylor felt there was little he could achieve by saying more.

Once again, however, a better indication of the feelings in the team was given by the less controllable actions of players off the field. After losing the Test match, the Australians gathered in the bar of the Taj Bengal Hotel in Calcutta to watch the pre-season Ansett Cup final of Australian rules football, played between North Melbourne and St Kilda. The Australian players, together with some Indian players and various other supporters, had a typical post-Test match night of drinking in the bar. Ricky Ponting, who supported North Melbourne, won a bet with St

Kilda supporter Warne over the result of the match. Afterwards, Ponting and some Australian followers were invited to a local nightclub. Like many in India, the Equinox club at the Peerless Inn Hotel was meant to be for couples only. An exception was made for Ponting and his mates, because they were the guests of Indian cricketers. Already well oiled from watching the football, Ponting drank more and allegedly made some unwelcome advances to a number of women. He denied having done so, but in his book *Punter* he later wrote that he had had so much to drink, he didn't recall very clearly what he had done. His advances and some unsavoury gestures led to his being ejected by security staff. He tried to return to collect a cap he had left behind, and was involved in another scuffle.

Ponting revealed none of this to his teammates the next day, when they rested in Calcutta. His scuffles only became known during the dawn flight from Calcutta to Bangalore another day later, when journalists showed the front page of a local paper, reporting the incident, to manager Steve Bernard. Shocked, Bernard sequestered Ponting with tour director

I Have A Problem . . . Ricky Ponting finally faces the press, MCG, January 1999. Mark Dadswell/Allsport

Rock & Roll . . . By now deeply suspicious of anything Indian, the tourists supervised pitch preparation for the third Test in Bangalore. Shaun Botterill/Allsport

Cam Battersby and Taylor at the Taj West End Hotel in Bangalore. Ponting admitted to the scuffles but denied having provoked them in the alleged manner. Bernard and Battersby acted promptly, fining and cautioning Ponting. Yet the story was so preposterous – an Australian Test cricketer being beaten up by security guards for no reason – that the Australian journalists on tour were under pressure from their home offices to flesh out the real story. I was able to contact witnesses from the nightclub, who reaffirmed that Ponting had tried to grope a woman, had shouldered another, and had made gestures with the fly of his trousers. It was behaviour that had clear similarities with that for which Ponting was again caught, in the Bourbon and Beefsteak Bar in Sydney's Kings Cross, a few months later. The pattern was evident, and Ponting would finally admit that he had to do something about it.

The incident probably helped the Australians unite for the third Test match. Tendulkar again flayed them in the first innings, blasting 177 from 207 balls, and Sidhu made 74. But India's total of 424 was disappointing. Slater, his position again on the line, went all-or-nothing in Australia's reply and hit 91 off 117 balls. Darren Lehmann, finally making his debut, 10,000 first-class runs and nine years after his appearance as 12th man in a Test match in Sydney as a 19-year-old, scored a fluent 52 as Steve Waugh's replacement at No 6. It was Mark Waugh's turn to suffer from the gastric complaint making its way through the team, but he responded with one of his finest innings, an unbeaten 153. Without the injured Srinath, India's pacemen posed little threat, but even so, Waugh's batting, in extreme heat and showing constant physical distress, was a treat. Kasprowicz then stepped up in the Indian second innings and ripped out five wickets, including Tendulkar and Azharuddin, as India collapsed for 169. Taylor, also in danger of losing his position, hit a sweet unbeaten century as Australia chased and caught the 194-run target with ease. It was their first Test match win on the mainland subcontinent since 1969, a morsel of consolation for the startling defeats in Chennai and Calcutta.

More important in the development of this team was the role this tour played in laying groundwork for the successes that followed. Even though many had found India a difficult and disagreeable country to tour, Australia's Test players finished the tour unanimous in the wish that they play more often on the subcontinent. Such was their improvement from the first to the third Test matches, that some believed Australia would have won a five-Test series. The fruits of their experience were to ripen six months later when they returned to south Asia on their tour of Pakistan. It was as if in order to come back and beat Pakistan, they needed first to lose in India.

Australia's one-day team also gained much from the 10 matches they played in India and then Sharjah. The 11 players who tussled with India in the finals of both tournaments were substantially the same 11 who contested the final three games of the winning World Cup campaign two years later. The only different personnel were McGrath and Reiffel, who were out in 1998 with injury.

Playing in barely tolerable heat and humidity in Kochi and Ahmedabad, and dodging missiles from the crowd in Kochi, the Australians built the team spirit and combinations that were to bear such dramatic fruit in England in 1999. So bad was the heat in Kochi, in a soccer stadium holding around 80,000 fans, that Kasprowicz had to leave the field with breathing difficulties and Damien Martyn was throwing up in the dressing room before batting at No 8. Darren Lehmann expressed a deep overall frustration when, after losing his wicket, he ranted about 'This shithole of a place!' as he removed his pads. But after losing to India in Kochi and Kanpur, Australia won the final in Delhi, thus entrenching their belief that in one-day cricket they could win the matches that really counted. The nucleus of their World Cup campaign – a fast-starting batting order, a steady, clever middle, and a bowling attack of pace and leg-spin – was set during this period.

The campaign did, however, have an immediate cost. Warne, already fighting the pain of his worn right shoulder, dived on it attempting a catch in the game against Zimbabwe at Delhi. He injured his rotator cuff and could not move his arm after play. Yet he picked himself up to contribute to the final, also at Delhi, and then to a five-match series in Sharjah. It was only when he returned to Melbourne that he realised how close he had been to damaging the shoulder permanently. He underwent serious surgery a week after his arrival home, and announced that he was to miss up to a year's cricket. In a symmetrical turn of fate, his absence was to open the way for the unlucky, 'invisible' man of the Indian tour. Stuart MacGill was about to burst into Test cricket. Briefly.

India in Australia, 1999–2000

By the turn of the century, Australia's gilded age in Test and one-day cricket had reached its apotheosis. As World Cup champions, they carried an air of invincibility into their home Test series with Pakistan and India. The latter encounter, fought out in Adelaide, Melbourne and Sydney, only highlighted what a different game Test cricket is when played at home. The Indians, so confident on their home turf, had a timidity about them on foreign soil that was hard to fathom. They had won just one away Test match in 13 years, against Sri Lanka in Colombo. By contrast, they were nearly unbeatable in India, as Australia had found.

This was not a one-off situation; it could be seen in other Test matches around the globe being played contemporaneously with the Australia–India series. The West Indies, who had only lost once at home in 27 years, were being humiliated by New Zealand in New Zealand. South Africa completed a run of 10 consecutive Test wins, all at home, with their massacre of England in Johannesburg in December 1999.

All teams struggled away from home, and all prospered on their own turf, except the recognised second-rank teams such as England and Zimbabwe. Even Australia, so powerful in the last decade of the 20th century, had an inconsistent record away from home. They had lost in Sri Lanka and India (twice), and drawn in the West Indies. So rare are away wins in Test series, however, that their defeats of Pakistan in Pakistan in 1998, South Africa in South Africa in 1997 and the West Indies in the West Indies in 1995 were what placed them above the ruck. Australia didn't have a great record overseas; it was simply that everyone else had a terrible one.

The Indians, Dr Jekylls at home, turned into Mr Hydes on tour. They lost their first match to Queensland, but showed some resilience to defeat a very poor NSW team at the SCG. Characteristically, they felt hard done by with regard to Australian umpiring. One of the reasons they had not toured Australia since 1991-92 was because of the dreadful decisions, nearly all in the home team's favour, that they suffered then. In the NSW match, umpire Darrell Hair clashed with stand-in captain Sourav Ganguly over the Indians' tendency to watch big-screen replays of contentious decisions, and then continue the protest. Just as the Australians had done in India, the Indians in Australia started to have the look of a team convinced in its own bad luck.

This conviction intensified during the first Test, in Adelaide. Tendulkar had reached 62 in the first innings in ominous style when Australian umpire Daryl Harper gave him out, caught at short leg off Warne, when the ball had hit only the pad, not the bat. In the second innings, Harper gave Tendulkar out for a duck, this time when the Indian master ducked into a McGrath bouncer. It was an unusual mode of dismissal, but side-on replays suggested Harper was correct, and the ball would not have passed over the bails. So Tendulkar got a bad one and a fair one. Nonetheless, the Indian players and media were sure that they had been robbed by local umpires, much as the Australians had felt in Chennai in 1998.

Low Blow . . . McGrath traps Tendulkar with the contentious bouncer, Adelaide 1999.
Ray Kennedy/Age

It was pointed out that India lost the game convincingly. Recovering from the loss of four early wickets on day one, Steve Waugh and Ponting scored centuries and Warne 86 as Australia piled up a big first innings. Tendulkar's and Ganguly's sixties were India's response, but Warne produced sustained accurate spells in both innings to soften the Indians up. McGrath and Fleming, with some accurate and intimidating pace bowling that showed up some of the Indians' frailties on bouncy wickets, mopped up in the second innings.

On the other hand, who is to say that the one umpiring decision against Tendulkar in the first innings did not change destiny? In Trinidad earlier in 1999, the West Indies had been thrashed after Brian Lara was given a poor decision in his sixties in the first innings. After the game, with the West Indies dismissed for 51 second time around, there was no suggestion that if Lara had been given the benefit of the doubt in the first innings, the West Indies might have turned the game around. Australia were unbeatable, weren't they? Yet in the next two Test matches, Lara showed that, on his game, he could beat the Australians single-handed. When such players are involved, there is no such thing as destiny or an inevitability of results.

Tendulkar scored a century in the second Test, in Melbourne, but again only Ganguly offered him notable support. Their top order was a shadow of what it had been in India 18 months previously. Sidhu, the key man, was gone, and the openers now were Sadagopan Ramesh and V.V.S. Laxman, silky strokemakers whose defensive techniques were unsuited to the challenges of Australian wickets. Rahul Dravid, so commanding at No 3 in India, seemed tied up inside himself with overly fierce concentration, and made little contribution when it mattered. Down the order, the omission of Mohammed Azharuddin had left India one top-class batsman short at No 5 or No 6. And in their bowling, the persistence of Srinath and Prasad was of limited influence because the Australians were playing Kumble much better at home than they had played him away. He had demoralised them in India, takng 32 wickets in four Tests, but on Australian wickets Kumble was unable to turn the ball significantly away from the bat. This allowed the Australians to play him as a slowish inswing bowler. He did extract some bounce, but not with the surprise effect he had enjoyed at home. When the Australians introduced a new young fast bowler, Brett Lee, in the last Test of 1999, India were outgunned. Lee bowled Ramesh with his fourth ball in Test cricket, becoming the first Australian to snare a wicket in his first over since leg-spinner Tony Mann in 1977-78, and took five on the day. He was selected again in the next Test, the dead rubber in Sydney, and took another four wickets on the first day. With McGrath and the unlucky Fleming, he routed the Indians in the first innings. Australia killed the contest in what was now a routine manner, piling up 5/552 in their first innings, Langer scoring a streaky but merciless 223 and Ponting an unbeaten 141. Kumble was ineffective on the former spinners' paradise; it found Warne in the same boat. For the first time, Warne played a Sydney Test match without taking a wicket. Partly this could be attributed to the improved pitch, partly to the Indians' fear of Lee's pace and McGrath's aggression, and partly to the wear Warne was suffering after some heavy bowling stints earlier in the summer.

Nonetheless, Australia strolled home to win by an innings, their seventh straight victory. It seemed, for the moment at least, that everything they touched would turn to gold.

Two Teams or One?

TAYLOR'S DIPLOMACY AND leadership skills, largely responsible for his keeping his job during 1997, let him down in the heat and strain of his last days in India in 1998. For once, he made a curious and ill-considered public statement. It was in the bowels of the Chidambaram Stadium in Bangalore, minutes after he had come off the field, his unbeaten century lifting Australia to their only first-class win of the tour and their first Test win in India since 1969. But his ongoing omission from one-day cricket since late 1997 was still eating him away. Like Healy, who was still saying he would vie for selection in the one-day team until he retired, Taylor yearned for reinstatement. In part, he still believed he could perform as a limited-overs opener, despite the success of Mark Waugh and Adam Gilchrist in partnership at the top. But of more concern to Taylor was the effect of having two national captains, a split which he felt detracted from the prestige of the office. Moreover, he felt the announcement of the seven changes to the Indian touring team, made on the eve of the second Test in Calcutta, had contributed to Australia's record defeat there. So in Bangalore, he gathered the five touring Australian journalists and said: 'We have to look at the set-up of Australian cricket. I don't think this is a settling process, having two different teams and different captains.'

It was the nearest Taylor ever came to a public tantrum. Certainly he was not in the habit of trying to dictate policy in public, but his exasperation with the situation prompted him to call for meetings with selectors, ACB officials and players during the off-season, to work out a more cohesive plan for the future.

He even said that stepping down from the Test captaincy, to play under

Steve Waugh's unified captaincy, was 'definitely a possibility'.

'I haven't ruled out still playing and not being captain. That's a possibility. I'm not saying I'd do that, but it's something to discuss. I've got to understand where other people are coming from. I don't make all the decisions in Australian cricket. I make less now than I did a year ago, when I was captain of both sides. I think that feeling has gone through the side. There are too many people who are not really sure where they're going at the moment in Australian cricket.'

He admitted he would find it strange playing Test cricket under another captain. Asked if he would feel comfortable, he said: 'I don't really know. You get a sense of ownership of the team, I suppose, having been captain for four years. I don't know how I'd go.'

There were recent precedents for an Australian captain to stand aside in this manner. After five years as captain, Ian Chappell played under his brother Greg in 1975–76 and 1979–80. And Greg Chappell played his last Australian summer under the captaincy of Kim Hughes, having led Australia from 1975–77 and 1979–83.

How serious was Taylor? His words renewed discussion of the so-called 'two teams' policy in Australia, with *The Australian*'s Mike Coward leading the lobby to remove what he described as the 'wedge' between the two teams. That night, Taylor and the team held their end-of-tour party at the Taj West End Hotel in Bangalore, at which they levied fines on players for various misdemeanours. Had they known of Taylor's words being transmitted back to the Australian players while they partied, they might have agreed to fine him personally.

His comments only became known a day later, after he and the Test-only players had flown to Australia and the one-day team had gone on to Kochi, in the southern province of Kerala. Once there, Steve Waugh and Geoff Marsh seethed over Taylor's comments. They felt he had undermined their difficult task in keeping their players 'up' for the remaining four weeks in India and Sharjah. Particularly hurtful was his remark about 'ownership'. Marsh reacted strongly, saying: 'Mark Taylor's got to accept that he's not going to play any more one-day cricket for Australia.'

It was the nearest the leadership had come to a real rift since the dark days of Taylor's slump. In the end, and this was unusual for any of Taylor's gambits, it was also futile. Malcolm Speed called Taylor and Waugh together in Melbourne during the following winter, they agreed that certain statements had been made in the heat and frustration of an arduous tour, and they emerged to tell the public that Taylor would play on as Test captain, Waugh as one-day captain, and they were one happy family again. Taylor's pressure had come to nothing.

'Some people thought I was heavy-handed,' he wrote later, 'forcing the issue too hard for personal reasons. It wasn't that. I was trying to do what I thought was best for Australian cricket. The Melbourne meeting cleared the air and I think all of us walked out of it reasonably happy ...

'... I found the situation of being in one Australian team and out of the other slightly embarrassing ... Suddenly, at a certain time of the cricket season, I became the disappearing man. It was demeaning. I was supposed to be a senior player, a senior figure in Australian cricket, yet I was rated not good enough to play one form of the game. My attitude was quite simple: that I didn't think the captain should be out of the team half the time. Yes, it hurt. I can say that now.'

A philosophical difference underpinned the argument. Taylor felt that the change of captains indicated that Australia were treating one-day and Test cricket as fundamentally different games. He saw a future where youngsters were to be streamed into one-day or longer cricket from their teens, and where the two Australian teams would have no common players. He didn't like the idea. Waugh, on the other hand, believed that the two games were essentially variants on the same code, and that there were no barriers to one player excelling in both. He could point to himself, his brother, Warne and McGrath as examples. Waugh, along with Trevor Hohns, felt that the 'two teams' idea had been blown out of proportion simply because one player – Taylor – was not in both. Waugh said Australia – and all international teams – had always selected some players in one game and not the other, and the fact that the captain was involved, this time, was immaterial.

There was merit in the Waugh–Hohns position, but at the same time Australia were trying to rebuild their one-day personnel and reshape their game in time for the 1999 World Cup. Their loss to Sri Lanka in Lahore in 1996 had been more than just a lost game. Sri Lanka's easy seven-wicket win had turned the compressed game on its head. The 1996 World Cup final had been a clash of one-day cultures, and Sri Lanka's had not just triumphed over Australia's – it had crushed it. Their ascendancy was reaffirmed when Australia toured the subcontinent later in 1996. Sri Lanka pulverised the Australians twice in Colombo, and then Australia lost their five games in the Titan Cup in India.

Taylor had even been one of Australia's better players in that series, scoring 39 (off 58 balls), 105 (his first one-day century, off 144 balls), 42 (74 balls), 38 (76 balls) and 78 (91 balls). He topped Australia's averages and aggregates. After eight years, he had finally broken through to be Australia's most effective one-day opener.

But it was too late. The game had changed under his feet. Australia's one-day plan, ever since Bob Simpson and Allan Border had engineered their World Cup win in 1987, had been to make it a bowler's game. They would try to bat first and bat smart, milking the ones and twos before hitting out at the end; yet no matter how many runs they made, they based their attack around their ability to defend their total in the field. Australia's one-day style revelled in high-pressure, low-scoring games. They felt that no matter how few runs they scored, they could always harass and harangue opponents into scoring fewer.

What the Sri Lankans were doing – along with the quicker-learning teams such as Pakistan, South Africa and India – was to turn one-day cricket back into a batsman's game. Sri Lanka preferred to bowl first, conservatively, but no matter how many runs they conceded, they believed their batsmen could overhaul the target. Instead of waiting until the final 10 overs to launch their attack, the Sri Lankans batted 'upside down', taking advantage of the fielding restrictions in the first 15 overs to score most of their runs. A classic example of this culture clash was when the teams met in Colombo for their Singer World Series match on 30 August 1996. Australia won the toss, batted first and squeezed out 228 – not an imposing score, but more often than not defensible. In reply, Sri Lanka made an extraordinary start, losing five wickets in their first 13 overs but still scoring 81 runs. Jayasuriya had hammered 44 in 28 balls. In past times, this would have set up a predictable platform for Australia's pressure with the ball. Instead, Sri Lanka found themselves needing 140 runs off 35 overs – only four runs an over. Sure, they had lost five wickets, but Aravinda de Silva and Roshan Mahanama were able to pace the innings along without taking risks. They won the match by four wickets, with 4.1 overs to spare.

By the end of the Titan Cup, Taylor argued that these results, which had now left Australia with a run of 8 losses in 10 games, were an aberration. Bring us back home, he said, and on our bouncier wickets our old plan will prevail once more.

It didn't happen. Even though the 1996–97 World Series turned out to be low-scoring, the team batting first scoring more than 200 only four times in 14 games, a circumstance which should traditionally have favoured Australia, the hosts failed to make the finals for the first time in 20 years. Pakistan won the series comfortably, but even the West Indians, whose tour had stuttered almost to a halt before Christmas, rebounded to win their last five qualifiers and tip Australia out of the finals. Significantly, the West Indians went with the new orthodoxy, promoting Junior Murray to the top of the order where he contributed 342 runs at 34.2 with a strike rate of 78.98, better than any other top-order batsman from any team. In high-scoring matches in Brisbane and Perth, Australia could not defend totals (281 and 269) that they had considered winning scores, at home, for the previous decade. And in a low-scorer in Hobart, Australia could not even chase down Pakistan's 149, despite Pakistan using such bowlers as Ijaz Ahmed (who dismissed Mark Waugh, caught down the leg side) and Mujahid Jamshed (whom Wasim Akram had never seen bowl before, not even in the nets).

Australia's crisis was mirrored – and, Hohns was beginning to believe, partly caused – by Taylor's. In eight innings that summer, Taylor made 143 runs at an average of 18 and a strike rate of 42. Continually, Australia were getting bogged down at the start, and their middle order was having to make up too much ground. In the field, Taylor was an anachronistically leaden figure at short mid-wicket, a creature from a bygone age. And his justification for keeping his place in the Test team during his slump – that the team was winning – could not hold in one-day cricket.

His dispensability was proven two months later, when he sat out the last five games of Australia's one-day series in South Africa. Under Healy's captaincy, Australia bounced back to win the series with a game to spare. And this was after their worst-ever run of one-day results – up to the fourth match in South Africa, Australia had won only six of the last 21 limited-overs internationals.

What Hohns noticed during that reversal was that Australia started winning their games when they put a dynamic, young pair of openers in to attack the bowling, Sri Lanka-style. Michael Di Venuto and Greg Blewett spearheaded Australia's up-off-the-floor wins in Durban and Johannesburg, and Adam Gilchrist was making his presence felt in the middle order. Di Venuto's 89 from 115 balls at the Wanderers and Gilchrist's 77 off 88 balls at Kingsmead were the wake-up innings for Australia's selectors. Both Gilchrist and Di Venuto, along with Stuart Law, Adam Dale and Brendon Julian, had been flown out to South Africa specifically as one-day players. Australia's series win designated this 'separate teams' concept as the way of the future.

When they moved on to England two months later, Australia faltered again, losing the one-day series 3–0. The touring schedule precluded their flying specialist one-day players to England, so it was the Test men who played that one-day series. Significantly, Taylor was back at the top for the first two games, scoring seven (from 16 balls) and 11 (35 balls). There was a clear line between the two approaches: youthful vigour, all-out attack in the first 15 overs meant victory; the old steady-as-she-goes way, with Taylor playing sheet-anchor, spelt defeat.

Taylor saved his Test career during the 1997 Ashes series, but the line had been ruled under his one-day future by the time the 1997–98 season was underway. In 1998 the ACB interviewed 35 leading players during the winter, and 28 said they believed separate teams should be chosen for one-day and Test cricket. The board further facilitated the new set-up by programming the coming season in discrete 'blocks' of Test and first-class cricket (October to early January) and one-day cricket (January–

February). The two-teams philosophy was becoming an international standard; visiting teams also wanted to be able to separate their one-day squad into an autonomous unit in preparation for the 1999 World Cup.

Amid some overheated speculation, Taylor was dropped from Australia's one-day team for the Cricket Academy's 10th anniversary match in Adelaide on 28 October 1997. The announcement was made on 15 October, when Taylor was in Brisbane with the NSW side to play Queensland in the season-opening Sheffield Shield match. Unusually, Taylor reacted with some anger to Robert Craddock's story in the *Courier-Mail* explaining Taylor's one-day omission as stemming from a 'loss of respect' from his fellow players. Craddock had it on good authority that as a one-day batsman and captain, Taylor had lost his teammates' support. As he had with Malcolm Conn in Port Elizabeth earlier in the year, Taylor flared up at a journalist who dared to put into print what his teammates were muttering behind his back.

Truer to form, Taylor came out that day and scored 124 for NSW. It was Edgbaston all over again. So bloody-minded was he that he ran out his one-day captaincy successor, Steve Waugh – one of the rare occasions when Waugh was ever run out.

There was another surprise to follow. Healy was duly selected for the Academy match, and smashed a typical 24 off 25 balls down the order, saving the senior team from an embarrassing loss. Healy's one-day performances had not deteriorated, as Taylor's had, and Waugh suffered a great shock when on 30 November 1997 Hohns called him during the Hobart Test match against New Zealand to say that the selectors had omitted Healy, along with Taylor, from Australia's World Series squad. Hohns's explanation was simple. Adam Gilchrist was firmly in the team as a batsman, and it would be a waste of a position to maintain Healy when Gilchrist could also don the gloves. Healy was not (contrary to some public opinion at the time) dropped for Gilchrist. Healy was dropped to make way for an all-rounder at No 7. Waugh's first task as Australia's official one-day captain, then, was to go to Healy's room at Hobart's Grand Chancellor hotel and give him the news. The entire team was sombre that night, but kept the news to themselves, allowing Healy to make a dignified – if pugnacious – statement the following day, when his omission was announced.

'I was very disappointed,' Healy said. 'I think I'm entitled to feel disappointed. I've been happy with my current form and past form in one-dayers, and the effort I've put into Australia's one-day games, so I think I can hold my head high. Everyone knows how much I enjoy playing for Australia.

'I definitely want to make it clear that I want to be considered as No 2. I am definitely available to play for Australia if required.'

Waugh called it 'probably the hardest thing I've ever had to do', to inform his closest cricketing friend of the decision. 'It wasn't a good start to the captaincy. He was very disappointed, because I guess he didn't think it was coming.'

It was a bitter pill for any senior Australian player to be restricted to one form of the game. Two seasons earlier, David Boon had said: 'I didn't want to even contemplate having to come into the team again as a "specialist" Test player. I don't believe that as a senior player, you can be one or the other. I've seen too many players regarded solely as limited-overs cricketers. I didn't want to go out the other way.'

At the time of his axing, Healy had played 168 limited-overs internationals since his debut in Pakistan in 1988, scoring 1764 runs at 21.00 and effecting a world-record 233 dismissals. His career strike rate of 84 runs per 100 balls was the best of Australia's long-term players. Even Taylor's record wasn't too bad, statistically. In World Series games in Australia, his career strike rate was 59.14. By comparison, Geoff Marsh's was 54.35, Desmond Haynes's 59.42, Richie Richardson's 56.45, and Javed Miandad's 57.89. But the game had moved on.

There were many ironies underlying Australia's experiment. Healy was told that he had to make way for younger blood, but the man who eventually took his place in Australia's 1999 World Cup win was Tom Moody, only eight months Healy's junior. While he made a sound contribution in some World Cup matches, Moody was no more consistently effective than the other all-rounders tested in Healy's No 7 spot – Shane Lee, Brendon Julian, Andrew Symonds and Ian Harvey. It could be argued that the omission of Healy weakened Australia's performance in the 1999 World Cup, because they did not get full value out of Gilchrist's batting, in part because he had also to take the burden of keeping wicket. The other leading teams in the World Cup used conventional wicketkeepers batting down the order. Pakistan's Moin Khan, South Africa's Mark Boucher and New Zealand's Adam Parore all gave good accounts of themselves. If anything, Healy's one-day career fell victim to Australia's perennial search for a genuine all-rounder rather than to the rise of Gilchrist.

The other irony was that Australia were to become world champions by reverting to a more old-fashioned variety of one-day cricket. On England's lush wickets, it was impossible for Sanath Jayasuriya and Romesh Kaluwitharana to come out and blast Sri Lanka to a repeat of 1996. Most opening batsmen struggled, and those who succeeded were the conventional straight-bat players such as Pakistan's Saeed Anwar, Zimbabwe's Neil Johnson, South Africa's Herschelle Gibbs, and Mark Waugh. Hysterical slogans such as '100 runs off 100 balls', which had excited the Australian fraternity during their attempted transition to a new style of the game, were left in the past. As often happens in cricket, philosophies and projects were forgotten in the competitive heat. But by winning the 1999 World Cup, Australia could boast that their 'two teams' policy had worked. If nothing else, their squad received an impetus each tour from the arrival of fresh faces. Yet in the World Cup win, it was their most old-fashioned tactics that worked best: McGrath with the new ball, Warne bowling great leg-spin, and Steve Waugh and Michael Bevan propping up the middle order. When the selectors chose their first team after the World Cup, to tour Sri Lanka and Zimbabwe, they recalled fast bowler Jason Gillespie to the one-day line-up: an admission that the things that work in Test cricket also work in the shorter game. Who knows? Had Taylor and Healy been there, they might have been match-winners.

The Captains

A MAN SAYS a lot about himself in the way he enters and leaves his job. Australian cricket captains of the post-Chappell era could be said to have defined themselves by their manner of assuming, and relinquishing, the leadership. Kim Hughes came to the job in a factionalised atmosphere, the shadows of Marsh, Lillee and Greg Chappell standing over him like buzzards waiting for his decay. Hughes's short and disastrous tenure came to an end in tears.

Allan Border had to be talked into the job in 1984–85. A decade later, he had to be talked out of it. Border's captaincy was always characterised by stubbornness and fight. He was obstinate about taking the role from Hughes, and then feisty in his decision to retire when his time had come. There was also an endearing modesty, almost a homeliness, about Border's character that was personified in his retirement. It was a messy affair. He felt he had been betrayed by the ACB when it held meetings, behind his back, with Mark Taylor, Ian Healy, Steve Waugh and David Boon after the South African tour of 1994. Taylor and the others contend that the captaincy was not discussed in these meetings, and that they were not 'job interviews' as such. 'There they talked to us about a number of issues,' Taylor wrote. 'AB and the captaincy were not among them. The question of whether he should or shouldn't play on as captain was not mentioned. There was one disquieting aspect: that Allan Border didn't get invited to those discussions. I think that was a mistake, and I suspect that he took it very hard. I had the feeling from then on that he had the "dirts" – whether with us or the board, I don't know.'

Yet it requires a certain disingenuousness to sustain the line that these

A Captain Says A Lot About Himself By The Way He Retires ... Mark Taylor makes a gentleman's exit, Sydney 1999. Craig Golding/Sydney Morning Herald

were not job interviews. These were meetings between the board and the only four players whose names would be raised in a ballot for the captaincy after Border. The future of Australian cricket was discussed. They were job interviews in everything but name. If Border felt so, he had moral right on his side. Then his somewhat rash announcement of the end – told to a media mate on a golf course – was typically Border. It was unplanned, it was messy, it was anything but slick. Allan Border would be remembered as the great fighting captain, the champion of adversity, who never quite knew what to do with himself when the fanfare was waiting.

Taylor was equally characterised by his ascent and retirement. After Border was gone, the appointment of Taylor was carried out with military precision. He won the ACB vote easily, having deputised for Border in 24 of the previous 26 Tests, led NSW and led Australia A on two overseas tours. He was the recognised first slip fieldsman, and had played a crucial role in counselling a troubled Shane Warne in South Africa. He was told of his appointment when visiting Peter Taylor at his farm near Moree.

Mark Taylor was flown secretly down to Sydney and Melbourne, not a word of his anointment leaking until the proper time. He gave an impressive first press conference, and was on his way. Before Taylor's first home Test match as captain, Gideon Haigh observed: 'Taylor holds a small circle enthralled as he responds fully, frankly and fairly to questions about the Pakistan tour ... It's like Taylor's playing himself in with the press, taking their pace, line and length. More than once it's observed: "Crickey, d'ya reckon AB would ever have done this?"'

Taylor's retirement, four and a half years later, was executed with similar gloss. He had found, on a New Year's holiday with his family to the north coast of NSW, that he had simply had enough of the physical and mental preparation necessary to go away and combat the West Indians in the Caribbean. His body and his mind told him it was over. He made his decision, and resisted the blandishments of the ACB and others who urged him to think again. Taylor, always decisive as a captain, was not to be swayed. As Australian of the Year, he was retiring at a moment when he would be appreciated most. He told the right people – Denis Rogers, John Howard – and kept his announcement secret until he addressed a packed press conference at Sydney's Sheraton on the Park. At the end of it, the media clapped and cheered him. He was driven away in a limousine. That was Mark Taylor: everything done just right.

The Waugh succession was smooth at first, on and off the field. He only had one serious challenger for the captaincy, Warne, who enjoyed support from the 'mafia' of former Australian captains in the Channel 9 box, some such as Ian Chappell and Richie Benaud seeing in Warne the image of their own aggressive styles. Warne had impressed as captain of the one-day team during Waugh's absence, his revved-up manner perfectly suited to the football-type atmosphere of the compressed game. He also had a fan in ACB chairman Denis Rogers, and in the Nine Network heir, Jamie Packer. Yet at board level, Waugh had a clear majority.

At first, in the West Indies, everything went Waugh's way. Australia dismissed a local selection for 55 on the first competitive day of the tour, won the next match inside three days, and crushed the West Indians in the first Test match. Waugh appeared to have inherited Taylor's fabled 'luck'. In the first Test, several wickets fell in the first over after bowling changes; it seemed that, like Taylor, Waugh was one step ahead of the game.

The truer test of Waugh's mettle was when things went wrong. When Brian Lara took Australia apart in Kingston and Bridgetown, all eyes turned to Waugh. Inevitably, the question was what would Taylor have done? Waugh confessed to difficulties trusting his instincts at these times. He certainly concentrated too much energy on Lara in Kingston, letting Jimmy Adams pad and paddle his way along unobtrusively, giving Lara essential support. In Bridgetown, Waugh's management of MacGill showed a demoralising lack of faith. On the second day, MacGill was hitting his stride for the first time in the series, dismissing Dave Joseph and troubling Lara. Yet Waugh took him off, replacing him with Gillespie. MacGill had been expensive against Lara, but was also likelier than Warne to take wickets. Australia needed wickets on the last day at Kensington Oval, but Waugh shunned MacGill, preferring Warne. His argument was that Warne's track record justified giving him the ball. His failure was a rare one.

Waugh appeared to recognise his error when he omitted Warne from the next Test, in Antigua. This was a courageous decision, from which even Taylor might have recoiled. Waugh was able not only to overrule his vice-captain in the selection meeting, but stand up afterwards and publicly accept responsibility. Other captains might have hidden behind their chairman of selectors. Waugh did not. The turning point in his captaincy was not so much that Australia won the Antigua Test and saved the Worrell Trophy, but that he had shown the strength to stand up to the charismatic leg-spinner and assert his will as captain.

Taylor had also asserted his will over a powerful ally. When the ACB interviewed him in 1994, he (along with the other candidates) expressed concern over the influence Bob Simpson wielded in Australian cricket. As coach and selector, Simpson unnerved some players, who felt inhibited about confessing problems to their coach if they thought he might turn those problems against the player at the selection table. As David Boon said, 'When he became both coach and selector, his power was enormous. I'm not breaking anyone's trust in saying that I know that some of the young blokes were scared to talk to him about certain aspects of their game ... Some cricketers, being mistrustful and superstitious at the best of times anyway, saw that if they were struggling and confided in Bob, their self-doubts might actually count against them when it came to picking the team.'

The set-up had worked in the Border years, primarily because Border wanted Simpson to share the load, but also because Simpson's instrumental role in lifting Australia from a poor cricket team into a very good one gave him a mandate to continue his work. When Taylor took over the captaincy, he asked that Simpson be stripped of his selector role. Simpson denied that the change had been imposed on him, saying in 1994-95: 'I'd had a long run of it and, with fourteen months in the job as coach ahead, I didn't feel like the extra work. I haven't noticed any difference this year between not being a selector and being one.'

But he was pushed towards the margins as soon as Taylor took over. In Pakistan, Taylor conducted the pre-match pep talks, which Border had delegated to Simpson. In the 1994-95 Ashes series, Simpson was increasingly in the background, assisting rather than directing the team. Taylor banned Walkmans, cards, books and mobile phones from the dressing room in the Perth Test of 1994-95. 'We're not trying to run blokes' lives for them,' he said. 'It's just that we want everyone to be involved in what's going on out in the middle.'

In the West Indies, Simpson was hospitalised with a clot in his leg, pushing him further towards the fringes of team preparation. His time in bed, sometimes sedated with drugs, led to the odd amusing story when the players went to pay him a visit. When Michael Slater visited, Simpson mistook him for Justin Langer: 'Lang, I'm so pleased to see you,' Simpson told Slater. 'Good on you.' Despite Slater's protestations – and his wish to earn brownie points with the coach – Simpson continued to believe he was Langer. Then, a day or two later, when Langer visited, Simpson exclaimed: 'Lang, a second visit! It's great to see you again.'

When Australia triumphed in the Caribbean in 1995, Simpson drew some fire with an article he wrote for the Fairfax press touting his own importance to their tactical approach and preparation. It was titled, 'They did it my way'. Simpson was criticised for apparently trying to hog the credit for a successful team. Yet the players would acknowledge their debt to Simpson's methods. Taylor, who eventually played a role in the board's decision not to renew Simpson's contract in 1996, was to say, when he (Taylor) broke the world catching record in 1999, that Simpson's drills and encouragement formed the foundation of his success. Steve Waugh acknowledged the same over his batting. Paul Reiffel said: 'I liked the way Simmo went about his coaching. I now realise he was very insistent on having things done his way, and I know that didn't sit well with some of the older players. I think that was because he always kept them on their toes and never allowed them to slip into the comfort zone that is sometimes the territory of automatic selections. Simmo was always ready to criticise anyone in the side who he thought needed it, senior or junior. Reputations didn't count for anything. As a young bloke you accept it; as an older player, you can sometimes be a bit sensitive.'

Even senior players, though, such as Boon, praised Simpson:

'... generally speaking, the more times you bowl, hit or catch the ball, the better you get at it – like a golfer hitting thousands of balls or a tennis player practising the same shot for hours. Simmo recognised the worth of this philosophy. He introduced fielding drills, seemingly thousands of them, many of them variations on old exercises. And the players began to look at the idea of practice in a new light ...

'I have always struggled with my subconscious. After a good summer, in my early years with Bob, I sometimes suffered from thinking: "I don't need any runs today, I've made heaps in the last six months!" Simmo, however, was a master at recognising such faulty thinking and was forever badgering me about it ... Of course, he drove everyone mad with it, but that was his job as coach.'

Simpson lost his job in 1996 after the World Cup in India and Pakistan. The players' attitudes speak loudest of the reasons. Nobody doubted Simpson's virtues, but he was an abrasive, domineering and sensitive character, and after a decade he was simply getting on people's nerves.

Taylor's old opening mate, Geoff Marsh, took over for the 1996 tour of Sri Lanka. The captain's ascendancy in the team structure was complete.

Marsh was a modest, avuncular figure in the team set-up, clearly subordinate to the captain. His role was to run practices, and to console and encourage players who responded to his low-key advice. He was a strong influence in improving the all-round games of Jason Gillespie, Michael Bevan and Adam Gilchrist. His modesty was an asset. Marsh was the first to admit that he might not be the most innovative or inspirational ideas man, so he called in experts from other fields – Australian Rules coaches, athletics and rugby motivators – to freshen up the team's attitude. He expanded the team's support network to include a psychologist, Sandy Morgan, a fitness consultant (Steve Smith, then David Misson) alongside the long-time physiotherapist, Errol Alcott, and oversaw the installation of a new computerised cricket analysis program operated by scorer Mike Walsh. Marsh kept clear of the political games in which Simpson had revelled, generally avoided getting his name in the newspapers, and was the perfect foil for the aggressive captain Taylor was turning out to be.

When Marsh had had enough in 1999, he was succeeded by Queensland coach John Buchanan. This signalled another tack. Steve Waugh obviously wanted more technical input from the coach, and some fresh ideas that would keep his men thinking. He fought hard for Buchanan, an unusually intellectual man (unusual for Australian cricket, that is) who could sustain an argument from beginning to end. He had not been any great shakes as a cricketer himself, which caused some to doubt him. But Waugh wielded the authority of his World Cup mandate, and had Buchanan appointed before the home series in 1999–2000. At time of writing it is still too early to judge Buchanan's effect, other than to note that Australia has not lost a Test match under him. As innovative as he is, Buchanan's methods still adhere to the basic Simpson model. There is no doubt that Simpson invented the international cricket coach and coaching's integrated approach to playing team cricket: 'In the Australian cricket team, each man is a cog in the wheel. If the team executive – the captain and vice-captain – decides on a course of action, it is up to the player to follow it without question. I know a lot of individual performances suffer in this way and sometimes it goes against the grain of the player concerned. But this is the only way the captain can work the team as a really efficient cricket machine.'

That dogma had been too stifling for Taylor, however. Taylor, Reiffel observed, was 'a natural captain. He wants to be captain, he likes to show that he is in command and he is happy enough to accept the responsibility for whatever happens out there. It might not sound terribly revealing, but it cannot be said of all captains ... The best thing about him is that he is honest and direct. If he has something to say to you – praise, advice, criticism, whatever – he'll come out and say it. So you always know where you stand. That's all you can ever ask of a captain. I don't need a captain to mollycoddle me. I respond best to one who tells it as it is, even if it is not always flattering. Mark does, and I think that's one of the keys to his success.'

Nobody ever doubted Taylor's enjoyment of the captaincy, and it was not long before he established his reputation for freakish luck. In 1995–96 against Sri Lanka in Melbourne, Taylor gave Ponting the ball when McDermott, McGrath and Reiffel couldn't get Chandika Hathurusinghe or Asanka Gurusinha. To that point, Ponting had taken two first-class wickets. He got Gurusinha immediately. He did the same for Taylor against the West Indies in Brisbane a season later, trapping Jimmy Adams. There were countless other occasions when Taylor made an unexpected bowling or fielding change, and it worked.

He recalled his reasoning:

My approach with the strike bowlers was not to bowl them for too long – a policy that admittedly had to be ditched at times when blokes like Warne and McGrath were all over an opposing team. The rule of thumb was that if they didn't come up with wickets in five or six overs, I would start to think about a change. I was always happy to try a Bevan or a Mark Waugh or a Ricky Ponting for two or three overs. The worst scenario might be no wickets and 15 or 20 runs. Meanwhile the "guns" – Warne and McGrath etc – would be freshening up, thinking about what they'd been doing and how they could go about getting the batsmen out next time around ...

'Often, in my experience, the part-timers would jag a wicket. The relaxation factor would have clicked in, the batsman thinking: "I've seen Warnie off ... geez, he was bowling well." The same applied with Glenn McGrath. A batsman relaxing just a fraction in such circumstances is then very vulnerable ...

There began to develop a mystique about him, reinforced by the phlegmatic figure he cut at first slip, chomping on his gum, always an island of calm. Bradman had said a captain must be 'a fighter; confident but not arrogant, firm but not obstinate, able to take criticism without letting it unduly disturb him, for he is sure to get it – and unjustly, too.'

Test player and selector John Benaud listed the ingredients of the perfect captain: 'Hell bent on winning; a sportsman; an entertainer; a psychoanalyst; a leader by example; a prophet; and lucky ... When you think about it, it's not often they all fall into place.'

In Taylor, they fell into place. In Taylor's first home series, Gideon Haigh watched closely the differences between Taylor and Mike Atherton. They were small but telling: 'If ever there was a case of two sides making their captains, the Ashes of 1994–95 was it. There's not a lot between Taylor and Atherton as batsmen and tacticians, but the former trusts his team while the latter doesn't and probably can't. Australia has brought Taylor out of his shell as a captain, England puts Atherton back into his.'

Haigh observed the way the captaincy fell on Taylor like a second skin at Sydney Airport for the third Ashes Test: 'Taylor stands to one side in the reflected glare of the television lights, waiting like he's at the non-striker's end. Nobody has to corral him or tap him on the shoulder, for within a few minutes he has tape recorders at his chin. Only when they click off does he take his trolley, and his pregnant missus Judi, and head for the car park.' Yet the genius for communication did not always comes naturally. Early in his captaincy, Taylor admitted to timidity when it came to addressing his teammates. 'A couple of times I've walked up to chat with an individual and had a lump in my throat,' he said, 'because I wasn't sure how it was going to go. I've got to talk to the players and tell them how I want them to play and how the team will play.'

Nor was his authority always unquestioned. Steve Waugh often thought he had better ideas standing at gully, but Taylor's forceful style regulated Waugh's opportunities to share those ideas. Warne also clashed with Taylor over tactics, as Reiffel recalled: 'Warney is the sort of bowler who is always making adjustments to his field, and he and Tubby do have their run-ins. They don't have a problem with each other about it. It's just the way they are, and the way it works on a cricket field. It's not always clockwork. As I said, Tubby generally gets his way.'

Taylor's legacy had few negatives. The temptation to seek a more balanced view, in fact, was only prompted by the tendency of some to so overstate the positives that it began to seem, by the time of his retirement, that Mark Taylor could walk on water and raise the dead. Nobody in their right mind would deny Taylor's greatness as a cricket leader; nor would anybody in their right mind say he was perfect. Perhaps it was not Taylor's fault, but the on-field behaviour of Australian teams, often bordering on unsportsmanlike and certainly boorish at times, did not improve during his time. Warne, Healy, the Waughs, Ponting and McGrath were all guilty of indiscretions. Maybe it was not coincidental that these were Australia's best players and those considered Taylor's successors to the team leadership. Taylor never showed bad temper on the field, as Border had, and sometimes he stepped in to put out a fire, such as the occasion in 1994–95 when he stopped Warne claiming a catch, off Atherton, which had bounced first. But more typically, Taylor turned a blind eye to what his players were doing. He did the right thing when directed by the umpires, but the Australian players understood that under Taylor they could do what they wished as long as they did not cross the official lines. Taylor left discipline in the hands of authorities rather than taking that role himself. He preferred to abdicate that area of responsibility. In doing so, he made the authorities' jobs more difficult.

Most of all, Taylor was able to convince himself that most of the verbal tactics his team used were not unfair. Reiffel explains the thesis:

Gamesmanship... is more subtle and so more effective. I don't know that you can even classify it as sledging. Ian Healy is brilliant at it. He might say something that is totally irrelevant to the game, or to anything, really.

He won't have sworn; he won't even have raised his voice. It's just chatter. But if it causes the batsman to stop and think about what Heals has said, it might distract him just long enough to make him give his wicket away. If that's sledging, I think it's good sledging.

Other teams also sledged. The Australians felt they bore the brunt of public criticism because they were simply less subtle about it. No doubt they were right. It takes two to have a fight, as the world learned, eventually, about the Sri Lankan team under Ranatunga. But most often, when two were having a fight, Australia was one of them. As Sunil Gavaskar said, 'Funny how in most of the storms involving cricket the Australians are somewhere in the picture.' In the late 1990s, sledging spread through the world, with England and South Africa having a particularly spiteful series in 1999–2000. But it was widely felt that teams were adopting these strategies in imitation of the Australians.

Taylor's informal blind-eye policy may have earned him some criticism, but the difficulty of his task was underscored by what happened after he retired. With the succession of Waugh, a master practitioner of verbal intimidation, the last restraints were taken off the Australian approach. In the West Indies, McGrath spat in the path of Adrian Griffith, an unsavoury incident on the very fringes of gamesmanship and decency. When Waugh's team toured Sri Lanka in August 1999, they refined the tactic of bearing down on a dismissed batsman, screaming in his face to celebrate a wicket. Fleming was disciplined for shoulder-charging a Sri Lankan batsman, and later in the summer, McGrath was cautioned again for charging into the face of Sachin Tendulkar after dismissing him in Sydney.

Teams evolve in the image of their captains, and under Waugh the Australians became an almost frighteningly aggressive force. The Pakistani team believed Ponting, McGrath and Fleming were out of control. Even the mild-mannered Adam Gilchrist was filmed telling Sourav Ganguly to 'fuck off' after he was dismissed in Melbourne. Waugh engendered a new style of hyperaggression that was as repellent, at times, as it was effective. By early 2000, his team was starting to mould itself into the shape of

Steve Waugh the batsman: obsessed, focused, indomitable, and without a trace of feeling for the way it looked or what means it used to achieve victory. Waugh told the story of when he was young and, racing his brother on scooters down a driveway at their Panania home, he stuck out a leg, which caused Mark to crash into a garage door. Steve thought the story amusing. It showed that he preferred to be a winner than a charmer. Accordingly, his objective was to lead a great team, not necessarily a nice team.

In taking over the entire leadership load from Simpson, Taylor probably undermined his ambition to stay Test and one-day captain. The incessant demands of the job eventually wore him down, and in his early thirties the lightness of touch, with bat and in the field, that were so essential to one-day success, began to desert him. The seeds of this decline had been clear as early as his first Test, in Karachi in 1994, when he made a pair.

'I paid a price, I think, that captains sometimes pay – and especially new captains. In that match my focus was all on getting the team "right". I was concerned that things should be in place exactly the way I wanted them, and with the side running the way I wanted it. I wanted to be a captain in control. People who know me will tell you that I'm not a great delegator. If something has to be done, my inclination is to get in and do it myself.'

Test selector John Benaud had seen the conflict coming as early as the debate over Border's successor: 'The suggestion came from Queensland, and a cynic might have been inclined to wonder whether it was intended to influence the eventual captaincy changeover from Border ... after all, if Taylor the vice-captain couldn't make the one-day team, how could he be captain of Australia? On the other hand, Queensland's Ian Healy, the wicketkeeper, was assured of a spot in both forms of the game ... It put Taylor under a great deal of unnecessary pressure to change his style. His non-slogging batting style was perceived as being wrong for what is touted as the fast form of the game. So you might wonder how two players of stodgy style, Geoff Marsh and Mark Taylor, can be so differently judged in the one-day arena.'

Eventually, the bitter Test and one-day split was the result. Taylor did not especially dignify himself with his running opposition to the plan, but on the positive side, he was at least speaking his mind, rightly or wrongly, and he influenced the ACB to make the very sensible change, in 1998, from mixing up the home Test and one-day seasons to separating them into discrete blocks.

Taylor's form slump kept causing ripples through the Steve Waugh era. Firstly, Waugh was so haunted by the saga that he made his own batting form an obsessive priority. Of course that was part of Waugh's character anyway, but in the early days of his captaincy he stated continually the need for a leader to hold his place first and foremost by scoring runs or taking wickets. Accordingly, he scored two brilliant centuries in the West Indies, often carrying Australia's batting, and he played his greatest one-day innings in 14 years against South Africa at Headingley. He scored a century in Zimbabwe and carried on into the home season of 1999–2000, hitting an even 150 against India at Adelaide, making himself the first batsman in history to score centuries against every Test-playing nation.

The other legacy of the Taylor slump was another kind of 'two teams' policy. For better or worse, the example of indulgence set in the Taylor decline was one that was applied, later, to other senior players. Warne was able to select himself, almost certainly too soon after his shoulder surgery, for the fifth Ashes Test in 1998–99 and for the West Indies tour. When Waugh was agonising over reversing that decision, he and Warne referred constantly to Taylor's slump. As Warne argued, 'If Tubby went 21 innings without making a score, why am I only allowed a couple of Tests before I start taking wickets?' Mark Waugh also lost form periodically through 1997 to 2000. He too appealed to the Taylor precedent. After failing throughout the 1997 Ashes series, he quipped: 'I've still got about 10 innings to go before they can drop me.'

For better or worse, double standards became a feature of team politics in those last years of the century. At various times, Warne, Mark Waugh, McGrath and Ponting were given preferential treatment over others who were not part of the inner clique. The counter-argument is that that inner clique was formed by success, and its members had earned their privileges. Waugh fought hard to sustain the impression of unity, writing as early as 1996 on Jason Gillespie's call-up: 'His situation takes me back to my first Test match, when I walked out to bat for my first Test innings. My first batting partner was Geoff Marsh, whom I had been introduced to the previous evening, and our conversation had involved maybe half a dozen words. But in this Australian side, making newcomers feel welcome is one of our strengths and I'm sure Jason will feel pretty much settled straight away. There may be titles such as "senior" players, but no one is more important than anyone else and every player's input is welcomed by all.'

That was certainly true for those new players who had the easygoing personalities that enabled them to slip neatly into the team fold. People like Ponting, Blewett, Gillespie, Gilchrist and Fleming were the type of men who fit the pattern. Others, such as MacGill, Scott Muller, Kasprowicz, Matthew Hayden, Lehmann, Bevan and Stuart Law, were never left with a quite unqualified assurance that they were to be shown the same faith at the selection table, on tour and at home, as were some of their teammates. Inevitably there were biases against some types of players. Under Taylor and Waugh, a belief persisted that Ponting was simply a better player than Lehmann and Bevan; that Gillespie was a better bowler than Kasprowicz. Time vindicated these decisions – or did it? If Lehmann, say, had been given a good run at Test level, as many chances as Taylor, Mark Waugh or Ponting, who is to say he would not have been an out-and-out star of international cricket?

Perhaps more remarkable was the Australian team's capacity to survive and prosper with this set-up. The unlucky players of the Taylor-Waugh era only appear so unlucky because they played so well when given their chances at Test level. Each of that selection of 'unlucky' men named above played vital roles in Australia winning Test matches: particularly MacGill, without whose bowling Australia would never have won the decisive Test in Pakistan in 1998 and the subsequent Ashes series. Under Taylor and then Waugh, the Australian team established its own winning tradition, into which new players could slip in and out and always make a contribution. When the team went onto the field all in baggy green caps, as it did for the first fielding session of each Test, every player was identically attired, without any seniority or faction. (To emphasise the deep roots of that tradition, however, it must be noted that the baggy-green ritual started not under Taylor or Waugh, but under Border. In a dire position in the third Test of the 1993 away series against New Zealand, having to take seven cheap wickets to win the game, the Australians made a pact to wear their baggy greens. They went out, all fired up ... and didn't take a wicket. The tradition was more successful in later years, even prompting some opponents, such as England and India, to imitate it.)

Much of the team's success can be put down to the natural talent of its constituent parts. But the role of leadership cannot be understated. What Taylor did was set in place an atmosphere of special confidence. Gideon Haigh wrote that it was 'Benaud who observed that tactical acumen was rarely a distinguishing factor in captaincy, and that the capacity to give orders and expect their execution depended more on the atmosphere a leader was capable of cultivating.'

Taylor's calm authority cultivated it, and Waugh's more democratic, individual style of leadership also cultivated it. Both faltered at the start, having to take teams to the toughest destinations for their first series, but both were quick learners.

At the start of 2000, the signs are that Australia has moved into the Steve Waugh captaincy with the same smoothness as the West Indies graduated from Clive Lloyd to Viv Richards in 1985. The new man has a new style, but the system keeps producing players of talent and the national team keeps refining them into players of fibre. Just as Lloyd's team built on its memories of humiliation in their Australian tour in 1975–76, the early teams under Taylor worked on a revenge mentality, a desire never again to lose. At the start of 2000, the challenge is different. Few of the team have lost series anywhere. Their challenge is not to avenge embarrassments, but to avoid ever experiencing loss.

After his last Test in Durban in 1994, Allan Border took David Boon aside in a hotel bar and said these words: 'When I've finished, I'll need you to do one thing. We've been doing it for a while, but now it'll be up to you to never, ever let these younger blokes know what it's like to get their backsides kicked week-in, week-out.'

In the ensuing six years, the battle-scarred veterans retired and the memories of defeat faded. By 2000, only Steve and Mark Waugh remained who had lost a series to the West Indies. Only Steve had lost to England. In 1994, the desire to ward off bad memories was a driving force in the Australian team. By the time Taylor handed over to Waugh, the message was different: rather than avoid reliving painful defeat, the leader's purpose was to ensure defeat never entered the frame. It is a different challenge altogether.

Further Reading

Matthew Engel (ed), WISDEN CRICKETERS' ALMANACK, John Wisden.
Gideon Haigh (ed), WISDEN CRICKETERS' ALMANACK AUSTRALIA, Hardie Grant Books.
Allan Miller (ed), ALLAN'S CRICKET ANNUAL, Allan Miller.
Mark Ray, BORDER & BEYOND, ABC Books 1995.
Paul Reiffel with Greg Baum, REIFFEL: INSIDE OUT, HarperSports 1999.
Darrell Hair, DECISION MAKER: AN UMPIRE'S STORY, Random House 1998.
David Boon with Mark Thomas, UNDER THE SOUTHERN CROSS: THE AUTOBIOGRAPHY OF DAVID BOON, HarperSports 1996.
John Benaud, MATTERS OF CHOICE: A Test Selector's Story, Swan Publishing 1997.
Ken Piesse, THE TAYLOR YEARS: Australian Cricket 1994-99, Penguin 1999.
Steve Waugh, STEVE WAUGH'S WORLD CUP DIARY, HarperSports 1996.
Gideon Haigh, ONE SUMMER, EVERY SUMMER: AN ASHES JOURNAL, Text 1995.
Mark Taylor with Ian Heads, TIME TO DECLARE, Pan Macmillan 1999.
Steve Waugh, NO REGRETS: A CAPTAIN'S DIARY, HarperSports 1999.

Index

Aamir Malik 20
Aamir Sohail
  accusations against Salim Malik 32
  matches: Australia 20, 21, 23, 24, 33, 35;
    South Africa 186; West Indies 64
  national captain 25, 26, 27
Aaqib Javed 24
ACA 202-22
Adams, Jimmy
  in Antigua 79
  culture of winning 42
  matches: Australia 46, 75, 76, 77
Adams, Paul 83, 87, 88
Akram Raza 19
Alcott, Errol 115, 246-7, 272
Allott, Geoff 224
Ambrose, Curtly
  photographs *68, 94*
  Antigua 79-80
  attitude to winning 65-6
  confrontation with Steve Waugh 47-8
  dismissal 70
  last Test appearance in Australia 71
  matches: Australia 49, 56, 59, 62, 63, 69, 77-8
  mutiny 52
  short-pitched bowling 50
Angel, Jo 5, 18, 19
Antigua Recreation Grounds 47
Arbab Niaz Stadium, Peshawar 31
Arthurton, Keith 49
Ashes, the 131-68
Astle, Nathan 223, 227
Asylum (Kingston nightclub) 72
Ata-ur-Rehman 24
Atherton, Michael 134-6, 138, 153, 156, 162-3
Australia
  in England, 1997 144-56
  in India: 1996 230-7; 1998 237-52
  in Pakistan: 1994 16-21; 1998 25-35
  in South Africa, 1997 82-93
  in Sri Lanka, 1996 195-201
  in the West Indies: 1995 40-51; 1999 73-80
Australia 'A' concept 140-2
Australian, The 30
Australian Cricket Academy 137, 138
Australian Cricket Board
  attendance at Lahore High Court 29
  Australian Cricketers' Association 202-22
  bribery affair 10, 12, 13, 14, 40-1 captaincy 266-7
  create heavy schedule 197
  finances 66, 213-14
  'media tips' to players 17
  one-day series 262, 278
  players' pay dispute 101, 110, 113, 153, 202-22
  series' marketing 139
  Sri Lanka and 170, 174, 182
Australian Cricketers' Association 202-22
Australian Industrial Relations Commission 211
Australian Rugby League 205

Bacher, Adam 86, 87, 90, 122, *123*, 124
Bacher, Dr Ali 86, 121
Barker, Lloyd 46
Basit Ali 7, 19, 22, 23, 24
Battersby, Cam 198, 199, 250
Benaud, John 273, 277
Benaud, Richie 177, 268, 280
Benjamin, Kenny 48, 49, 50, 52, 59, 67
Benjamin, Winston 48, 50
Bernard, Steve 53, 202, 249-50
Berry, Scyld 59
Bevan, Michael
  Australia 'A' team 141
  debut 17
  earnings 209
  Marsh's influence 272
  matches: India 198, 230, 234; Pakistan 18, 19, 20, 21; South Africa 87, 92; Sri Lanka

179; West Indies 56, 58, 61, 62, 66, 67, 68, 69, 191
selection 97
sledged by English side 135
Bichel, Andrew 71, 92
Bird, Dickie 19
Blake, Martin 64, 94
Blewett, Greg
  photograph 68
  fearlessness 51
  matches: England 106, 108, 142, 162; India 245, 247; New Zealand 225; Pakistan 24, 36, 37; South Africa 85, 87; West Indies 49, 59, 63, 67, 70, 74
  one-day series 262
  selection for Ashes 141
Boon, David
  Border's plea 280
  bribery affair 5, 11
  Cullinan and Warne 111
  dropping of 54
  form 133
  matches: England 138; Pakistan 16, 18, 24; West Indies 39, 47, 49
  one-day series 264
  players' pay dispute 216
  Simpson as coach 269-70, 271
  swansong century 178
  view of West Indies team 72
Border, Allan 40, 52, 81, 135, 204, 216, 266-7, 280
Border-Gavaskar Trophy 229, 230
Botham, Ian 139
Boucher, Mark 29, 81, 265
Bouts, Trent 200, 201
bowling styles
  reverse swing 18
  short-pitched 45
Boycott, Geoff 143
Bradman, Sir Donald 31, 33, 273
bribery affair 1, 5, 10, 12, 13, 14, 40-1 *see also* match-fixing
Bridgetown, Barbados 76
Browne, Courtney 40, 49, 50, 60, 62
Buchanan, John 272
Burdett, Les 66
Burns, Gary 219, 220
Butcher, Mark 157, 160

Caddick, Andrew 152
Cairns, Chris 222, 224, 226, 227
Campbell, Ryan 158
Campbell, Sherwin 42, 45, 58, 59, 61, 62, 68, 77, 79
captaincy 267-81
Centurion Park, Pretoria 90
Chanderpaul, Shivnarine 52, 58, 61-2, 63, 67, 69, 187

Channel 9 112-13, 203, 209, 217, 218, 268
Chappell, Greg 37, 96, 99, 104, 139, 258
Chappell, Ian 23, 193, 258, 268
Chauhan, Rajesh 245
Chevell, Kevin 32
Collins, Pedro 75, 77
Collymore, Corey 79
Colombo, Sri Lanka 181, 184-5, 195
Commins, John 83
Conn, Malcolm 2-3, 8, 30, 67, 98, 99, 100, 115, 263
Cook, Simon 225, 226, 227
Cooray, B. C. 198
Cornell, John 'Strop' 208, 221
Coward, Mike 56, 248, 258
Cowper, Bob 33
Cozier, Tony 52
Craddock, Robert 43, 95, 101, 215, 263
Crane, David 69
Crawley, John 157
Croft, Robert 108, 157
Crompton, Alan 9, 12, 41, 105
Cronje, Hansie
  photograph 89
  ball-tampering 112-13
  bowling incident 123-4
  feelings about winning 122
  leadership 81, 127, 130
  loss to Australia 118
  matches: Australia 84, 92, 110, 111, 119; Pakistan 186
Cuffy, Cameron 67
Cullinan, Daryll 81, 92, 111-12, 113, 126, 186
Cumberbatch, Clyde 74

Daily Telegraph (London) 106
Daily Telegraph (Sydney) 106
Dale, Adam 79, 92, 246, 262
Davis, Steve 113, 123
DeFreitas, Phil 134, 135, 137, 142
de Silva, Aravinda 175, 188, 190, 193, 195, 201, 261
Dev, Kapil 185
Dharmasena, Kumara 180
Di Venuto, Michael 92, 262
Dodemaide, Tony *214*
Donald, Allan
  bowling Waugh 50
  greatest desire 110
  matches: Australia 81, 84, 85, 88, 114, 117
  World Cup, 1999 129-30
Doull, Simon 224, 227
Dowling, Graham 172, 175
Dravid, Rahul 245, 248, 255
Dujon, Jeffrey 51
Dunne, Steve 172

Ealham, Mark 147, 149

Edwards, Jack 51
Egar, Col 6, 7, 11, 86
Elliott, Matthew
  photographs *55, 61*
  century in Antigua 76
  character of 54–5
  collision with Mark Waugh 60
  first Test runs 58
  form in Port Elizabeth 100
  Gloucestershire game 105
  maiden Test hundred 148
  matches: England 108, 150, 151, 162; South Africa 83, 84, 114; West Indies 53, 56, 62, 74, 78
Emerson, Ross 173–7
Emery, Phil 21
England in Australia
  1994–95 131–44
  1998–99 156–68
Erskine, James 153, *203*, 203–22

Fakhruddin G. Ibrahim 22
Feroz Shah Kotla ground, Delhi 231
Fleetwood-Smith, Chuck 26
Fleming, Colin
  disciplined 276
  matches: Pakistan 20, 26, 27, 29; West Indies 192
Fleming, Damien 19, 43, *166, 191*
Fleming, Stephen 222, 223, *223*, 224, 227
Fletcher, Keith 137
Frank Worrell Trophy 23, 35, 39, 40–2, 49, 52, 69, 75, 78, 80, 96
Fraser, Angus 158

Gaekwad, Anshuman 239
Ganguly, Saurav 197, 232, 253–5, 276
Gatting, Mike 137
Germon, Lee 189
Gibbs, Herschelle 49, 83, 120, 126, 127, 128
Gilchrist, Adam
  hyperaggression 276
  international debut 236
  Marsh's influence on 272
  matches: Pakistan 36, 37; South Africa 92, 120
  one-day series 262, 263
  preferred 93, 102
  Western Australian match 56
Gillespie, Jason
  Marsh's influence on 272
  matches: England 150, 153, 160; India 237; South Africa 86, 87, 88; Sri Lanka 35; West Indies 63, 74, 75, 76, 77–8
  team welcome for 279
  Test debut 59
Gooch, Graham 158–9, 162
Gough, Darren 108, 134, 138, 149, 157, 166

Graveney, David 150
Gray, Malcolm 183
Greenidge, Gordon 42, 51
Griffith, Adrian 57, 69, 276
Group 4 182
Gujranwala (Pakistan) 21
Gurusinha, Asanka 171, 178, 179, 193, 273

Hair, Darrell 70, 172–7, 182, 253
Halbish, Graham 9, 12, 41, 175, 206–13, *213*
Harper, Daryl 253
Harper, Roger 187
Harris, Chris 189
Harrity, Mark 137
Harvey, Ian 138
Hathurusinghe, Chandika 273
Hayat, Khizar 171
Hayden, Matthew
  first Test century 66–7
  form in Port Elizabeth 100
  matches: South Africa 83, 91; West Indies 53, 62, 69, 71
  reprimand 141
Headley, Dean 149, 157, 164, 165, *166*
Healy, Ian
  photograph *180*
  cricketer: captaincy 196, 262; century against England 160; dismissals 29, 90, 149; earnings 209; media contract 218–19; one-day series 169, 263–5; position in team 56–8; retirement 37; strengths 50; suspension 91; 100th Test 120
  matches: India 198, 245; New Zealand 226; Pakistan 5, 17, 19, 20, 21; South Africa 88–9; Sri Lanka 180; West Indies 39, 46, 59, 61, 63, 66, 68, 70, 74, 76, 78, 191
  Playing for Keeps 199
  relations with players: leadership 28–9, 93, 101–4; Mark Taylor 96; sledging 275; West Indies 45
  views on Indian opponents 27
Hegg, Warren 163
Hick, Graeme 138–9, *140*, 160, 162, 163
Hindu, The (newspaper) 237
Hitchcock, Cole 101, 103
Hogg, Brad 196, 232, 234, 236
Hohns, Trevor 37, 100, 103, 119, 126
Holding, Michael 61
Hollioake, Adam 134, 152
Hollioake, Ben 134, 152, 157
Hooper, Carl
  in Antigua 79
  matches: Australia 40, 42, 45, 49, 58, 60, 62, 63, 67
  plotting of 48, 51
  walk out 52

Horne, Matthew 227
Hudson, Andrew 28, 186
Hughes, Kim 258, 266
Hussain, Nasser 107, 151, 157, 161

Ijaz Ahmed
  photograph *26*
  matches: Australia 33, 35, 37, 64
  match-fixing 7, 14, 35
  one-day cricket 261
  'The Axeman' 24
India 229–56
  in Australia, 1999–2000 252–6
India. Third Test in Bangalore (photograph) *250*
International Cricket Council 4, 13, 22, 173, 177
Inzamam-ul-Haq
  photograph *26*
  matches: Australia 5, 19, 20, 23, 37; West Indies 64
  match-fixing 7–8

Jacobs, Ridley 77
Jadeja, Ajay 189, 197
Javed Miandad 189
Jayasuriya, Sanath 179, 183, 188, 193, 200, 201, 261
'John' ('Pinky') the bookmaker 1, 11–13
Johnson, David 53, 232
Jones, Dean 8, 107, 215–16
Joseph, David 77
Joshi, Sunil 197, 231
Julian, Brendon 43, 45, 162, 262

Kallis, Jacques 81, 83, 87, 114, 117, *118*
Kalpage, Ruwan 180
Kaluwitharana, Romesh 171, 178, 179, 188, 200, 201
Kambli, Vinod 198
Kanitkar, Hrishikesh 243
Kapoor, Aashish 231
Kasprowicz, Michael
  Ashes tour 103
  matches: England 107, 154; India 246, 247, 251; South Africa 114; West Indies 62
Keane, Patrick 9, 17, 210
Kensington Oval (Bridgetown) 45
Khizar Hayat 19
Kingston (Jamaica) 72
Kirsten, Gary 81, 86, 111, 114, 120, 128, 186
Kitchen, Mervyn 90
Klusener, Lance 81, 83, 129–30, 227
Knott, Alan 29
Knox, Malcolm (photograph) *xi*
Koslowski, Michael 59
Kulkarni, Nilesh 242
Kumble, Anil 231, 233, 234, 237, 244, 255

Lahore High Court 3, 29
Lane, Tim 102, 215
Langer, Justin
  advice to Taylor 107
  in Antigua 79
  attitude to touring India and Pakistan 28
  century in Antigua 76
  flies home 91
  form in Port Elizabeth 100
  Gloucestershire game 105
  matches: England 161; India 255; Pakistan 27, 32, 35, 37; South Africa 21; West Indies 62, 66, 74
Lara, Brian
  photograph *57*
  Antigua 79–80
  batting form 64, 65, 66
  captaincy 48
  double century in second Test 73–6
  incident at SCG 61
  Jamaica and Barbados in 1999 42
  matches: Australia 40, 45–6, 47, 49, 50, 58, 59, 62, 63, 68, 254–5; Kenya 187; South Africa 189
  performance in Bridgetown 77–8
  plotting of 51
  talks to media about sledging 69–70
  team's reliance on 52
  Waugh's captaincy 269
Law, Stuart 190, 191, 198, 235, 262
Laxman, V. V. S. 243, 248, 255
Lee, Brett 255
Lehmann, Darren 27, 250, 252
Leroy, Peter 59
Lewis, Chris 142
Liberation Tamil Tigers of Elam (LTTE) 184, 185
Lillee, Dennis 37, 96
Lloyd, Clive 61, 73, 75
Lloyd, David 158–9, *159*

McCague, Martin 134
McDermott, Craig
  death threats 182
  international cricketer of the year 131
  last matches 183, 186
  matches: England 136, 138, 141, 143; Pakistan 5, 16, 17, 19, 23, 24; Sri Lanka 170, 178, 180; West Indies 43
McDonald, Ian 40–1, *132*, 137
MacGill, Stuart
  photograph *164*
  bowling 25–6, 79, 124
  matches: England 159, 160, 163, 167; India 240, 247; New Zealand 223; West Indies 75, 76, 78
  Waugh's captaincy 269
McGrath, Glenn

Index 287

photograph *254*
Antigua 79-80
bowling style 143-4
career top score 59
in Colombo 199
earnings 209
fearlessness 51
in India and Pakistan 28
matches: England 146-7, 150, 153, 154, 160, 163; India 253-5; New Zealand 225; Pakistan 16, 17-18, 24, 26, 27; South Africa 21; Sri Lanka 170, 179, 201; West Indies 46, 58, 61, 62, 63, 74, 75, 76, 77-8, 121
peak form 131
reprimanded 141, 276
in West Indies 44, 45
McIntyre, Peter 232, 235
McLean, Nixon 67
McMillan, Brian 81
Mahanama, Roshan 201, 261
Malcolm, Devon 134, 135, 137, 142, 153
Malik Mohammed Qayyum, Justice *3*, 13, 25
Manjrekar, Sanjay 242
Marks, Neil 100, 104, 136
Marsh, Geoff
 photograph *145*
 characteristics as coach 84, 271-2
 concern over Warne's weight 115
 conflicts with Taylor 102-3, 235-6, 258-9
 drops Warne 78
 excitement at Gilchrist's century 120
Marsh, Rod 29, 37
Marshall, Malcolm 51, 53, 73, 122
Martin, Ray 109
Martyn, Damien 141
match-fixing 1, 4-8, 13-14, 18, 21, 25, 35, 158, 189 *see also* bribery affair
Matthews, Craig 83
Matthews, Greg *214*, 215
May, Tim
 photographs *205*, *213*
 Australian Cricketers' Association 204-12
 bribery offer from Salim Malik 4-6 fears about safety 22
 matches: England 139; Pakistan 18 retires 25
McMillan, Brian 83, 90
McMillan, Craig 223, 224
McMillan, Keith 88
Miller, Colin 26-7, 29, 35, 79, 160
Miller, Keith 68
Misson, David 272
Mitchley, Cyril 90, 91
Mohammed Azharuddin 232, 236, 237, 239, 248, 251
Mohammed Rafiq Tarar 36
Mohammed Wasim 37, 64

Mohammed Zahid 32, 64
Mohsin Kamal 104
Moin Khan 8, 21, 24, 33, 65, 265
Mongia, Nayan 232, 233, 236, 244, 245
Moody, Tom 216, 264
Morgan, Sandy 272
Mujahid Jamshed 64-5, 261
Mullally, Alan 157, 163
Muller, Scott (photograph) *36*
Muralitharan, Muttiah 169, 172-8, 193
Murray, Junior 62, 63, 261
Mushtaq Ahmed
 matches: Australia 5, 17, 19, 24, 32, 33; West Indies 64
 match-fixing 8
 spin-bowling 23-4, 159

Nawaz Sharif 36
New Zealand 202-28
 in Australia, 1997-98 222-8
News Limited 205-6
Nicholson, Matthew 158, 160, 163, 165
Nine Network 112-13, 203, 209, 217, 218, 268
'No Whinge, No Wine Tour, The' (newsletter) 28

Odumbe, Maurice 186, 187
one-day games 260-1
Oppenheimer family 83
O'Regan, Rob 9-10, 12, 13
Otieno, Kennedy 186

Pakistan
 in Australia, 1995-96 21-4
 in Australia, 1999-2000 35-8
 grudge match 1-15
Pakistan *before the third Test, Australia v Pakistan, Karachi, 1998* (photograph) *31*
Pakistan Cricket Board 22, 25
Pakistan India Lanka Committee 185, 204
Pakistani butchers and cricket optimists, Peshawar, 1998 (photograph) *30*
Pakistani match-fixing inquiry in 1998 158
Parke, Trent 54
Parker, Peter 113
Parore, Adam 222, 225, 265
Perry, Nehemiah 78, 79
Philpott, Peter 159
PILCOM (Pakistan India Lanka Committee) 185, 204
players' pay dispute 101, 110, 113, 153, 202-22
Pockock, Blair 224
Pollock, Graeme 84, 85
Pollock, Shaun 81, 83, 93, 114, *121*, 121-2, 123
Ponting, Ricky

photograph 249
Ashes tour 103
Australia 'A' team 141
behaviour 248–50, 276
maiden Test century 151
matches: England 150; India 243, 246, 254–5; New Zealand 224, 225; Pakistan 33; South Africa 114, 126–7; Sri Lanka 273; West Indies 56, 58, 62, 77
Punter 249
Test debut 171
Premadasa Stadium, Colombo 199–200
Prime Minister's XI 62, 161
Pringle, Meyrick 83
Prue, Terry 112
Punchihewa, Asa 183

Rackemann, Carl 43
Raju, Venkatapathy 245
Raman Subba Row 91
Ramaswamy, V. K. 224
Ramesh, Sadagopan 243, 255
Ramiz Raja 24
Ramprakash, Mark 154, 157, 158, 161, 164
Ranatunga, Arjuna
  photographs *175, 176, 180, 181*
  behaviour 172, 180, 197
  comments by and about 183, 192, 199, 200
  matches: Australia 169, 171, 193
  receives the Cup 194
Ranatunga, Dhammika 196, 200
Ranatunga, Sanjeewa 183
Randell, Steve 4, 114, 123, 175
Ranjan Madugalle 124
Rashid Latif 7, 19, 21, 22, 24
Rawalpindi Cricket Association 31
Ray, Mark 12, 30
Reed, Ron 185
Reid, John 5, 19, 38, 141
Reiffel, Paul
  photograph 57
  assessment of Simpson 271
  Australia 'A' team 141
  comments on team morale 109
  death threats 182
  greatest one-day win 192
  matches: England 146, 147, 149, 150; New Zealand 227; South Africa 118; Sri Lanka 178; West Indies 41, 44, 45, 50, 57, 58, 62
  omission in Port Elizabeth 99
  overstepping crease 177
  players' pay dispute 217
  wicket preference 98
reverse swing bowling 18
Richards, David 6, 7, 11, 206
Richards, Viv 46, 51
Richardson, David 81, 117, 124

Richardson, Richie
  Australian tactics 50
  career end 192
  leadership 48, 51, 52
  matches: Australia 40, 45, 47, 49
  shoulder injury 42
Ritchie, Greg 50
Rixon, Steve 136, 222, 223, *223*, 228
Roberts, Andy 48, 52
Robertson, Gavin
  in India and Pakistan 28
  matches: India 240, 243, 244, 245, 247, 248; Pakistan 35
Roebuck, Peter 32
Rogen Communications 17
Rogers, Denis 9, 30, 40, 101, 174, 200, 207–22

Sabina Park, Kingston 47, 73
Saeed Anwar 18, 19, 20, 26, 32, 36
Salim Malik
  photograph 26
  bribery affair 15–16
  double century 20
  Lahore High Court inquiry 29–30
  matches: Australia 21, 24, 27, 32, 35
  match-fixing 1, 4, 5–6, 7, 13, 18, 35
  Pakistan Cricket Board inquiry 22, 25
  perceived lack of courage 23
Salim Pervez 11
Samuels, Robert 58, 59, 61, 69
Saqlain Mushtaq 8, 37, 64
Sarfraz Nawaz 8
scandals
  bribery affair 1, 5, 10, 12, 13, 14, 40–1
  match-fixing 1, 4–8, 13–14, 18, 21, 25, 35, 158, 189
Schultz, Brett 83
SEL (Cricket) Pty Ltd 208
Shahid Afridi 28, 64
Sharp, George 246
Shoaib Akhtar 32, 37–8
short-pitched bowling 45
Sidhu, Navjot Singh 188, 244, 245, 248, 250
Simmons, Phil 42
Simpson, Bob
  bribery offers, and 4, 6, 7, 11, 40
  character as coach 269–71
  circulates questionnaire 43–4
  death threats 182
  era ends 194–5
  hospitalised 46
  record falls 33
Sims, Graem 5
Singer World Series 11, 197, 260
Sinhalese Sports Ground, Colombo 14–15
Sivaramakrishnan, Laxman 240
Slater, Michael

Index 289

in Antigua 79
Ashes tour 103
centuries 74, 135, 142, 160, 167
dropping of 53-4, 99, 197
fearlessness 51
India 232, 241, 243, 247, 250
matches: England 139, 143; Pakistan 16, 19, 27, 32, 35, 36, 37; South Africa 21; Sri Lanka 171; West Indies 46, 47, 49
media contract 218-19
partnerships with Taylor 133
sledging 38, 69-70, 275, 276
Smith, Mike 150, 151
Smith, Steve 84, 272
South Africa 81-130
  in Australia, 1997-98 110-25
Speed, Malcolm 8-9, 29, 174, 207-8, 211-12, 217, 259
Sports and Entertainment Limited (SEL) 208
Sports Illustrated 32
Sri Lanka 169-201
  in Australia, 1995-96 169-84
Sri Lanka in Lahore (photograph) *194*
Srinath, Javagal 237, 247, 255
Srinivas Venkataraghavan 46
St George's Park, Port Elizabeth 86
Stewart, Alec 152-3, 156, 158-9, 161, 163, *164*
strike 101, 110, 113, 153, 202-22
Stuart, Anthony 96
Such, Peter 157
Symcox, Pat 111, 114, 120, 122

Tamil Tigers of Elam (LTTE) 184, 185
Taylor, Jack (MT's son) 104
Taylor, Judi (MT's wife) 100, 104, 105-6
Taylor, Judy (MT's mother) 107
Taylor, Mark
  photographs *xi*, *33*, *34*, *72*, *94*, *121*, *132*, *147*, *181*, *214*, *238*, *267*
  captaincy: appointment to 267; conflict with Marsh 235-6; decision on follow-on 136; decision to declare 1-2, 32-5; decision to send in opposition 86; end of the Taylor years 167-8; first year 132-3; fourth-innings pattern 137; leadership 28-9, 237, 273; sledging, attitude to 275; team performance 248
  cricketer: back injury 196, 230; batting form 17, 31, 64, 82, 90, 91-2, 93-110; biggest Test win 89; century India 251; earnings 206, 209; Edgbaston century 151; greatest one-day win 192; 100th Test 160; leadership 60; media contract 218-19; one-day teams 91-2, 169, 257-65; record catches 167
  matches: England 139; Pakistan 20, 23, 24, 32, 35; South Africa 21, 120-1; Sri Lanka 171; West Indies 39, 46, 49, 50, 56, 58, 62, 66, 68, 69
  relations with players: Brian Lara 70; Ian Healy 224; Michael Slater 53-4, 133
  scandals: bookmaker affair 30; bribery affair 1-2, 5, 10, 12, 40-1
  Time To Declare 6, 14, 33
  views: on one-day cricket 66; of Simpson as coach 271; on team 51; on training in West Indies 44-5; of Warne 72; of wicket 47; on winning in the Caribbean 42
Taylor, Peter 267
Taylor, Tony (MT's father) 107
Taylor, William (MT's son) 104, 106
Tendulkar, Sachin
  photograph *254*
  charged at by McGrath 276
  comes to the wicket 241-2
  matches: Australia 187, 188, 197, 244, 245, 250
  study of Australians 239-40
  umpires, and 198, 253-5
Thompson, Patterson 67, 68
Thomson, Jeff 38, 64
Thorpe, Graham 107, *140*, 142, 147, 150, 153, 154, 157
Tillekeratne, Hashan 171, 180
Tudor, Alex 157
Tufnell, Phil 142, 154
'two teams' policy 257-65

Upton, Paddy 110

Vaas, Chaminda 171
van der Merwe, Peter 245
Venkatesh Prasad, B. K. 235
Vettori, Daniel 223

Waight, Dennis 65
Walkley Award 3
Walsh, Courtney
  in Antigua 79-80
  argument with Waugh 70
  bowling style 51, 71
  captaincy 43, 48, 52, 65-6
  matches: Australia 47, 49, 57, 59, 63, 67, 77, 78
Walsh, Mike 272
Wanderers Ground, Johannesburg 84
Wankhede Stadium, Mumbai 187
Waqar Younis 8, 17, 18, 19, 21, 22, 23, 24, 65, 189
Warne, Shane
  photographs *9*, *118*, *170*, *195*, *214*, *241*
  cricketer: Australian Cricket Board 51; Australian Cricketers' Association 206; bowling form 116-17, 124, 125-6;

captaincy 268; career 55-6, 85, 117-18, 132, 136, 171, 239-40; dropped 78-9; earnings 209; injuries 25, 194, 246-7, 252; media contract 218-19; self-selection 165, 278; weight 115-16, 244
matches: England 107, 138, 139, 143, 149, 151, 153; India 187, 242, 248, 254-5; New Zealand 190, 227; Pakistan 16, 18, 19, 20, 23, 36; South Africa 87, 113, 114, 128-9; Sri Lanka 180, 193; West Indies 46, 50, 57, 58, 62, 64, 66, 68, 71, 74-8
relations with players: abuse of and by 69, 148, 152; batsmen 28; Brian Lara 70; Daryll Cullinan 111; death threats 182; English team 159; Glenn McGrath 59; Mark Taylor 101; Matthew Elliott 54; pitches 99; safety 22, 185
scandals: bribery affair 1, 8-9, 30, 40-1, 158; 'John' the bookmaker 11-13; match-fixing 1, 4-6; O'Regan's criticisms 10
Warne, Simone (SW's wife) 126
Wasim Akram
alleges sledging 38
captain 16, 35
matches: Australia 17, 18, 19, 20, 21, 24, 29; India 189; West Indies 64
match-fixing 7, 14, 189
withdrawal 31-2
Waugh, Mark
photographs 9, 57, 61, 89, 123
cricketer: Australian Cricket Board 51; career-best India 230; career-high England 141; centuries 98, 117, 171, 187, 190; collision with Elliott 60; dropping of 54; innings India 251; loss of form 278; strengths 50
matches: England 136, 143, 151, 153; India 245; Kenya 186; New Zealand 226; Pakistan 18, 19, 20, 27, 32, 35; South Africa 88; Sri Lanka 179, 180; West Indies 49, 56, 58, 67, 69, 71, 75, 76
relations with players: fears about safety 22; Glenn McGrath 59; Pat Symcox 122
scandals: bribery affair 1, 3, 30, 40-1; faces Lahore High Court 29; fines 8-9, 158; 'John' the bookmaker 11-13; match-fixing 4, 5-6, 21; O'Regan's criticisms 10
A Year To Remember 225
Waugh, Steve

photograph *214*
captaincy: and batting 278; Buchanan appointed 272; first series 35, 78; one-day 258-9; succession 268
cricketer: 5000 runs 92; Australian Cricketers' Association 206; bowling incident 123-4; caught out 67; centuries 149, 160, 179, 254; disciplinary fine 198; dropping of 54; earnings 209; media contract 218-19; one-day matches 126-8, 192, 201; run out by Taylor 263; strengths 50; 100th Test match 117; World Cup matches 16, 184
matches: Antigua 79-80; England 163, 165; India 231-2, 233-5, 254; New Zealand 226; Pakistan 17, 18, 19, 23, 27, 32, 37; South Africa 21, 85, 88, 90, 114; Sri Lanka 178, 183; West Indies 39, 40, 46, 49, 57, 58, 62, 63, 75, 76, 77
match-fixing scandal 5-6
relations with players: Brian Lara and Courtney Walsh 70; Curtly Ambrose 47-8; Glenn McGrath 59; hyperaggression 276-7; Mark Taylor 101-2; Shane Warne 269; sledging 276; West Indies team 45
views: on fast bowling 49-50; on fourth Test 66; on losing 280; on South African team 82-3, 119; on touring the sub-continent 28, 199, 239
World Cup Diary 174
Webster, Rudi 75
West Indies 39-40
in Australia, 1996-97 51-73
West Indies Test, Sydney, 1996 (photograph) *60*
White, Craig 134
Wilkins, Phil 4, 7
Willey, Peter 70, 118, 231
Williams, Stuart 45, 52
Wilson, Paul 246, 247
Wisden Australia 12, 32
Woolmer, Bob 88, 110, 113, 127, 130
World Cups
1996 184-95
1999 14, 125-30

Young, Bryan 223
Young, Shaun 154

Zahid Fazal 20